MORE ADVANCE PRAISE FOR *FROM ALCHEMY TO IPO:*

"*From Alchemy to IPO* combines the unique wisdom of a biotech insider with a real enthusiasm for innovative science. It offers pragmatic advice for the novice and fascinating insights for the aficionado."
—Dr. Stan Crooke, CEO, ISIS Pharmaceutical

"Cynthia Robbins-Roth provides the insight of an industry insider in this entertaining account of the rise of the biotechnology business. As a former bench researcher, long-time journalist, and consultant to the industry, she understands both the science and the business of biotech, and does an excellent job of conveying both to her readers."
**—Donald R. Johnston, Vice President/
Group Publisher, BioWorld Today**

"*From Alchemy to IPO* is a very important tool for seasoned biotech entrepreneurs as well as researchers considering a move into the biotech business sector. I plan to show this book to everyone who has a question about how biotech works."
**—H. Michael Shepard, Ph.D., Chief Scientific
Officer, NewBiotics, Inc.**

"To those who believe the Internet bubble is unsustainable, Robbins-Roth offers a battle-tested view for investing in biotechnology."
—Constance McKee, CEO, Xavos Corporation

from
ALCHEMY
to
I P O

from ALCHEMY *to* I P O

The Business of Biotechnology

CYNTHIA ROBBINS-ROTH, PH.D.

PERSEUS PUBLISHING
Cambridge, Massachusetts

Many of the designations used by manufacturers and sellers to distinguish their products are claimed as trademarks. Where those designations appear in this book and Perseus Publishing was aware of a trademark claim, the designations have been printed in initial capital letters.
A CIP record for this book is available from the Library of Congress.
ISBN: 0-7382-0253-3
Copyright © 2000 by Cynthia Robbins-Roth, Ph.D.

Perseus Publishing is a member of the Perseus Books Group

Text design by Jeff Williams
Set in 11-point Janson Text by the Perseus Books Group

1 2 3 4 5 6 7 8 9 10—03 02 01 00
First printing, March 2000

Perseus Publishing books are available at special discounts for bulk purchases in the U.S. by corporations, institutions, and other organizations. For more information, please contact the Special Markets Department at HarperCollins Publishers, 10 East 53rd Street, New York, NY 10022, or call 1-212-207-7528.

Find us on the World Wide Web at http://www.perseuspublishing.com

This book is dedicated to my wonderful children, Austin and Alexandra. As biotech heads for the outer reaches of our galaxy, I fully expect to see them leading the charge.

CONTENTS

PREFACE

As we head into the new millennium and into biotech's third decade, the industry is undergoing a resurgence of energy. The AMEX Biotech Stock Index performance has caught up with the Standard & Poor's 500 Index performance for the first time since 1993 and shows no signs of stopping. The top 100 public companies represent more than $200 billion in market capitalization. Biotechnology is poised to provide another incredible run for investors.

Even more important, there are 65 new drugs on the market that came from biotech labs and another 140 in final stages of the regulatory process. Every day, the industry labs generate more information about how our bodies work, in sickness and in health, down to the single-molecule level. For the first time in history, it is possible to design new treatments for diseases such as Alzheimer's disease, Lou Gehrig's disease, breast and prostate cancer, and heart disease—and aim those drugs directly at the molecular causes of the disease. More effective drugs, with fewer nasty side effects, will be possible because of biotechnology.

But wait—there's more! Most of us think of biotech as medicine or genetically engineered crops. In the next 30 years, biotechnology may make it possible for humans to reach the stars and to change the environment on other planets to become more hospitable to human life. Computers based on the human brain, spacecraft using cell-like signaling pathways and genetic information encoding structural and functional molecules to evolve in new environments, transgenic crops able to generate enough food in spacecraft environments to feed a crew, drug discovery tools rapid enough to help astronauts deal with unknown organisms on other planets—all of this is in early stages of development today.

Those impatient Wall Street analysts and day traders demanding that biotech move at Internet speed are doomed to miss out on the great investment returns and the chance to participate in something a bit more world shaking than the next on-line pet food company.

It's very true that biotech investing is not for the faint of heart. Individual stocks and entire chunks of the sector have taken investors for heart-pounding roller coaster rides—sometimes based on fundamental issues, and sometimes based simply on faulty responses to press releases. Many investors have little knowledge of the process that takes a new discovery from the lab bench to the marketplace. Given the complexity of the science, how can an innocent bystander hope to decipher the code for a great company versus a not-so-great company?

This book is designed to give you a close-up view of the thrills and chills of the biotechnology industry—what makes it so compelling, and what makes it one of the most risky sectors for investors. You will meet some of the innovative entrepreneurs who created this industry back in the late 1970s, when everyone insisted it wasn't possible to start new pharmaceutical companies. The risks they took and the value they generated make the Internet start-ups look like wimps.

You will also get a guided tour through the mysteries of the drug development process (just what the heck is Phase II and why do we care?), the convoluted funding trail from venture capital through that all-important initial public offering (IPO), a tutorial in why biotech stocks behave the way they do, and a checklist for picking out the companies most likely to succeed—without getting a Ph.D. in biochemistry first.

My great hope is that you will also gain an understanding of the incredible power of biotechnology to change all of our lives—our health care, our food, our clothing, our earth-bound industries, our space program, our personal lives. The first person you will meet is Betsy Patterson, an oncology nurse who saw her entire family affected by the ability of a new biotech drug to change the course of her own cancer.

You'll hear directly from the entrepreneurs and business leaders who went against common wisdom and lived to tell the tale, and from the bankers and venture capitalists who were captivated by the new technology and its ability to revolutionize a stodgy business.

The biotech world will never be an easy place for investors—high upside potential is inevitably coupled with high risk. But it is one of the most personally rewarding market segments in which "doing good while doing well" is a key drawing card.

As we begin the 21st century, literally hundreds of new biotech projects begun in the last decade are poised to power into the marketplace. This explosion will fuel opportunities for investors and employees alike, and we will all benefit from the products. As Craig Taylor of Alloy Ventures says so succinctly, "Soon everyone will be communicating all the time, anywhere, with beautiful color monitors, but parts of their bodies will need fixing."

Biotech's Golden Age lies ahead.

ACKNOWLEDGMENTS

After spending more than a decade writing a 38-page monthly newsletter, running a daily biotech news service, producing a quarterly biotech industry magazine, and writing columns and articles for the general business press, I figured, "How hard could it be to write a book about the emergence of the biotech industry?"

Okay, so I was just a little naive. This was definitely a labor of love, with the emphasis on *labor*. But as it turned out, the toughest part of all was not gathering all of the information. The tough part was figuring out how the heck to condense and organize an incredible amount of information and great stories—what to leave out—into something that innocent bystanders would read and enjoy.

The patient and talented editing of Jacque Murphy, my incredible editor at Perseus Books, helped me beat this growing monster into a book. It turned out that the two of us were independently searching for each other, each wanting to help create a way to tell the story of biotech to the public. Jacque's assistant, Arlinda Shtuni, got stuck with the job of dealing with all of the last details—tracking down decent graphics, reminding me to get my last bits and pieces in, and riding herd on the reviewers.

I especially want to acknowledge with deep gratitude all of those industry insiders who willingly spent hours sharing their personal stories and thoughts about the creation of the biotech industry and its continued growth. Their shared vision makes the excitement and creative fervor of the early days of biotech come alive and did a lot to stoke my optimism about the future.

These folks include Howard Birndorf, Jim Blair, Robert Blum, Bill Bowes, Brook Byers, Farah Champsi, Ron Cohen, Stan Crooke,

Stephen Evans-Freke, Jim Gower, Fred Frank, Tom Kiley, Louis Lange, Jan LeCocq, Patricia McGrath, Constance McKee, Stelios Papadopoulos, Betsy Patterson, George Rathmann, Michael Shepard, Craig Taylor, Henri Termeer, and Richard van den Broek. While these folks got quoted directly in the book, there are many more people who have spent time talking with me over the years about the biotech industry than I could ever list here. I am so grateful for their insights and comments, which have helped me form a more clear picture of this growing sector.

A very important member of the industry insider group, one who did more than anyone else to mold my perception of biotech as *the* place to be, was Robert Swanson. He led all of us into this new era of putting biology to work for humanity and gave us all a great example of true entrepreneurial leadership. The lessons I learned at Genentech in the early days formed my own philosophy of management and team formation, which were inflicted on my innocent staff in my own entrepreneurial endeavors. We will miss him terribly.

I'd also like to thank Dan Goldin, the NASA Administrator, whose incredibly stirring keynote speech at the 1999 BIO International Annual Meeting introduced me to the concept of "biotech in space" and the crucial role of biotech beyond medicine. That talk led me to the NASA Ames Astrobiology Institute in Santa Clara, California, and discussions about biomimetic computers, transgenic crops to support space stations, and evolvable intelligent spacecraft—very cool stuff that will keep me occupied for the next decade!

Karl Thiel, Editor in Chief of DoubleTwist.com and my former managing editor at BioVenture, did an incredible job of pulling together the sections on the new technology of tools for genomic studies, combinatorial chemistry, and agricultural biotechnology. He has brought quality biotech reporting to the Internet.

Elizabeth Moyer's comments on the trials and tribulations of product development were invaluable in ensuring that my readers would get a realistic view of this integral process. Our discussions also helped outline ways in which investors can look for clues about companies through their clinical trials, without the need for attending medical school.

My business partner, Carol Hall, and her incredibly useful BioVenture Consultants' *Stock Report* provided reams of important data and analysis for this book. Carol has managed over the past 11 years to drag me, kicking and screaming, to a point where I actually appreciate the value of financial data as a great tool for figuring out what companies are *really* up to (just don't quiz me on convertible subordinated debentures).

It would have been impossible to pull together all of the data on the industry without the help of many people willing to share their personal archives and databases with me. I particularly want to thank Don Johnston and his team at BioWorld, who gave me free access to their incredible historical and current information on the biotech industry; the sales and marketing team at IDEC, who introduced me to Betsy Patterson; Marie Kennedy at Genentech; Carl Feldbaum and his team at the Biotechnology Industry Organization; Alan Mendelson of Cooley Godward; the biotech team at Wilson Sonsini Goodrich and Rosati; Mark Edwards at Recombinant Capital and Jennifer Van Brunt, editor of Recombinant Capital's *Signals Magazine;* Dr. Robert Longman at Windhover Information; and Dr. Mark Dibner at the Institute for Biotechnology Information.

My version of the biotech timeline was compiled with much flipping of the pages in my tattered copy of the biochemists' bible, *Principals of Biochemistry,* edited by Albert Lehninger (Worth Publishers Inc.) and in *Northern California's Bioscience Legacy,* published in 1991 by the Bay Area Biotechnology Center, San Francisco, California.

And finally, I want to thank my family for putting up with this editorial process for the past year. Their support and encouragement, and my mother's wildly enthusiastic editing, made this a great experience.

part one

THE ROOTS OF BIOTECHNOLOGY

— 1 —

BIOTECH IN
THE BEGINNING

THE HEART OF BIOTECH

Fourteen years ago, Betsy Patterson was a 34-year-old single mom
with three kids ages 5 to 10. She was a registered nurse in oncology
working on the bone marrow transplant unit, where cancer patients
go to replace the marrow cells destroyed by cancer treatments. She
was reminded daily just how terrible cancer could be.

And then she found her own lump.

Betsy was diagnosed with non-Hodgkin's lymphoma (NHL), a ma-
lignant growth of immune system cells that begin to form tumors in
lymph nodes and throughout the body. NHL, a deadly cancer that affects an estimated 250,000 Americans, is growing at a rate second
only to lung cancer. About 55,500 new patients will be diagnosed in
this country this year, and 25,000 will die of the disease. There is no
cure for most patients, and only 60% of patients treated with the conventional treatments—toxic radiation and chemotherapy—are still
alive 5 years after diagnosis.

Because there were no other symptoms, she and her doctor adopted
a "wait and see" approach. Betsy did very well for 9 years. Her lymph
nodes would periodically balloon up but then disappear before she
even had time to see the doctor. She remarried, and life went on.

But in 1995 things changed. Betsy enrolled in graduate nursing
school—the stress level went up. Within weeks, tumor-filled lymph
nodes were popping out all over her body. A biopsy showed that her

lymphoma had kicked into overdrive. Her doctor suggested immediate chemotherapy, and she entered a 9-month Phase II clinical trial protocol with two drugs—fludarabine and mitoxantrone.

Chemotherapy works by killing off rapidly dividing cells, such as tumors. Unfortunately, there are lots of healthy cells in our bodies that also divide rapidly—hair follicles, the cells lining the digestive tract, the bone marrow cells that produce red blood cells to carry oxygen, and the immune system's white blood cells. During chemotherapy, your hair falls out, your mouth develops ulcers, your gut loses the ability to absorb food properly, your red cell count gets so low that there is not enough oxygen getting to your organs, and your immune system loses the ability to protect you from infection. Some drugs damage the kidneys and the heart. Most lymphoma patients die not of the direct effects of their disease, but of complications of the treatment. Chemotherapy is essentially a race to kill the tumor before the treatment kills the patient.

Betsy's doctor told her that fludarabine was not associated with extreme toxicity—he expected her to keep her hair, and her job, throughout the 9-month protocol.

But to Betsy, it felt as though the treatment was killing her pretty quickly.

"The chemo was very tough on my veins and I felt pain with each infusion burning up my arms. Within days of the first treatment, I was sick as a dog, with uncontrolled nausea and vomiting."

Within 3 weeks of the first treatment, Betsy got another unpleasant surprise.

"The drugs were so toxic to my ovaries that they just stopped producing hormones. I went into abrupt menopause and all the wonderful things that means—constant hot flashes; loss of sexual libido; major physical changes; serious night sweats that would soak the bed, my nightgown, and my poor husband; and my periods ended. Sleep was totally disrupted for both of us. Nobody had warned me about this effect. These were major quality-of-life problems for me and for my family."

At the end of the 9-month protocol, she began replacement hormone therapy. At that point, her body felt and looked like that of a much older woman. The hormone therapy, which she will need to take for the rest of her life, helped return some of her body to normal. But some of the induced changes are permanent.

The drugs used to control the continuous nausea and vomiting caused problems themselves, particularly drowsiness. By the last 3 months of the protocol, Betsy was taking such high doses that she was in bed 22 of every 24 hours.

The physical effects of the chemotherapy also caused emotional trauma.

"I felt totally worthless. I couldn't work. It became completely impossible to walk to the mailbox. I tried to go to the grocery store and had to sit down in the middle of the aisle because I was too weak to get to the end. I lost about half my hair; what was left was ugly! I had no energy to put on makeup, no libido, couldn't work. I felt that by not bringing home a paycheck, I was not contributing to the family.

"The feeling of being worthless can be so monumentally devastating that it overshadows the cancer. I felt they took away my life with that treatment, and there were times when I wanted to die to get away from this."

The good news was that Betsy finally went into full remission. The bad news was that her life was completely changed. She tried to go back to nursing part time 6 weeks after the treatment ended but couldn't summon the energy. She was completely debilitated. She finally had to give up her job to focus on getting healthy enough to enjoy life again.

It was an uphill battle. And the chemotherapy left behind a few more surprises—diabetes, a severe folic acid deficiency that contributing to anemia, and arms so weak from nerve damage that Betsy couldn't drive. For about a year after the chemo, her sense of taste was altered so much that she couldn't eat meat or drink tapwater. Betsy spent much of her time researching her ailments and looking for ways to treat them.

This effort was beginning to pay off when a small spot showed up on a chest scan in mid-1998, 18 months after she had finished the chemotherapy. "I could feel myself going back down the tubes. My husband had gotten a great job offer in South Carolina, and all I could think was how in the world I was going to fit in that awful treatment with finding a house and getting my kids and husband situated. I decided to wait till we moved to start treatment. I found a new doctor and told him right up-front—no more toxic chemo, no bone marrow transplants. I had found some information on Rituxan (IDEC Pharmaceuticals' new cancer treatment) and wanted to try it."

Rituxan is a monoclonal antibody—a genetically engineered version of the antibody molecules made by our immune systems to fight off disease. Rituxan travels through the body and sticks to a protein found only on mature B cells, the immune system cells that go bad in NHL. No other cell types, not even younger versions of B cells, carry that protein. This allows Rituxan to bind to the lymphoma cells and cause the rest of the immune system to actually kill the bad guys—without affecting normal, healthy parts of the body. This means that the drug does not cause the nasty side effects that Betsy experienced with chemotherapy.

When the Food and Drug Administration gave IDEC Pharmaceuticals the okay to market Rituxan in November 1997, it became the first new drug approved in a decade for NHL, and the very first monoclonal antibody treatment approved for cancer. Rituxan is one of the great biotechnology success stories. It changed Betsy Patterson's life.

"I started Rituxan in December 1998. After two treatments, the chest pain from that swollen lymph node went away completely. CT scans a month after I finished the first treatment showed a 35% response in my tumor." The nodes in her neck were completely gone, and those in her back and groin were disappearing and no longer painful. CT scans in June prior to her second dose continued to show a substantial reduction in her tumors.

This great response was not accompanied by toxicity. And there were few side effects. "Even with the second treatment, I had very little toxicity—no nausea at all, and within 2 weeks I could feel my energy coming back. In August, I went to Snowmass, Colorado, with my husband. We rented bikes, and I convinced my husband to try a 12-mile ride to Aspen! This was incredible to me, after all those months of barely being able to get out of bed."

Betsy was put into a maintenance protocol, where she will receive Rituxan every 6 months regardless of disease progression.

"My quality of life with Rituxan is wonderful. I'd be willing to take it every 6 months for the rest of my life. Being well lets me and my husband carry on with life and also helps my kids. This disease and the treatments—they just spiral to affect so many people, not just the patient. My kids don't have that fear in their faces they had when I was going through the chemo. They don't have to put their lives on hold because I am sick. My daughter was ready to leave her home and job and come live with me when I started the Rituxan, because she remembered how wiped out I was from chemo. But that didn't need to happen. My daughter is getting married in the fall, my son is in the process of getting engaged. I can work about 20 hours a week. Life is so full."

Biotechnology has completely changed the way we discover and develop new drugs and has allowed us to help patients with previously untreatable diseases. Stories like Betsy's are one reason so many people have invested their time, money, and careers in biotech.

SETTING THE SCENE

Back in the late 1970s and early 1980s, conventional wisdom dictated that we wouldn't witness the emergence of any new pharmaceutical companies. The cost of creating the infrastructure and supporting all the R&D was astronomical, and no new company could possibly compete with the existing powerhouses. Syntex and Marion Labs had been the last new pharmaceutical companies created—back in the 1950s.

Biotech changed all that. Much to the surprise of those in the know, a group of hardy entrepreneurs not only built new pharma companies—they created an entire industry based on new science, an innovative approach to management, and some incredibly creative financing ideas.

Pre-biotech, big pharma's traditional approach to drug discovery consisted primarily of targeting lots of small organic molecules at enzymes or cell surface receptors sitting in test tubes, and looking for compounds that stuck. These initial "hits" became the basis for a massive medicinal chemistry assault, looking for ways to tinker with the molecular structure to generate a drug that both stuck to the target and had the characteristics of good drugs.

The dream drug was potent when taken orally, remained active in the body long enough to allow once- to thrice-daily pill taking, didn't generate toxic metabolites once exposed to the body's biochemistry, and didn't muck up normal body functions.

The problem with this approach was that scientists didn't really know enough about the details of how the body worked and what caused many diseases. And they didn't have ways to ensure that their drug candidates would act only on the desired target. As a consequence, most drugs treated only the symptoms of disease—pain and swelling in arthritis, for example—without stopping the cause of the disease.

Also, drugs aimed at one disease target inevitably interacted with other enzymes or receptors throughout the body, causing nasty side effects. For example, the most potent drugs for rheumatoid arthritis are also the most dangerous for the patients—and even they are not able to stop disease progression or reverse the joint damage.

These limitations of the drug discovery process, coupled with the cost and risk of new drug development, helped create a focus in the 1970s on "me too" drugs—drugs that imitated successful therapeutics already on the market. The blockbuster drugs, generating $500 million to $1 billion in annual revenue, were few and far between. Those that did exist—such as SmithKline's Tagamet, Bristol-Myers's Capoten, Syntex's Naprosyn, and Glaxo's Zantac—were due to lose their patent protection in the mid-1990s. This was destined to leave a huge revenue gap for these companies, and not much was in the product pipeline to replace the lost proceeds.

As we enter the new millennium, drug companies have continued to struggle with the driving need to fill their product pipelines with innovative new pharmaceuticals. There is also an ongoing need for more effective therapies aimed at diseases affecting the largest numbers of patients, including cancers, cardiovascular diseases, and neurology disorders such as Alzheimer's disease.

The big pharma companies need these drugs to ensure the double-digit revenue growth demanded by their shareholders, and to ensure that their products will be used in today's managed-care environment, where drugs must justify their cost.

The emerging biotechnology industry has provided answers to some of these tough problems and has evolved into the research and development force supporting the drug industry. But biotech is not just an outsourced research division for big pharma.

The top nine biopharmaceutical companies with products on the market posted 12-month sales of almost $6 billion at the end of the first quarter of 1999. Biotech has provided most of these new products. Amgen Corp. (Thousand Oaks, California) accounted for almost half of the total with its two "recombinant" protein products, Epogen for stimulating production of red blood cells and Neupogen to drive growth of immune system cells in cancer patients. The pipeline is crammed full of more than 300 biotech products in clinical trials, each heading toward the marketplace.

Dr. Stelios Papadopoulos, managing director at PaineWebber, points out, "People have not focused on the fact that biotech products have been incredible successes. These new companies have managed to outdo the practitioners of the art at their own game. Biotech develops new products to sell into markets dominated by huge multinational companies that are better financed. These young companies walked into a mature market and succeeded; the intellectual property of their products dominates the market."

But onlookers need to remember that most product candidates never reach the market. And without new products, there is no certainty of survival even for large companies. In fact, the continual surge of big pharma mergers followed by shedding of infrastructure over the latter part of the 1990s has demonstrated just how irrelevant size is. Once the patents protecting the blockbuster products are gone, there is no certainty for any company that's dependent upon a single drug.

The huge challenge facing biomedical companies of all sizes is coming up with enough breakthroughs to sustain earnings growth. It's remarkable that the very smallest biotech companies have demonstrated the potential to carve a place for themselves out of nowhere by coming up with true innovation. You don't encounter these circumstances in many established industries. Imagine a small upstart trying to take on General Motors. But a tiny biotechnology company with a novel diabetes treatment could make the entire insulin market obsolete. That's the allure of biotechnology.

How did this new sector emerge seemingly out of nowhere?

BIOTECH'S BIRTH

The U.S. federal government and the National Cancer Institute (NCI) declared war on cancer in the 1970s and spent enormous sums to fund cancer research. An estimated 11% of all federal R&D dollars was poured into basic biomedical research, and the NCI dominated the National Institutes of Health budget with a whopping $989 million spent annually on cancer research by 1981.

I was a postdoctoral fellow back in 1980, slaving away in an immunology lab at the University of Texas Medical Branch in Galveston, waiting for a grant to come through that would send me to Switzerland. My lab, along with most of the departments of microbiology and human genetics/biochemistry, was grappling with the question of how the human immune system worked to protect people from cancer and serious infections—and how to make it work better when it failed.

My mentors at Texas, Dr. Benjamin Papermaster and Dr. Howard Johnson, were part of a small international network of researchers at the forefront of the relatively new area of immunotherapy. Their labs were trying to isolate the specific proteins used by the immune system cells to communicate with each other and to signal attacks on tumors or virally infected cells. Once we had them purified, we could study how they worked—and hopefully put that information to use treating patients.

This sounds straightforward, but in reality it was a huge task. The only way to get enough of these proteins—termed *lymphokines*—was to grow big flasks of immune system cells (isolated from volunteers' blood) and trick the cells into thinking they were under attack. This stimulated the cells to dump their lymphokines into the tissue culture medium in which they grew.

Unfortunately, the proteins we cared about were present in only tiny amounts and were surrounded by huge amounts of irrelevant proteins made by the cells. It was extremely difficult and time-consuming to collect enough of any one lymphokine to study. Most experiments were done with preparations containing many other proteins, making it tough to figure out which activities belonged to which protein.

Nonetheless, experiments in animals and early, very primitive, clinical studies with terminal cancer patients made it clear that lymphokines had very powerful anticancer and antiviral activities. There was evidence that these proteins played key roles in inflammatory diseases such as arthritis; in transplant rejection, asthma, and allergies; and in the lethal systemic response to serious infections.

Scientists and physicians all over the world became very excited about the potential for using lymphokines to treat patients whose own immune systems were not up to the task. We found ourselves tripping over the BBC camera crews and journalists from all the major newspapers while trying to get to the lab.

In spite of all the "Cancer Cure!" headlines in business magazines and major newspapers, and the wrenching phone calls from patients and their families, we all faced one crucial roadblock. Nobody could make enough of these important proteins to treat even a fraction of the patients who could benefit. It took weeks to make enough for just animal studies. The race was on to discover an efficient way for lymphokines to become part of the therapeutic arsenal.

NEW OPPORTUNITIES IN SCIENCE

In the fall of 1980 the science world learned the answer—it was biotechnology.

I was invited to give a seminar on my research at a small company in South San Francisco, named Genentech. The seminar room, which doubled as the library, was full of young scientists in T-shirts and jeans.

This same band of motley characters had already used the newly developed tools of genetic engineering to create novel breeds of microbes that could be grown in huge vats and would happily crank out grams of human proteins. The process involved using molecular tools to "cut and paste" the genetic code for human proteins into bacterial cells, which would then read the code and make lots of the desired protein.

Biotech's genetic engineering was the answer to the supply problem. We were able to make as much of the lymphokines as we needed to study and to treat patients. By 1980, the Genentech team had also used this approach to make somatostatin (a hormone that turns off secretion of other hormones in the brain), insulin (thus ending the use of pig and cow insulin, which had caused allergic problems for diabetics), and growth hormone (previously available only from cadaver pituitary glands).

From my perspective, it was even more interesting that Genentech's team had produced recombinant thymosin alpha-1, a previously elusive hormone involved in immune system development, thought by some to have significant clinical potential. All of the academic research groups were still trying to purify thymosin away from the other proteins made by the immune cells so that they could study its specific actions in the body.

In 1980, the Genentech team would also notably add alpha and beta interferons to its catalog of cloned proteins. Interferons are vital: They're proteins that can improve the body's natural response to disease and slow the rate of growth and division of cancer cells.

From a business perspective, the technology of genetic engineering made it commercially feasible to develop these proteins as pharmaceuticals. Thanks to biotechnology, a whole new world of therapeutic development opened up. Most first-generation biotech companies focused on immune modulating proteins—interferons, interleukins, tumor necrosis factor (my personal favorite protein), and hepatitis virus proteins for vaccines. They also worked on other proteins with known activities in the body—tissue plasminogen activator to break up blood clots in heart attack victims, erythropoietin (EPO) to stimulate red blood cell production, glucocerebrosidase to correct the genetic defect causing Gaucher's disease.

These multisyllabic proteins and hormones are biology jargon, but the tools and methods invented by Genentech and other early biotech companies provided the building blocks for new drugs and treatments that were previously unavailable. The techniques were also the beginning of today's much-publicized mapping of the human genome.

Biotech also effectively opened up an appealing new career alternative for biological scientists. Up until the 1980s, researchers on the biology side of science had very few opportunities outside academia. The big drug companies hired biochemists and cell biologists, but the word in the postdoc world was that Ph.D.'s made far lower salaries than M.D.'s—and had to wear dress-up clothes to the lab.

Being a typical postdoc, I joined Genentech because they were willing to pay me twice my postdoc salary (a pitiful pittance) and let me do the research I wanted to do, surrounded by really smart people— and all without having to waste time writing grant proposals or change my science nerd wardrobe.

Genentech and its biotech brethren created a new haven in which to do innovative science without the trappings of the big pharma environment, and away from the crazed politics of government-sponsored academic research. Although academic colleagues decried the abandonment of campus for an industrial setting, the migration was on.

2

GENENTECH

The Leader of the Pack

First-generation biotech firms revolutionized how drugs were made and also created a new kind of company environment. The focus was on productivity, not established corporate behavior. Scientists were supported by management and touted as the key ingredient for success. Of course, part of this shift was because these start-ups lacked sales and marketing groups, so just about all they *had* was science.

This new environment was engineered by people like Genentech CEO Bob Swanson, who carried the entrepreneurial spirit generated in Silicon Valley in the 1960s and 1970s into the biotech babies. The financial backing for biotech came from a new generation of venture capital funds springing up in the San Francisco area, including Kleiner & Perkins, U.S. Venture Partners, and Asset Management.

Eugene Kleiner and Tom Perkins formed Kleiner & Perkins in San Francisco in 1972, with its first office in Embarcadero Center (in the downtown financial district). Kleiner & Perkins first entered the biotech world with an investment in Cetus Corp., started near Berkeley, California, in 1971 by founders Ron Cape and Peter Farley. Both Cape and Farley had training that straddled science and business. They were joined by Dr. Donald Glaser, a Nobel Prize-winning physicist and molecular biologist, and Moshe Alafi, one of biotech's great entrepreneurial investors and the early chairman of Cetus.

Cetus was a classic early biotech company, convinced that the best approach for success was to do everything imaginable, including genetically engineered bacteria for alcohol production, vaccines and therapeutic proteins, and a new approach to fermenting microbes and making antibiotics. This broad vision was encouraged by its investors: Standard Oil, National Distillers, and Shell Oil, all looking for diversification of their core businesses, the chic corporate activity of the 1970s.

In a sense, Cetus's early business strategy is what led to the creation of several key competitors. Many of the early investors and board members got frustrated with its "all over the map" approach and decided there had to be a better way. One of those frustrated investors was Bob Swanson.

"Cetus was very exciting, a new thing—the merger of biology and engineering—but management was not focused at all in terms of the business opportunity," remembers Brook Byers, a partner with what is now Kleiner Perkins Caufield & Byers.

Swanson started nosing around at the University of California–San Francisco campus and ran across the work of Drs. Herb Boyer and Stan Cohen.

Boyer, a biochemist based at the University of California at San Francisco, collaborated with Cohen at Stanford, building on years of research conducted in many labs, to create the first example of deliberate genetic engineering. The two met at a 1972 conference in Hawaii, where Cohen heard Boyer's present on using "molecular scissors" to cut out genes and splice them into another organism's DNA. Boyer's approach was simpler than the methods previously used, making the potential for applications much broader.

The two researchers met in a Waikiki Beach deli and emerged with a plan to use a Boyer-discovered enzyme and Cohen's genetic delivery device, termed a *plasmid*, to cut and paste a gene from one organism into another, in order to read the gene and make a needed protein. By mid-1973, the collaborators had created a "recombinant" strain of *E. coli*, a common bacterium, that kept dividing and reading out a gene that originally came from toads.

"Recombinant DNA technologies" are genetic engineering procedures used to join together DNA segments from different origins in an environment outside a cell or organism. It's a technique perfected by Cohen and Boyer and used as a basis for much of the scientific progress that biotechnology has made in cloning cells and drug production.

Niels Reimers, head of Stanford University's technology licensing group, convinced the scientists to apply for patents covering this recombinant technology.

Long before the patent showed up in the outside world, the first scientific publications emerged from the labs of Cohen and Boyer onto the pages of the November 1973 issue of the *Proceedings of the National Academy of Sciences.* That paper caught the attention of Bob Swanson, who was looking for a better way to build a company.

Swanson picked up the phone and called Boyer, and they ended up meeting for a beer at Churchill's, a Bay-area bar on Masonic at Geary Street. Based on that conversation, Boyer and Swanson formed a partnership in January 1976 to create a business plan for Genentech (short for *genetic engineering technology*). This first meeting is immortalized in bronze in front of the main Genentech research building in South San Francisco.

About that same time, Brook Byers was working for Asset Management, a venture firm based in Palo Alto, California. Byers, an electrical engineer and physics major out of Georgia Tech, liked working with Asset's founding partner, Pitch Johnson, but wanted to live in San Francisco. "At the time," says Byers, "there were only about a dozen young associates working with the venture funds in the area. We all knew each other. I moved in with Bob Swanson in a place on Broadway at Fillmore, with a view of the Golden Gate Bridge."

Although the two spent some of their free time double-dating, the rest was spent talking, reading, and thinking about biotechnology. "Bob was definitely way out there ahead of everybody. He started writing the business plan for Genentech around then, which he had me proofreading."

That business plan must have been compelling. Swanson left his current job at Kleiner & Perkins to start Genentech. Boyer converted $500 cash and a half interest in their partnership into what became 1 million shares each prior to the 1980 initial public offering (a 14.3% stake each). Deciding to change its original bet and follow its junior partner, Kleiner & Perkins sold its stake in Cetus and invested $100,000 in Swanson and Boyer's venture.

Swanson was fiscally conservative and incredibly innovative from the beginning. He started Genentech as a virtual company out of the K&P offices, and put together the first contract research deal with an academic group that gave the biotech company product rights. According to Byers, the concept of using venture funding to generate what is known as the "proof of concept" data—experimental results supporting the founders' belief that their technology will work—originated with Swanson's arrangement to have the initial experiments carried out in the labs of Herb Boyer at the University of California at San Francisco (UCSF) and Keichi Itakura and Art Riggs at City of Hope National Medical Center in Duarte, California.

Swanson had some help putting together those contract research agreements. Through the network, he had been introduced to Tom Kiley, a law partner at Lyon & Lyon, a law firm specializing in intellectual property law. Kiley was not your stereotype lawyer, which probably explains his willingness to work with an impoverished start-up in an unproven area.

Says Kiley, "I represented all kinds of clients, including Ms. Nude USA, who was being sued for trademark infringement by Miss USA, as well as George Zweig at Cal Tech—one of the guys who discovered the quark. I liked Bob and was intrigued by the idea of biotech. Bob didn't have a lot of money, so I tried to stretch cash by sleeping on his couch while other clients put me up at the Stanford Court and the Fairmont."

The proof-of-concept work was not all smooth sailing, as Kiley remembers. "When the gene got assembled for somatostatin and was hooked up to express, they got nothing! No protein got expressed. The anxiety level was so high that Bob checked himself into the hospital. But then it turned out they had to protect the expressed protein from proteolytic degradation. The team used another protein to protect the somatostatin—and it worked!"

Ironically, scientists Riggs and Itakura had tried to get federal funding for the work, but the reviewers doubted they could do it in the 3-year grant time frame and also doubted the scientific merit. Genentech funding did it in 9 months, and Philip Handler, President of the National Academy of Science, called it a scientific triumph of the first order.

When this first project showed that in fact genetic engineering could induce microbes to make foreign proteins, the founders and their financial backers moved the company into its own labs in a South San Francisco warehouse—proclaimed "The Industrial City" in huge cement letters emblazoned on the San Bruno mountains nearby.

Swanson found Genentech's new home through his roommate, Byers. "I had a friend in the real estate business with Cabot Cabot &

Forbes. They had an empty warehouse in South San Francisco, and I convinced him to put in some tenant improvements."

That favor paid off for Byers, also. Through helping Genentech, Brook Byers got to know Tom Perkins and Eugene Kleiner and co-invested in Tandem Computer with them. In 1977, Byers was invited to join K&P as a full partner—a major kudo. Kleiner Perkins Caufield & Byers, and especially Byers, went on to become one of the leading VC (venture capital) firms in the emerging biotech industry.

LIFE IN A START-UP

Little was done to disguise the original use of Genentech's first building—fancy decor and lots of glass would have to wait for product revenues. The sole source of food in-house was a vending machine. Working at Genentech in those early days was a lot like being in academic labs—it was not uncommon to work 7 days a week, 12 or more hours a day. Almost all of the scientists were right out of academia, with no industry experience. We were all driven by the science and the sense that what we did could make a profound difference to patients.

I still remember the in-house seminar in the early 1980s where the head of clinical development for Activase, Genentech's innovative heart attack drug, showed some of the first images of blocked blood vessels opening up after treatment. The message came through loud and clear—Genentech's research was keeping people alive, people who otherwise might have died. That was an incredible impetus.

Another huge motivator was the guy at the top of the organization, Bob Swanson. Many of us working at the bench late at night would look up and find Swanson striding in the lab door. He knew our names, knew what project we were working on, listened attentively to our descriptions of project status, and asked smart questions. That strong sense that the guy at the top knew and appreciated what we were doing kept the labs lit up far into the night.

Swanson had set up a company that focused on results. He allowed huge freedom for researchers to set their own hours and encouraged the staff to play as hard as it worked. Visitors would frequently be subjected to *Star Trek* scenarios coming over the PA system in the evenings and had to watch out for quarter-pitching contests in the halls. The managing director of German-based Bayer, in town to negotiate product rights, found himself subjected to a weird-out duel

between scientists "Wild" Bill Holmes and Mark Matteuchi that led
to their standing in the cafeteria line, Holmes dressed in his girl-
friend's wraparound skirt and Matteuchi with half his beard and mus-
tache shaved off—the rest still in place. The Japanese business
development contingent got to catch Holmes dressed as Christ and
dragging a cross down the hall, whipped on by Matteuchi dressed as a
centurion. Somehow, both groups got over their concern about the
mental status of these scientists and signed up for hefty corporate alliances with Genentech.

Friday "Ho-Hos" were a companywide carousing, hosted by different groups within the company and often with a theme. Although
Swanson was never seen during business hours without his carefully
tailored shirt and tie, there are those who would kill for a copy of the
tape of him dressed in a grass skirt and singing "The Duke of Earl"
with the Genentech rock band.

To understand the environment within entrepreneurial companies,
whether high-tech, biotech, or no-tech at all, look to the leaders.
Their attitude is what shapes the corporate culture. Bob Swanson sin-
gle-handedly drove Genentech into existence, coupling strong business instincts with a love of the science and a willingness to step off
the usual CEO pedestal to do whatever it took to keep the company
moving forward.

Another biotech entrepreneur, Dr. Jan Le Cocq, put the glamour
into perspective during a phone conversation during the early days at
Icos Corp. (Bothell, Washington). Le Cocq started out as one of the
early biotech investment bankers, then joined Amgen president
George Rathmann as CFO in his first post-Amgen venture, Icos, before heading up her own biotech start-up, Gryphon. "You go from
the sublime to the ridiculous in a start-up. Everyone has to wear
many hats, because there are never enough people. Today I went from
a board meeting where we discussed crucial strategy, then back to my
office to make the decision about what plants to have in the lobby. It
sounds crazy, but someone had to make the decision—and that someone was me."

During the late 1980s, venture capitalists began sponsoring gray-
haired senior managers from big pharma to run biotech firms instead
of enlisting executives with science backgrounds. Their idea was to
jump-start the management team with decades of experience, strong
industry networks, and résumés that looked really good in offering
memoranda.

The downside of this strategy quickly became clear—many of these CEOs had been spoiled by their years in the big leagues. They found it difficult to function in an environment that lacked the perks—secretaries who took dictation, hordes of minions, big travel budgets. These execs had never had to deal with raising money, working with the press, negotiating with bigger and stronger corporate partners, or handling concerned shareholders—some of the most important relationships for any biotech company. In most cases, their previous firms had entire departments of people dedicated to keeping Wall Street, reporters, and shareholders far away. And of course, their big pharma firms were always in the driver's seat when it came to deal making.

Says Jim Gower, former Genentecher and two-time biotech start-up CEO, "Biotech execs need to be able to do whatever it takes. I remember when Bob Swanson was touring some Japanese businessmen through the Genentech halls. In the midst of discussing some high-level project, he stopped to fix a leaky sink and never dropped a beat in the conversation."

This same entrepreneurial drive was seen in many of the other young biotech firms around the United States. But Genentech was always something special, and always the leader.

THE GENENTECH IPO

The biotech world changed October 14, 1980, when Blyth Eastman Paine Webber and San Francisco boutique bank Hambrecht & Quist took Genentech Inc. public.

Although Cetus had been founded before Genentech, the South San Francisco company was really the first to focus all of its attention on using the tools of the new biology to create products. Essentially, Genentech was the first biotechnology company to successfully scale up protein manufacturing from small quantities used for research to the much larger quantities needed for clinical trials and marketing. All of the general press focus on Genentech's interferon and its cancer-fighting properties created a fertile ground for this new offering. *Time* magazine, *Forbes*, and *The Saturday Evening Post* all proclaimed interferon the hottest thing going on in cancer research.

At the time, none of the players would have predicted the incredible response that Genentech's IPO (initial public offering) would generate. Stephen Evans-Freke, one of biotech's most innovative financiers, remembers his first look at Genentech as an incredible "Aha!" experience.

"Sometime around 1978, Eugene Kleiner took Bud Coyle, the senior banker at PaineWebber, and myself, a lowly associate banker, to spend a day at Genentech. Back then, they had about 20 employees in a warehouse building. I had had no exposure to molecular biology before that, but after spending the morning, it was like light bulbs going off. I loved it, nothing could keep me away."

Evans-Freke found himself sitting in on the first discussions about an IPO for Genentech, where the bankers and the company management tried to come up with a market valuation for this new company. "At the pricing meeting, Swanson was told he could price the shares at $40. He said, 'Let's leave something on the table for the investors,' not realizing just how much he was leaving. None of us had the faintest idea that the offering would be as hot as it was."

The two banks and Genentech management closed the offering book with 1 million shares at $35 each—an incredible amount for a company with no products on the horizon until 1984 (insulin), a brand-new technology, and so many potential pitfalls that the front cover of the offering memorandum is emblazoned with "HIGH DEGREE OF RISK"!

Pharmaceutical industry analysts who were used to basing market valuation estimates on rational things like projected sales and earnings were completely trampled by the market. Wildly enthusiastic investors ran the stock all the way up to $89 per share within 20 minutes of free trading through the market makers—a record for an IPO. The stock closed out its first day at $70 per share—more than doubling Genentech's market capitalization in 24 hours as a publicly traded company.

This amazing IPO opened the floodgates, convincing other little biotech start-ups that big money was in the offing. From the perspective of Genentech, the day's activities suggested that the company had left a lot of money on the table by pricing its IPO stock at $35. The companies that followed right after didn't make the same mistake.

Senior Lehman Brothers banker Fred Frank remembers getting a call in 1973 or 1974 from Alejandro Zaffaroni, who then was involved with Cetus. "They were thinking about taking Cetus public, with its eight staff scientists. I said it was totally absurd, a big mistake for many reasons, but the call got me interested in what they were up to. I learned a lot about the people and the science and began to see biotech as the future. Biotech created a whole new corporate universe—it was quite fabulous!"

TABLE 2.1 Biotech's First Generation

Company	Date of IPO	Gross Amount Raised
Genentech (now part of Roche Holding)	10/80	$35M
Cetus (now part of Chiron)	3/81	$107M
Genetic Systems	4/81	$6M
Ribi Immunochem (now part of Corixa)	5/81	$1.8M
Genome Therapeutics (formerly Collaborative Therapeutics)	5/82	$12.9M
Centocor	12/82	$21M
Bio-Technology General	9/83	$8.9M
Scios (formerly California Biotechnology)	1/83	$12M
Immunex	3/83	$16.5M
Amgen	6/83	$42.3M
Biogen	6/83	$57.5M
Chiron	8/83	$17M
Immunomedics	11/83	$2.5M
Repligen	4/86	$17.5M
OSI (formerly Oncogene Sciences)	4/86	$13.8M
Cytogen	6/86	$35.6M
Xoma	6/86	$32M
Genzyme	6/86	$28M
ImClone	6/86	$32M
Genetics Institute (now owned by American Home Products)	5/86	$79M

Genentech's rocket ride IPO changed Frank's mind about the viability of biotech IPOs. The market gave a clear indication that it was willing to place a high value on this totally untried company, lacking products and at least a decade away from product revenues. (A clear echo of this phenomenon can be seen in Internet stocks of the late 1990s.)

Says Frank, "I called Cetus that day, and we raised $120 million instead of $35 million." Amgen made it out the door in June 1983 and added $39.55 million to its coffers.

In classic Genentech overachiever mode, the company managed to outdo its biotech brethren by doing a second IPO in July 1999 after Roche Holding (Switzerland) bought all outstanding Genentech shares in June 1999 at $82.50 a share and then spun out 17% back to investors. The July 1999 IPO opened at an astounding $97 a share and raised $1.94 billion for Roche. That was the third-biggest stock offering of 1999—behind only Goldman Sachs ($3.7 billion) and the Pepsi Bottling Group launch ($2.3 billion).

Genentech's big splash did more than excite investors. It drew the attention of science and business entrepreneurs who were looking for something innovative to sink their teeth in. One of those heeding the siren call was Stelios Papadopoulos, Ph.D., now Managing Director and Head of Health Science Investment at PaineWebber. Papadopoulos went on to become one of the top bankers in biotech, along with Evans-Freke and Frank.

"It really started for me in 1980 with the Genentech IPO. I was a physicist doing structural biology. When I came into the lab and saw the article about the Genentech IPO, I got a feeling it was a big thing. If I wanted to get out of the lab and do something more business-like, maybe this was the way to do it! That IPO may be the second most important event for biotech, following the Cohen-Boyer invention of genetic engineering. It showed that you could actually finance this business in the public markets."

THE GENENTECH TEAM:
ACADEMICS AND CORPORATE MAVERICKS

The scientific team was built around a strong core of molecular biologists and organic chemists, led by Genentech's first full-time employee (in early 1978) and übercloner, David Goeddel. The company became populated with great scientists in the entire range of disciplines needed to encompass drug discovery and development. But Goeddel remained the key driving force for the molecular biology component until 1991, when he left to start a new company, Tularik.

Meanwhile, Swanson's business background was paying off in the form of a nucleus of executives focused on making Genentech a financial success, not just a scientific winner. He recruited executives who were just as fired up about building a new kind of company as the scientists were. The first members of the team were Tom Kiley, enticed onboard in 1979 as VP and general counsel; Robert Byrnes, VP for marketing; and Fred Middleton, VP for finance and administration and CFO.

Kiley, as introduced above, had come from the law firm Lyon & Lyon. Byrnes had been VP for marketing and sales at the McGaw Division of American Hospital Supply (a lab that provided several key execs to the biotech world) and had worked at Abbott and Eli Lilly & Co. Middleton and was a former McKinsey consultant before moving to Genentech. Jim Gower, former senior vice president at Genentech, was one of the early managers recruited into the young biotech firm, joining in February 1981. Gower had taken over Bob Byrnes's position at American Hospital Supply when Byrnes left for the risky start-up. He was intrigued with Byrnes's tales about the new world of biotech, but he, too, thought it was nuts to try to start a new pharmaceutical company.

In spite of his doubts, Gower decided to give it a shot. "I was 32 and wanted to build companies. I had come out to visit with the Genentech scientists and really thought they were onto something cool. The atmosphere was invigorating, refreshing compared to big pharma."

Another of the important team members was Patricia McGrath, who helped pull together the nuts and bolts of the financial operation at Genentech. McGrath had moved from accounting giant Peat Marwick to a small computer company in Silicon Valley, Logical Machine Corp., first as controller and then at its Byte subsidiary. Byte was the first company to build a business around retail computer stores, and it was an uphill battle. Pat spent a lot of time with Shirley Clayton, Logical's loan officer at Bank of America—who also was loan officer for another struggling start-up: Genentech. Clayton knew McGrath might be in the market for a new job, based on Logical's cash problems. Clayton also knew that Genentech's CFO, Fred Middleton, could use some help.

McGrath got talked into making the switch to biotech in 1979, when Genentech had about 20 employees. Her first task was putting in the infrastructure for a finance department—paying the bills, keeping track of the budgets (a new concept for most of the scientists at the time).

Gower remembers the early business meetings as pretty chaotic. "We had lots of ideas of where the company could go, but it was hard to make cohesive plans at first."

But the team finally coalesced. Says Gower, "It was a case of having enough people willing to forgo preconceived notions. The key was that Bob hired very strong people. There was nobody who was uncomfortable expressing opinions and arguing with Bob. Swanson hired people who were strong, and he listened to them. It was just hard to convince him. Genentech in the early days was all academics and corporate mavericks—people who succeeded in spite of themselves."

A New Approach to Business Strategy

One of the early challenges for Genentech and its first-generation brethren was focusing on a successful business strategy. Many of the early biotech firms were so excited about all the potential applications of this new technology that they were trying to go after everything at once—human health care, animal health care, agricultural uses, and industrial chemical programs.

This was in part a bid to reduce the high risk of developing human pharmaceuticals. Between the risk of the new technology and concerns about how the FDA (Food and Drug Administration) would react to these new drugs, many company execs and investors were looking for a quicker, less risky path to product revenues. Agriculture and industrial applications were seen as faster, cheaper routes because of the perceived lack of regulatory agency interference and the avoidance of the time- and dollar-consuming clinical trial process.

Not surprisingly, this nonfocused strategy did not work for anyone, and most companies backed away from the "do everything" approach by the late 1980s. But many of the first-generation biotech companies, including Chiron, Cetus, and Allelix, tried to encompass a broad range of programs. Even today's industry leader, Amgen, had a business plan that initially included chicken and pig growth hormone, specialty chemicals, and my personal favorite—indigo dye.

A look at the 1981 Genentech annual report reflects Swanson's interest in building three businesses: industrial chemicals (improved enzymes for food processing and production of organic chemicals, engineered microbes for producing specialty chemicals) and animal health (pig growth hormone and cow interferon), along with human health care.

Says PaineWebber's Papadopoulos, "Initially, Genentech wanted to address all the needs of the world. It had its 1982 GenenCor joint venture with Corning Inc. working on food processing and other industrial enzymes (bought by a joint venture between Eastman Kodak and Cultor Ltd. in 1990), its HP-GenenChem instrumentation venture with Hewlett Packard (since disappeared), and the ever-popular cow interferon program. Amgen and the others were just as bad. Thank God they all shed that stuff and focused on drugs."

In a top-level meeting at the Silverado resort in Napa, California, Gower and his business colleague Gary Steele went through the rationale for each of the projects. They pointed out that in fact it re-

quired the same amount of resources to get any of these programs going, so it would be smarter to aim for those with the best return potential for Genentech. "Chemicals are a commodity business;
agriculture and veterinary products are a bit better, especially products for companion animals, but pharmaceuticals win hands down for
return on your investment. It wasn't until after 1983 that Genentech
focused exclusively on human health."

Papadopoulos agreed with this analysis. "In the early to mid-80s, it
became clear that the only meaningful game was pharmaceuticals.
Most companies abandoned their chemicals, industrial applications,
and ag/vet businesses. Ironically, agricultural biotech is coming back
in the late 1990s with massive funding and acquisitions by the large ag
chemical and seed firms, but the technology has been developed
enough to offer something valuable now."

Gower and his colleagues also pushed for a change in business development strategy. In 1978, Genentech had sold worldwide rights to its
recombinant human insulin to Eli Lilly & Co. and had sold all rights to
its human growth hormone to AB Kabi, then the world's largest sup-
plier of cadaver-derived growth hormone. Hoffmann-La Roche
bought the marketing rights to Genentech's interferons in 1980. Lilly
received FDA approval to market Genentech's insulin—the very first
biotech therapeutics to reach the marketplace—in late 1982.

These deals were important to the young biotech company in two
key ways. First, having respected big pharma players pay for marketing rights to Genentech products gave potential investors some confidence that the technology was real and valuable. Second, the deals
gave Genentech cash to support its growth. Swanson was able to
show net income in 1979, 1980, and 1981—pretty impressive for a
young biotech firm, and immeasurably comforting for shareholders.

Making these corporate deals was not always simple. In the 1980s,
most of big pharma hadn't yet bought into the idea that biotech could
deliver marketable products. Eli Lilly & Co. was the first pharmaceutical leader to grasp the importance of the biotech product revolution.
It was used to working with protein products, thanks to its insulin
business, and understood the vagaries of product development for biologics as well as the more conventional small molecules. But the fact
that big drug companies lacked awareness of biotech's potential wasn't
always negative.

Says Papadopoulos, "In many ways, the most important thing for
biotech in the '80s was that big pharma didn't wake up. Its series of

denials of the value of the technology were essential for the biotech industry getting enough time to mature. Risk capital became available to support the companies, and big pharma allowed it to happen passively." Eli Lilly, Roche, and Schering-Plough were the only big pharma companies to really place major bets on biotech products, partnering with Genentech for insulin (Lilly) and interferon (Roche) and with Biogen for alpha interferon (Schering-Plough).

"At first, big pharma argued that the science just wouldn't work," points out Papadopoulos. "Then insulin was approved in 1982, so clearly the science worked. Then they said it was impossible to manufacture these protein drugs in a commercially feasible manner, but the biotech firms solved those problems. Next they argued through the mid-1980s about patentability of recombinant versions of naturally occurring proteins—but the U.S. Patent Office came through. Big pharma argued that injectable drugs couldn't be the basis of a big business, because the market was limited. But Amgen's huge market capitalization is based on two injectable drugs, Epogen and Neupogen. The final argument was that biotech companies could never market drugs as well as big pharma. But by October 1985, Genentech was marketing human growth hormone [HGH], having recruited 75 sales reps from big pharma companies. HGH was approved Friday, October 19, and on Monday these guys showed up at work. They were the first sales reps with laptop computers."

Papadopoulos remembers, "In March 1987, when Eli Lilly launched its version of growth hormone, everyone expected Genentech to buckle. But it didn't happen—Genentech is outselling them still."

Other biotech players have shown that same ability to play with the big boys and win. For example, Agouron Pharmaceuticals got approval for its AIDS drug, Viracept, in December 1997. Viracept was the fourth entrant in its drug category, marginally better than the products that proceeded it from Merck, Abbott, and Roche. Even though Agouron had never sold a product before and had to build its sales force from scratch, the company became the market leader in volume and dollars in less than 2 years.

Big pharma assumed that once the biotech companies got into small-molecule drugs, big pharma's powerful in-house medicinal chemistry programs would allow it to take over. But again, biotech hired the best talent away from big pharma and set up its own in-house groups.

According to Papadopoulos, "Basically, the denials of big pharma throughout the '80s allowed the biotech evolution to happen. If big pharma had had half a brain, there never would have been a biotech industry."

DEAL EVOLUTION

Essentially all of the corporate partnering deals of the '80s involved replacement proteins—using genetic engineering to make recombinant versions of proteins normally made by the body. It was only in the 1990s that broad-based technology deals became commonplace.

Ironically, the more actual data there were, the harder it was to partner a project. Remembers Gower, "Selling gamma interferon was easy, but selling TPA (Activase, for heart attacks) was harder because more was known about it. We hadn't even cloned gamma when we did the deal. Everyone thought it would be a miracle cure for cancer, and there were no data to refute that because there were not much data." Many of the animal studies published by other groups turned out to have been generated by impure mixtures of proteins.

With that first interferon project, "Big pharma was skeptical of whether we could even clone the protein," says Gower. "So we set up the deal with benchmarks—they paid as we made progress. Other biotech companies originally asked partners for reimbursement of expenditures. Genentech was the first to ask for an upfront licensing fee and benchmarks for payments—if we don't hit them, you don't have to pay us."

By end of the 1980s, people were focusing their interest away from molecular biology techniques and onto actual products created by those techniques. "In the early '80s, most of the folks running big pharma were medicinal chemists who didn't believe that biotech had any practical role in pharmaceuticals. They didn't believe in proteins as profitable drugs, or in molecular biology as a tool to make drug targets. They wanted to work on targets isolated from human tissues," says Gower.

Even once big pharma saw the approach as valuable, they didn't always bring in the best talent to create that capability in-house. With each ensuing technical glitch, there was greater resistance to the technology. The complex biological gamishes researchers worked with meant it was not uncommon to reach the conclusion of a long project thinking you had cloned an important therapeutic protein, only to find that you had actually cloned one of the most common proteins in the blood.

You can't actually see proteins when you are trying to isolate them. Rather, you use biochemistry tricks to try to separate the protein you want from the other molecules that make up the vast majority of the sample by size, electrical charge, and other biochemical characteristics. Every now and then, nasty surprises show up. According to Gower, one pharmaceutical lab got into a fight with Genentech over who had cloned urokinase, an important enzyme, only to find to their chagrin that they had in fact created something entirely different.

While big drug makers were contemplating dipping their big toe into genetic engineering, Genentech and its fellow biotech upstarts put that time to good use. Many of biotech's scientific leaders were recruited from academia, lured by the chance to do academic-style research in an entrepreneurial biotech setting. Says Gower, "I thought Genentech's science lead would last maybe a few years, but it lasted all decade! That allowed us to build the industry in that decade. It was much harder for big pharma to build the right group in-house."

In spite of the value of corporate partners, Gower and others were convinced that it was time for Genentech to make the switch from being an R&D boutique to being a real pharma company—which meant selling drugs. Genentech retrieved the U.S. marketing rights to human growth hormone in 1983, obtained FDA approval in late 1985, and saw revenues eventually reach $214 million by 1998—the company's top revenue producer to date. The company has followed up with Activase, a successful heart attack drug; Pulmozyme, to block the serious lung infections suffered by cystic fibrosis patients; and Herceptin, a monoclonal antibody that attacks aggressive forms of breast cancer.

Even today, most biotech companies follow this same path of evolution: beginning as a R&D house, using partners for late-stage clinical development and marketing, then retaining more rights with the next product, and finally retaining all manufacturing and marketing rights. This phase is essential. The public markets have provided a huge boost in market cap to biotech companies that are able to progress to selling their own products.

TABLE 2.2   Selected Genentech Milestones

1976
Robert Swanson and Dr. Herbert Boyer founded Genentech.

1977
Genentech produced the first human protein (somatostatin) in a microorganism (*E. coli* bacteria).

1978
Genentech became the first true biotech company to go public. The market response was unprecedented—the company raised $35 million and saw its shares leap from $35 a share to a high of $88 after less than an hour on the market.

1982
First recombinant DNA drug hit the market: human insulin (licensed to Eli Lilly Co.).

1984
First laboratory production of recombinant Factor VIII, the blood-clotting factor needed by many hemophiliacs. It allowed patients to get the needed protein without blood transfustions—which were a source of HIV contamination. Genentech licensed Factor VIII to Bayer.

1985
Genentech's first drug, Protropin® (growth hormone), became the first recombinant pharmaceutical product to be manufactured and marketed by a biotechnology company.

1987
Genentech brought its second product to market—Activase®, a recombinant tissue-plasminogen activator (TPA), to treat heart attack patients.

1988
Genentech and Roche Holding Ltd. of Basel, Switzerland, completed a $2.1-billion merger. (Actually, Roche bought about 65%, didn't buy the rest until mid-1999, and then turned around and resold a big chunk on the stock market—made a couple of billion bucks!)

Genentech's hepatitis B vaccine—licensed to SmithKline Beecham Biologicals S.A.—received FDA approval.

1993
Pulmozyme®, recombinant human DNAse, approved to treat cystic fibrosis.

Genentech's bovine growth hormone—licensed to Monsanto Corporation and distributed under the name Posilac—got FDA approval.

1995
Activase approved to treat acute ischemic stroke or brain attack.

(continues)

TABLE 2.2   Selected Genentech Milestones *(continued)*

1997

Genentech and partner IDEC Pharmaceuticals launched Rituxan® for non-Hodgkins lymphoma. This was the first genetically engineered monoclonal antibody approved to treat cancer. Rituxan is aimed at a protein found on the surface of these cancer cells and thus avoids the toxic side effects of conventional cancer treatments.

Genentech entered into agreements with Alteon, Inc., for the continued development and marketing of Pimagedine, an advanced glycosylation end-produce (AGE) formation inhibitor in Phase III clinical trials to treat kidney disease in diabetic patients. The agreements also include rights to second-generation AGE formation inhibitors, in pre-clinical development.

Genentech collaborated with LeukoSite, Inc., on the development and commercialization of LeukoSite's LDP-02, a monoclonal antibody to treat inflammatory bowel diseases.

1998

Genentech marketed Herceptin®, a recombinant monoclonal antibody, to treat patients with metastatic breast cancer. This product is aimed at a protein, the Her2/neu receptor, expressed only on certain cancer cells, and thus avoids the toxic side effects of conventional cancer treatments.

3

THE AMGEN STORY

Today, Amgen Corporation of Thousand Oaks, California, is the top biotech company in the world, with annual revenues topping $2.7 billion, three products on the market, and more than 5,000 employees. But Amgen was a latecomer to the biotech party. Its genesis is found in the frustration of another early Cetus Corporation board member, Bill Bowes.

In the early 1970s, Bill Bowes was an investment banker for Blythe & Co. (which later merged with PaineWebber and took Genentech public). Bowes was enamored of the innovative technology emerging from the growth companies of Silicon Valley and helped bring early-comers such as Ampex, Memorex, and Hewlett-Packard public. That enthusiasm for technology was part of what hooked him on biotech when he was asked to sit on the board of Cetus Corporation.

"My boss had raised some seed money for Cetus and asked me to join their board in 1972 or 1973. I became progressively more unhappy there. I thought they weren't recruiting great scientists and were too busy doing deals with big oil and big booze who were hoping biotech would yield cheaper manufacturing methods. I finally left their board the summer of 1978. I figured there was a right way to do biotechnology, and I intended to find it."

Bowes waited about a year, then started to poke around Bay area academic centers in the summer of 1979, looking for leading scientists who were not yet affiliated. When he reached Stanford, an introduction from fellow venture capitalist Sam Wohlstadter eventually led him to Dr. Winston Salser, an entrepreneurial scientist from UCLA who pieced together Amgen's scientific advisory board.

A scientific advisory board (SAB) is made up of the individuals who supply the initial scientific and business expertise and eventually take some role in running the company. Amgen's SAB included top researchers in molecular and cell biology, immunology, protein biochemistry, and organic chemistry. One of the early members was Dr. Leroy Hood, who went on to cofound Applied Biosystems and who is now William Gates Professor and chair of the Department of Molecular Biology and head of the Institute for Quantitative Systems Biology at the University of Washington in Seattle. Amgen was built in Thousand Oaks, California, close to its SAB members at UCLA, UC-Santa Barbara, and California Institute of Technology. The clean air and relatively cheap housing was also a drawing card for the young scientists whom the founders hoped to lure to Amgen.

While Salser was building the SAB, Bowes was building the initial investor team. This group included GC&H Investments—the investment fund of Bowes's favorite Silicon Valley law firm, Cooley Godward, along with fellow VCs Sam Wohlstadter, Moshe Alafi (cofounder of Cetus and Biogen, who had also lost faith in the Cetus team), and Franklin "Pitch" Johnson, who was a former Harvard classmate and friend of Bowes. Other seed investors were Donald R. Longman and Raymond F. Baddour, chairman of the chemical engineering department at MIT. This group along with the founding team of George Rathmann, Winston Salser, and Joseph Rubinfeld, contributed about $81,000 in seed financing plus a loan of $75,667 (paid back by the company).

The next critical ingredient in building Amgen was locating the right CEO. Right about then George Rathmann came into town to do some work for Abbott Laboratories.

In the mid-1970s, Dr. George Rathmann, division VP of R&D at Abbott, found himself increasingly intrigued by the new molecular biology techniques starting to show up in the young biotech companies. He began exploring the potential for partnering with companies like Cetus and Genentech to bring the science into Abbott. He'd first heard about biotech in the late 1970s when his cardiovascular product manager, Dr. Phil Whitcome, had started talking about the exciting new gene-engineering technology being developed by his former professor, Winston Salser, at UCLA's Molecular Biology Institute.

Rathmann says, "Whitcome was a visionary about recombinant DNA—I was skeptical but decided to put it to the test. I was tired of finding FDA-mandated signs warning of toxic agents in our factory working on the hepatitis B program. So I decided we should be working with the hepatitis surface antigen to make diagnostic kits. A group at Abbott said the cost would be too great to synthesize the protein with genetic engineering, so I took a sabbatical in Salser's lab to learn about the technology."

Rathmann remembers trying to convince the Abbott board to invest in the biotech approach being perfected by Genentech. The board wasn't interested. Like many established companies, Abbott believed the cost of creating new drugs was too high, only fundable from an existing revenue stream. Nobody realized that they could raise enough independent capital to fund the development. Meanwhile, Amgen's venture investors were becoming concerned about who would run this company. They courted Rathmann. Convinced that Abbott would never develop the new technology as aggressively as he would like, he joined Amgen in October 1980.

Says Bowes, "It took 6 months to persuade Rathmann to leave Abbott and a great house on a lake, and to convince his wife, who hated California."

Rathmann suddenly found himself running a start-up. "I got to learn about the field, and to run a company doing it. It was the most exciting thing I ever did! With this concept of recombinant DNA, you could make any biological molecule in any other species—grow the other species up in reactors and make as much as you wanted. There was the possibility of making anything from plants, viruses, and so on."

Within 4 months, Rathmann and his founding investors closed a Series A $19-million private round—a huge amount at the time for a company with no revenues and no products even on the horizon. The round included $5 million from Rathmann's old employer, Abbott. Abbott's participation, according to Rathmann, was prompted by Abbott president Kirk Raab (who later joined Genentech as president). "It was the first time that a very conservative company had invested like that, which encouraged the VCs to follow right behind," says Rathmann. Other key participants in the round were Tosco, an oil-shale-refining company interested in microbial approaches to oil recovery, and Rothschild. U.S. Ventures (Bowes's newly formed venture fund) and Asset Management also invested another $720,000 in the Series A financing.

According to Rathmann, the large-scale need for insulin was the real motivator for big pharma to finally take this technology seriously. It was clear the supply of animal insulin would be depleted in the future. This presented a huge business opportunity for insulin production—even better if it was human insulin, because the animal version caused allergic reactions in diabetics.

"When interferon was cloned in 1980 and published in *C&E News* by Charles Weismann, it was clear that some complicated molecules could be made. Within 6 months, Genentech and others had the full interferon gene cloned. It was the first evidence that you could make very complex proteins with this approach. Interferon is about fourfold more complex than insulin, which is a small protein. As time went by and we figured out the manufacturing process, it all became less scary."

FUNDING AMGEN

Another important participant in this $19-million financing round was Jim Blair, representing the venture arm of Rothschild Inc. Blair, a Ph.D. in electrical engineering, came to Wall Street in late 1969 to work with Charlie Lea, at a merchant bank, F. S. Smithers. Smithers was small but very innovative. It had evolved from the family fund that seeded IBM back in 1914 and had invented bond trading.

Two years later, Lea moved to New Court Partners, a $40-million venture fund managed by the Rothschild family but funded by institutional investors like General Mills, AT&T's pension fund, and big insurance companies. This structure was almost unheard of in the late 1960s and early 1970s. Back then, the venture business was primarily a family-driven business—the Rockefellers, the Smitherses, the Whitneys, and so on, investing their family funds and managing those investments directly.

Part of the reason for the sudden shift in source of funds was two important changes in tax law and investment law. First, back in 1969, the tax laws were changed so that capital gains lost their special status and were taxed at the same rate as ordinary income. Says Blair, "This completely stalled new company formation, because there was no incentive to get into long-term investments." In 1978, Congress adopted a tax law that gave back the tax advantage to capital gains.

Another important event occurred in the late 1970s when the Department of Labor changed the rules that had previously made it illegal for pension funds to invest in venture funds. The idea was that it was far too risky a thing to do with innocent bystanders' money. Folks running the venture funds could be personally liable if any of the investments failed. Only wealthy families who were investing their own money could actively participate in these early venture activities.

By changing the law, the Department of Labor made it possible for the big institutional investors to participate in venture investing on behalf of their clients without fearing for their own financial future. This was truly the beginning of the current venture capital industry.

Blair points out, "It's amazing how people's behavior changes when you take punishment away!"

By 1978, the biotech market had started to take off, and Blair's colleagues raised another fund. As New Court gained a good reputation, it got a flow of deal opportunities coming in the door. One of those deals was Minneapolis-based Molecular Genetics. Remembers Blair, "We didn't know anything about that area; we were investing in companies like Cray Research, Federal Express. They told us it was a lot like Genentech. We said, 'What's Genentech?' We liked the novel approach, off the beaten path, but we didn't have the skills to evaluate the technology. There were no business people associated with the company—it was not clear how it would become a business."

Nonetheless, biotech would slowly but surely ooze into New Court's universe. Victor Rothschild, who came over to the States every quarter for board meetings, held a Ph.D. in biophysics, had done research at Royal Dutch Shell Group, and was a great friend of Sydney Brenner, one of the scientists creating this new world. Victor proposed adding a scientific advisory board to New Court that included Brenner to evaluate the science, and in 1980 Rothschild set about raising a UK fund to invest in the new area—just in time for Amgen.

Says Blair, "George Rathmann, Bill Bowes, and Pitch Johnson gave us a spellbinding presentation about how this new company, Amgen, would be able to raise all the money it needed to develop its first product, which would come out of one of six categories being pursued. They were raising $19 million and figured they needed to do two more rounds, one from a corporate partner and one from the public, to raise $60 million total and be off to the races. Abbott was contributing $5 million. I called Kirk Raab at Abbott and got great validation of the concept. So New Court committed to $3 million. We were the largest institutional investor in the company."

By the end of 1983, Blair and his colleagues were finding that they were pouring more and more of their time into active participation in the strategy and management of their portfolio companies. They also found themselves in the midst of a culture clash between the biotech entrepreneurs and Wall Street's pinstripes, who tended to have more of a passive "put your money on the table, move onto the next investment" approach.

Blair was convinced that active investment was crucial for smart biotech investing. "One of the early problems we found was a lack of good businesspeople in these companies. Even Rathmann was a scientist's idea of a businessman, and a businessman's idea of a scientist. The investment opportunities were so science-driven that the absence of business made it tough to support investing."

Blair started thinking about the kind of investment organization that would be most effective in this new biotech world. "I wanted partners with industrial skills sets in operations and scientific management, not investment skills." That desire became the genesis of Domain Associates. By mid-1985, Blair had pulled together a group of four partners who were managing the Rothschild asset funds and continued to raise U.S. institutional funds. Domain went on to become a dominant player in the biotech venture world—and remains so today. And Blair's support of Amgen—financial and strategic—continued to be important to the growth of that young company.

Rathmann used the first $19 million in funding to bring in the team that would run Amgen's R&D. Dr. Noel Stebbing, former biology director at G. D. Searle, was recruited away from his post as head of Genentech's biology department to become Amgen's VP of scientific affairs. The research director slot was filled by Dr. Dan Vapnek, a professor of genetics at the University of Georgia who did a sabbatical with Herb Boyer up in San Francisco. Gordon Binder left his post as VP of United Geophysical Corp. (subsidiary of Bendix Corp.) to become VP and chief financial officer—he eventually succeeded Rathmann as CEO.

Former Abbott employees were lured away to beef up the new company's management. Phil Whitcome, who had first introduced Rathmann to the joys of biotech, joined Amgen as manager of strategic planning (and later went on to found Neurogen Corp.). Robert Weist, former patent counsel and senior strategic planner at Abbott, came onboard as VP and general counsel.

From Rathmann's perspective, the downside of this awesome financing round was a stodgy board of directors stacked with investors and some big pharma reps. All the big guys were cranky about the concept of creating a new pharmaceutical company and wanted to stick with the R&D boutique idea.

TABLE 3.1   Amgen Product Development Programs (1983)

Human therapeutics:	Antivirals: • Consensus alpha interferon • Gamma interferon • Hepatitis B vaccine
	Cell growth regulators: • Erythropoietin (red cell growth factor) • Epidermal growth factor
Human diagnostics	• DNA-based assays • Immunoassays
Animal health care	Growth regulators: • Chicken growth hormone • Bovine growth hormone • Growth-hormone-releasing factors
	Vaccines: • Porcine parvovirus • Transmissible gastroenteritis virus
Specialty chemicals	Manipulation of gene clusters: • Indigo from glucose • Acetaminophen

Rathmann is pretty upfront about his confrontations with the investors on his board and his view of their shortsightedness. "For 3 years, I was barred from making statements at the board meetings about how Amgen should become a pharmaceutical company, about using Genentech as a model for anything, about being science-driven—the board wanted us to say 'market-driven'—and about this idea that the company had to pick one thing to focus on. My position is to keep the product portfolio broad. If you pick one thing as your best bet and it works, great! But if it doesn't work, you're dead!"

According to the Amgen IPO offering memorandum, Rathmann won that argument. The company chose four major markets—human therapeutics, human diagnostics, animal health care, and specialty chemicals—and went on to list 14 projects falling into all of these categories.

The list in Table 3.1 demonstrates some important realities of the biotech world. As mentioned, first-generation companies wanted to be all things to all markets. Today, you would never find a funded company this broadly spread.

But equally important is the lesson that science works in unexpected ways, taking you down unexpected pathways. Amgen and the other early biotech firms were sure that the immune system proteins would propel them into the big pharma realm. That turned out to be an unfounded hope. Interferons never did much for Amgen. Infergen, its consensus interferon, finally reached the market in October 1997 to treat chronic hepatitis C and hit $16 million in 1998 sales revenues. All of the animal health products and specialty chemicals disappeared from the annual reports. The big winners turned out to be EPO, Amgen's first blockbuster product—approved in June 1989 and generating 1998 sales of $1.4 billion—followed by Neupogen (not even identified when Amgen went public, approved in January 1991 and turning in 1998 sales of $1 billion).

Even the VCs wanted Amgen to focus. Jim Blair, then senior VP with Rothschild's venture group, joined the board in August 1981. Says Rathmann, "Jim kept saying, 'You need to focus—pick one program! We want you all [the different biotech companies in his portfolio] working on single goals, but different goals.' I said, 'Give us the $150 million we need to take a project all the way to the marketplace, and we'll focus.' Not surprisingly, Blair was unwilling to commit the funds."

Bill Bowes remembers, "In those days, everyone had their own ideas about where biotech could go. An early Amgen investor, Tosco, was an oil company that hoped for bugs to get oil out of shale cheaply. We went in every direction but used other people's money for all but therapeutics. Abbott paid for the diagnostics program, and specialty chemicals fell to Eastman Kodak and Tosco; some chicken company paid for chicken growth hormone. We cloned the firefly light source, luciferase. But nobody wanted to pay for it, so we dropped it."

A major reason for Rathmann's drive to diversify had to do with the incredible risk of drug development—something most of his board knew nothing about. Amgen, like most of its first-generation biotech buddies, thought that replacement proteins should have less development risk and require less development time. But even so, Rathmann knew that the only way to tell the successful drugs from the failures was to get them into the clinic, which costs vast sums of money.

Riding the Wall Street Roller Coaster

Genentech, Biogen, and Cetus were the visionary companies that set the example Amgen followed in the early days, says Rathmann. He especially admired Bob Swanson's ability to spend only $11 million between founding and the October 1980 IPO, while managing to complete the alpha interferon cloning project.

In pulling together the Amgen business plan, "We basically plagiarized the Genentech offering memorandum. We had more cash in hand than Genentech when we raised the $19 million, and their $35-million IPO seemed like a huge amount of cash. We were going to spread the $19 million over four years. Then Cetus raised $105 million the next spring. That completely changed our spending pattern."

The financing environment was hot enough that Rathmann got the board's okay to spend faster. In the fall of 1982, after being in business about one year, Amgen had cash in the bank to fund just one more year of activity. Lehman Brothers' top banker, Fred Frank, suggested that Amgen do one more private round of financing and get each investor to bring in $4 million each at 20% premium and raise another $19 million.

A good idea, says Rathmann, but "not one person on the job agreed to put in one penny or induce others to invest! We had very little to talk about that was different from the first round. We had not discovered much at that point: We had made gamma interferon using the published Genentech gene structure; the Epogen program had two people in it and was not yet successful."

The "potential relationship with a major company" touted in the IPO document was with Dow, which Rathmann says had a supply of urine, from the Italian army. Amgen's team had hoped to use this urine to generate a large supply of the natural protein EPO for generating gene sequence information to drive the cloning forward. But it turned out that healthy humans don't spill much EPO into the urine. Amgen's researchers had a supply problem.

"Amgen was in a race. We had an adviser on our scientific advisory board who had EPO from patients' urine stored in his fridge. Our folks worked on cloning from that. About six other companies were in there trying and failing to get the EPO gene sequence. Amgen's board and management thought we needed to stop the project because all the other companies couldn't get it—so it must be impossible. But the Amgen scientists kept going and were successful, and suddenly we were in the EPO business!" remembers Bowes.

There was a lot of coveting of urine in the 1980s at biotech companies. Many important proteins can end up in the urine. At one point, Genentech researchers semijokingly planned placing piles of sawdust

in corners at the weekly beer blasts to collect tissue plasminogen activator protein for the Activase project.

With products still in early development, past investors were recal-
citrant. Rathmann and his team decided to aim for corporate partners
to take up the slack. He had two-person teams heading to Japan and
Europe monthly. Unfortunately, the Japanese market was unwilling
to take a chance. And big pharma companies in the United States and
Europe did lots of tire kicking, but nobody was willing to send a
check. By December 1982, Amgen execs had visited all the potential
partners to no avail. The company was running out of money.

Finally, the team decided to go public. "We went to the board
about doing an IPO in the spring," says Rathmann. "They thought it
was nonsense to contemplate going public when we were nowhere
near the clinic with a product and had a lawsuit pending with Abbott."

The lawsuit had to do with Abbott's right of first negotiation in the
human health care arena, gained when it invested in the initial $19-
million round. Amgen had an interested potential partner, Jim Clark,
then at Allied Chemical, who was willing to pony up $19 million in
R&D funding over the next 5 years. Rathmann was having trouble
getting Abbott to start the 120-day clock so that he could talk with
Allied Chemical. "Abbott played hardball," says Rathmann. "We had
to resolve this before going public. We negotiated with Abbott to see
if they would be willing to follow Allied's deal, finished negotiations
in March, then filed the IPO based on an Abbott deal for $19 mil-
lion."

Amgen raised $43 million in June 1983 with the help of chicken
growth hormone, a diagnostic deal with Abbott, and underwriting by
Smith Barney, Dean Witter, and Montgomery Securities. The timing
was close—Amgen hit just as the financing window popped open and
then closed. Bio-Technology General, California Biotechnology (now
Scios), Immunex, and Biogen made it out while the market was hot,
and Amgen just squeaked through before the market's enthusiasm for
speculative stocks disappeared.

Once the financing window closes, almost nothing can pry it open.
Rathmann remembers that Bill Rutter, chairman of Chiron Corp., ac-
cused Amgen of closing the window and forcing Chiron to go with an
IPO that was half the size and half the price that the company had
planned for. The window wouldn't open again for biotech until 1986,
making for a long lean time.

Just as with the nasty down market in the late 1990s, the 1983–1986 market was not necessarily caused by any fundamental problems with the biotech companies. A huge number of computer and biotech firms had rushed into the receptive markets in early 1983, and frenzied investors got caught up in the race to generate vast short-term returns in stocks that by their very nature could not generate such returns. Shareholders' disappointment and lack of focus on company fundamentals led them to turn a cold shoulder on the entire technology group.

Amgen was not exempt from this death spiral. Remembers Rathmann, "We went out in a brief euphoria, had a hard sell in June at $18 a share. The first trade was at $16.50, and we were down to $9 within 3 months. People had signed on at the IPO because they expected a near-term uptick. When it didn't show up immediately, they unloaded the stock. Smith Barney placed the stock with investors who were bad biotech investors—they were 'flippers' hoping for a quick win and so dumped any stock if it started to drop."

Rathmann and his fellow biotech CEOs spent the rest of 1983 and the ensuing couple of years learning that their former financing smugness was false.

Within 18 months of the IPO, Amgen's stock went down to $3.75. That was a dark time for Amgen, with discussions flying fast and furious about how to hold on long enough for the products to come through. Other companies interested in acquiring Amgen's expertise for cheap came sniffing around, including a Swedish company, Fermenta AB.

"Fermenta got very interested in Amgen and wanted to take us over. It was a Swedish company run by an Egyptian who was putting together an industrial combine with help from the Swedish government and had bought Farmitalia. They also bought Tosco's Amgen stock and wanted to expand their position, but then their own company blew up."

Amgen's shareholders today should breath a sigh of relief that no takeover ever occurred. The stock price slowly recovered as the public markets became more receptive once again to small cap stocks and technology plays.

Meanwhile, Amgen was running out of cash again. By late 1985, Amgen had worked hard on structuring an R&D limited partnership but couldn't do it without decent stock performance to entice investors. Finally, by early 1986, the public markets were showing signs

TABLE 3.2   Amgen Revenues and Net Income

Year	Revenues	Net Income
1998	$2.7 billion	$863.2 million
1997	$2.4 billion	$644.3 million
1996	$2.2 billion	$679.8 million
1995	$1.9 billion	$537.7 million
1994	$1.6 billion	$319.7 million*
1993	$1.4 billion	$383.3 million
1992	$1.1 billion	$357.6 million

*Includes a one-time charge related to the Synergen acquisition.

of opening again. OSI and Repligen went public, and Amgen stock bounded up to a high of $15.50 a share.

That was a turning point for the company, says Rathmann. "We sold stock to SmithKline at a premium in exchange for a deal in porcine somatotropin, then sold 2.3 million shares at $15 a share in March 1986. By June, the stock price was up to $26, and we began to see clinical progress in the EPO project and in consensus and gamma interferon, hepatitis vaccine, and IL-2; we were in Phase III trials with Epogen by the end of 1986 and raised $75 million for the company at $34 a share in April 1987."

Today Amgen remains a biotech industry leader. With 5,500 employees worldwide, its three leading products currently are:

Epogen—the recombinant version of a human protein that stimulates the production of red blood cells and is used in the treatment of anemia associated with chronic renal failure for patients on dialysis.

Infergen—a bioengineered, non-naturally-occurring Type I interferon used in the treatment of chronic hepatitis C virus.

Neupogen—a recombinant human-granulocyte-colony-stimulating factor used to prevent infection in cancer patients undergoing certain types of chemotherapy and bone marrow transplants.

4

AN EXCEPTION TO EVERY RULE

Genzyme

While biotech was fighting to convince big pharma of its value in the late 1970s and early 1980s, another sector of the business, the plasma-processing industry, was taking a closer look at this new technology. These companies, which included Baxter and Cutter Laboratories, collected donated blood and isolated clinically useful proteins to re-sell. These proteins included life-saving blood-clotting factors for he-mophiliacs, antibodies for passive immunization, and albumin for surgery and trauma patients who had lost a lot of blood and needed to replace the missing volume.

Henri Termeer was head of the blood fractionation group at Baxter back then. His company was looking for new ways to produce those proteins already in its pipeline, to get away from human donors. Bax-ter had plasma pheresis centers throughout the world in major cities, but the company had concerns about the people who were willing to sell their blood on a regular basis. Hepatitis C had not yet been iden-tified, and HIV was just being discovered—both of these diseases, along with the known hepatitis strains, represented major threats to the safety of the blood supply. This concern was raising serious issues around using human tissues as sources for therapeutic proteins.

These safety concerns made biotech a perfect partner for the plasma fractionation companies. With recombinant technology, it would be possible to manufacture all of the blood proteins in a nice, sterilized fermenter, far away from dangerous viruses.

Termeer was evaluating potential biotech partners for Baxter when he started getting courted by the "headhunters" working for the young biotech industry. Experienced health care executives willing to take the leap into these untried companies were few and far between. Execs showing any sign of interest found themselves literally barraged with phone calls about potential jobs.

Genzyme Corp. in the Boston area won over Termeer in October 1983. His Baxter mindset had a powerful impact on Genzyme, which to this day is very different in structure from its biotech brethren.

Termeer liked Genzyme's initial business plan, which included access to immediate product revenues, and was impressed by the scientists who were involved. The company had been started by scientists from the New England Enzyme Center and had bought a small diagnostic enzyme company in the UK that had annual sales of about $1 million. It was a big change for Termeer. The fledgling company had only 11 employees, could pay him about half his Baxter salary, and moved him into a small office opposite Boston's infamous Combat Zone.

A new group of venture capitalists got involved with Genzyme just as Termeer was joining—including David Leathers of Rothschild's BIL fund and his adviser, Dr. Sidney Brenner of Cambridge University, along with Montgomery Securities' venture fund, Oak Ventures, and Advent's Boston office. The scientific advisors were very actively involved, meeting with Termeer each weekend to come up with Genzyme's business strategy.

Says Termeer, "We looked at the other companies and came up with a strategy that is still the underpinning of what Genzyme does now—a diversified business, a plan to try to get profitable as soon as possible, all financed through product sales or selling equity rather than through corporate partnerships. This would give us off-balance-sheet benefits and still avoid being dependent on other companies that might change their strategic plans. To this day, we still have no major partners."

When visitors came to tour Genzyme in the early days, the first thing they saw was the shipping department, not the labs. Termeer and his team set up a subsidiary that sold glycoproteins, cytokines, and other reagents for research use. The company made deals with Immunex, Biogen, and academic researchers to get access to their reagents. Termeer proudly points out, "That business sold last year for $65 million and was very profitable. The combination of participating in the market while trying to affect that market was powerful. We were participating in the enzyme diagnostics business while developing new sets of reagents to support new assays."

Genzyme has always been at the forefront of using novel financing methods and corporate structures coupled with judicious acquisitions to keep its engine running. One of the most interesting methods has been the company's use of "tracking stocks." This approach was first used by General Motors in 1984 and 1985 to create a class of shares linked to its Electronic Data Systems and Hughes Electronics subsidiaries. The objective of tracking stock is to allow investors to focus on the performance of a business or program within a larger organization, while it still remains part of the parent company for tax purposes.

Genzyme distributed tracking stocks for its Molecular Oncology, Surgical Products, and Tissue Repair divisions as tax-free dividends to its shareholders. These shares then began to trade independently. This approach let Genzyme find specific investors interested in specific parts of the business while retaining the technology and products within the parent company.

It's also a nice way to showcase new technology without exposing it to the nasty public markets during a down cycle. Because the shares are distributed to parties already knowledgeable about the parent company, they should also be somewhat up to speed on the new technology. Since they get it as a tax-free distribution, there is no urge to sell the stock off. And the creation of the new stock puts the new technology more firmly on the radar screen of Wall Street analysts, who perhaps missed it while it was buried inside the parent company.

It remains to be seen how well Genzyme's tracking-stocks method will do for shareholders, but other biotech companies have followed Genzyme's lead.

DOING IT DIFFERENTLY

Genzyme's first big leap of faith into the therapeutics arena was Ceredase—a replacement protein product to treat Gaucher's disease. Gaucher's disease is a genetic disease affecting a very small number of individuals—estimated at less than 10,000 total cases. The patients have genetic mutations that cause the loss of a key enzyme needed to break down molecules called *glycosphingolipids*. These weirdly named molecules are important components of cell membranes, especially in the nervous system. The mutation causes a buildup of the glycosphingolipids inside cells, damaging the cells and mucking up their ability to function properly. The kidney, liver, heart, and spleen are all damaged, and patients usually die within the first decade of life.

The small number of patients meant that big pharma was not interested in developing "orphan" products to treat this fatal disease. But Genzyme, with its expertise in enzymes, was confident that it could find a way to manufacture enough replacement enzyme to treat these patients.

Before the company developed the recombinant production process, the scientists had to extract the enzyme from its naturally occurring source—human tissue. It turns out that placenta has a high level of the enzyme, and so company scientists began driving around to hospitals to pick up placentas from the labor and delivery suites and lugged them up to the 15th floor in Boston's garment district.

Recalls Termeer, "It took a huge effort to get through the clinical trials—we had to collect 22,000 placentas to treat one Gaucher's patient for a year. We were able to do this through a partner. After World War II a company called Pasteur Merieux developed a way to make albumin from placenta fluid. They developed some brilliant manufacturing techniques, including some originating from the wine industry."

When concerns about viral contamination of products derived from human tissues arose, Pasteur stopped making albumin, and the plant was idle until Genzyme came along. Thanks to the hardy nature of the enzyme, the manufacturing process could include harsh treatments that removed any viral contamination without hurting the enzyme activity.

Very few groups thought Genzyme's approach could be commercially feasible. "The FDA thought we were out of our minds, but we got them onboard. Within 3 years of Ceredase's 1991 market launch, it was made obsolete with our rDNA version, Cerezyme," remembers Termeer. Meanwhile, Genzyme proved that a profitable business could be built around these so-called orphan drug indications. The company reported Ceredase/Cerezyme revenues of $126 million in 1993, which grew to $400 million in 1998.

Termeer sees Genzyme as the last of a rare breed—a successful, broadly diversified biotech company. He points out that even Chiron

Corp., which retained its strategy of going after therapeutics, vaccines, diagnostics, and ophthalmics, started focusing more in the late 1990s. But Genzyme continues with its diversified strategy, which includes:

- therapeutics for genetic diseases including Gaucher's, chronic kidney failure, blood-clotting disorders, thyroid disease, and multiple sclerosis
- a surgical product business that includes medical devices and gene/cell therapy programs aimed at cardiovascular disease
- a tissue repair business working on biological products for orthopedic injuries, severe burns, and chronic wounds
- a transgenic animal business that produces recombinant proteins and monoclonal antibodies for other companies
- a molecular oncology business focused on new therapeutic approaches for cancer
- a genetic testing business
- a diagnostic products business

It remains to be seen whether Genzyme will continue to use diversification successfully. But it certainly seems to be working now—the company ranks eighth in biotech market capitalization ($3.2 billion as of November 1999), with total sales in all divisions of $693 million. With nearly 600 products and services already on the market, Genzyme General has a solid, profitable revenue base. The division also has a broad research-and-development pipeline intended to maintain a high rate of earnings growth.

5

THE OTHER BIOTECH

Monoclonal Antibodies

Most of the biotech firms getting Wall Street's attention in the early 1980s were developing recombinant protein therapeutics. But there was another important technology being developed within the biotech universe—monoclonal antibodies.

Antibodies are proteins that are made by your immune system to recognize invading microbes and other bad elements, like tumor cells, and then stick to them. This binding action acts like a neon sign to the rest of the immune system, recruiting it to attack and destroy the dangerous targets. Your immune system makes many antibody proteins that recognize slightly different parts of the invader. Some of these antibodies are better than others at recognition and binding very tightly to the target.

Research and clinical scientists realized that the exquisite recognition capability of individual antibodies might be valuable in many applications. But, as was the problem with cytokines, it was very difficult to get enough of any specific antibody protein to study or to use. The breakthrough came in the mid-1970s, when Georges Kohler came to work with Cesar Milstein at the Medical Research Council (MRC) Laboratory of Molecular Biology. Milstein had been experimenting with making hybrid cells of fused rat and mouse cells, which he termed *hybridomas*.

Kohler was looking for a way to make enough of specific antibodies to study the genetics of antibody specificity. He tried fusing a single antibody-producing cell with a myeloma cell—an antibody-producing cancer cell—and ended up with an immortal cell line pumping out bunches of the same antibody. This preparation of antibody proteins all aimed at the same target and all possessing the same structure is termed *monoclonal antibodies*.

Monoclonal antibody technology allowed scientists to grow huge vats of pure antibodies aimed at selected targets. This technique in turn let them use the target recognition and tight target binding of monoclonal antibodies to design new diagnostic tests and therapeutics. The therapeutics became known as magic bullets because they were injected into the bloodstream and then headed straight for their disease target, carrying a deadly payload. It was revolutionary.

HYBRITECH

Although the technical discovery that fueled monoclonal antibody development came from the UK, the first company (and many of those that followed) created to exploit this important technology was based in the United States, in the thick of the emerging California biotech corridor. Hybritech was founded in 1978 by venture capitalist Brook Byers; Dr. Ivor Royston, a professor at the University of California-San Diego (UCSD); and one of Royston's hybridoma-making researchers, Howard Birndorf.

In typical scientific fashion, the creation of Hybritech was serendipitous. Back in the mid-1980s, Royston was an oncology fellow working on cancer research in the Stanford lab of Dr. Ron Levy, and Birndorf worked with Royston. Dr. Leonard Herzenberg, a professor in the genetics department at Stanford, had spent a sabbatical in the lab of Dr. Milstein and learned how to make hybridomas, the cell lines that pumped out monoclonal antibodies. Says Birndorf, "Len came back and taught the technique to a woman in his lab, who taught me. I started talking with Ivor about how to apply this technique to myeloma."

Myeloma is a cancer of the antibody-producing immune cells, where a single B cell goes crazy, multiplies out of control, and starts pumping out tons of a single type of antibody—in essence, a naturally occurring producer of monoclonal antibodies. Classic cancer treatments would wipe out the entire immune system, leaving the patient vulnerable to infection. Birndorf and Royston figured that a monoclonal antibody aimed only at the B cell run amok would have a better chance of slowing the cancer without killing the patient.

By 1977, Royston had moved to his own lab at the University of California at San Diego. He asked Birndorf to come run the new lab. Birndorf made the move and within months had a 200-square-foot lab up and running in the VA Hospital. "I bought all the equipment, hired some folks, started doing hybridoma research on immune cells and lymphoma cells. But I was unfulfilled. I was making $15,000 a year as a senior research associate and had hit the ceiling—I couldn't go higher without going back to school for a Ph.D."

Birndorf kept lamenting his situation to Royston, and eventually their conversation turned to discussions of setting up a company. The idea was to use their expertise in monoclonals, still a rare commodity, to make monoclonals for research use to replace the polyclonals currently being used. Polyclonal antibodies are made by injecting an animal with the molecule you want to detect. The animal's immune system pumps out many different antibodies, all of which recognize different parts of the target molecule. Some stick tightly to the target; some are not as useful.

The advantages of monoclonals included better quality control and the ability to manufacture one monoclonal preparation that would stick really tightly to the target. Birndorf and Royston thought there was a real commercial opportunity and decided to give it a shot.

But where to get the money? Says Birndorf, "I bought a book on how to start your own business and wrote a five-page business plan. I figured we needed about $178,000 to buy equipment, rent lab space, hire some people, and start making antibodies. I had no idea where you got money for something like this, so I went to Chicago, where I knew some commodities traders. They all thought this was cool stuff, but it was way beyond their ability to judge if this was good business. I went to Michigan and met with some wealthy friends of my parents but ran into the same problem."

But then the biotech social club came to the rescue. Royston's wife, Colette, a former nurse at Stanford, had at one time dated Brook Byers, the VC whose fund had provided seed capital for Genentech. Royston met with Byers, who was interested in learning more. Byers remembers being approached in May 1978 by Royston and Birndorf about building a company around the new technology. At the end of the visit, waiting in a bar for Byers's plane at the San Diego airport, the researchers were amazed to hear that Byers's company, Kleiner & Perkins, had decided to give them $300,000 if they passed the due diligence test.

Says Byers, "We met in San Diego and scribbled ideas on place-mats. I spent the next three months doing due diligence. When I flew to England to meet the MRC folks, I found that Milstein had not filed patents for making hybridomas. He felt that it should stay pure science." By the time the due diligence was done, the partners had broadened the proposed company's scope to include diagnostics and maybe therapeutics along with the original research reagents.

In October 1978, Kleiner & Perkins invested $300,000 in seed money to start Hybritech. Byers says, "I told Howard that if he could make monoclonals to hepatitis B in 6 months, then we'll blast forward. Howard did it in two months! He set up the lab and hired folks in 1 week and was working with the mice himself. I was the acting president and chairman of the board. That began a partnership between Howard and myself that has lasted for 21 years so far, and seven companies."

Birndorf remembers, "We closed the deal October 18, 1978. The next day was Howard's last day at UCSD. Monday, October 23, I became the first Hybritech employee—VP of everything. The plan was that Ivor would stay at UC and be a consultant to the company. I opened a bank account, had lined up a lab to lease, and found myself sitting in an empty office next to a bare lab with a desk, chair, telephone, and scientific catalogs. By December, I had hired four or five people and completed the first proof of principal experiments making monoclonals to the hepatitis B antigen."

In January 1979, the collaborators found out that they were not the only folks to have noticed the potential commercial value of monoclonal antibodies. They heard rumors that a competing company was being started by Ted Greene, part of the biotech fan club from Baxter (which included Genzyme's Termeer). Byers convinced Greene to instead become CEO of Hybritech in March 1979, and Birndorf became VP of operations.

That crucial addition of experienced management was a turning point for Hybritech, and for the entire San Diego biotech sector. Greene spearheaded creation of an updated business plan, raised a few more millions to fund the development work, and began recruiting from established firms the management team that would in later years create many of the key San Diego biotech firms. Greene brought in Tom Adams as head of research and development, David Hale to run marketing and business development, David Kabakoff as head of diagnostic research, Dennis Carlo as head of therapeutics, and Cam Gardiner as head of marketing.

Hybritech went public in 1981, raising around $12 million, followed by a $33-million secondary offering in 1982. Its first product, a detection kit for IgE, was approved right around that time, and the company went on to commercialize many other important diagnostic tests and reagents—all based on the new monoclonal technology. This technology completely revolutionized clinical lab medicine, moving it away from enzyme-based tests to rapid antibody formats. But the first therapeutic monoclonal antibody would not be approved until 1998, when Hybritech's cousin IDEC Pharmaceuticals got FDA approval for Rituxan to treat non-Hodgkin's lymphoma.

Birndorf, Royston, and Byers have a lot to be proud of. The team pulled together to create and grow Hybritech to enough value that Eli Lilly & Co. bought the company in 1985 for an unprecedented amount of money—$375 million. This was the first truly lucrative biotech buyout ever and only the third buyout of any size for this industry. The management team, often with financial backing from Byers, later got involved with second- and third-generation companies in San Diego, including Genta, Gen-Probe, Amylin, Nanogen (where Birndorf is now chairman and CEO), Gensia (since split into Sicor and Metabasis Therapeutics), IDEC, Immune Response Corp., Corvas, and Pyxis.

"The initial Hybritech folks were true entrepreneurs who did it again and again. Dozens of companies came from Hybritech. We are one of the reasons the San Diego industry has flourished," says Birndorf. "GenProbe was bought by Chugai in 1989 for $110 million, IDEC has a huge valuation now, and Pyxis was bought for $900 million by Cardinal Health. Huge shareholder value was created by this original team."

Birndorf's most recent venture is Nanogen, an innovative company combining semiconductor technology and molecular biology to create devices that measure DNA arrays. Birndorf sees Nanogen's future as taking mechanical processes in the lab, like bacterial culturing, and reducing all the steps from sample to answer into miniaturized electronic processes.

PRODUCT WOES

The roller coaster ride experienced by the biotech firms trying to develop monoclonal antibody products is a good illustration of the collision between Wall Street expectations and scientific reality. The first-generation companies made two faulty assumptions:

- Any product based on a protein already made by the body should be easy to make into a product.
- Once the new technology part (cloning, making the monoclonal, etc.) is done, the rest of product development will be simple.

The fallacy of these two assumptions has been proven over and over again in the biotech industry. The first-generation biotech companies focused on replacement proteins as products—insulin, interferon, interleukin-2, tumor necrosis factor. These are all proteins with known functions (or so we thought) in the body, and it seemed straightforward to believe that clinical development should be without the usual surprises experienced when new drugs first go into humans. After all, there shouldn't be any unexpected side effects, and these proteins should be completely safe—right?

Unfortunately, the early companies forgot a basic point. Although the proteins were based on naturally occurring proteins, we were delivering unnaturally large amounts of them via unnatural routes. The early clinical studies to prove the anticancer properties of interleukins and interferons were fraught with serious adverse effects as the body tried to handle large systemic doses of proteins normally seen in very localized concentrations.

The biotech industry and its big pharma partners have spent considerable time retracing their steps and figuring out how to deliver these replacement proteins to maximize the therapeutic benefit and minimize problems.

Also, the researchers assumed that once the "new science" part was done, the hard part of product development was over. In fact, cloning and tricking cells into making the therapeutic protein were just the beginning.

The companies were forging trails through unknown territory—no pharmaceutical companies, other than those selling growth hormone and insulin—had experience purifying and characterizing large amounts of protein.

And it happened that the cells used to make these recombinant proteins for commercial use turned out a slightly different version of the proteins than did the cells in our bodies. Slight differences in three-dimensional shape and in the sugar molecules stuck on the finished

recombinant proteins led to potentially major differences in therapeutic activity in people. It also turned out that bacteria stuck an extra
amino acid on the end of each protein chain, which sometimes caused
an allergic reaction in patients treated with the recombinant version.
Companies had to develop methods to remove the extra amino acid.

In the case of monoclonal antibodies, the unexpected stumbling
blocks delayed product success for almost 20 years after Hybritech's
founding in 1978. Everyone was so sure that monoclonal antibodies
would be able to zoom in on cancer cells throughout the body and deliver chemotherapy payloads to kill them on impact. After Hybritech's
founding, there was a surge of new monoclonal companies, including
Centocor, Biotherapeutics, Genetic Systems, Invitron, Synbiotics,
and Xoma, all created to exploit this exciting new technology. Even
big biotech firms like Genentech and Cetus built strong in-house
monoclonal groups. But the real impact of this technology was not
felt on the stock market until November 1997, when IDEC Pharmaceuticals (San Diego) and its partner, Genentech, got FDA approval
for Rituxan, the first monoclonal antibody approved to treat cancer.

What happened?

The first stumbling block was the reality of cancer biology. To create a therapeutic monoclonal, you have to have a target at which to
aim it. It turned out to be a lot tougher than expected to find proteins
that showed up only on the surface of tumor cells, which could be
used as disease-specific targets. Having a monoclonal that can't tell
the difference between normal, healthy cells in your body and the tumor cells would be a major problem.

Once you found a tumor protein to aim at, it was really hard to get
enough of the monoclonal and its payload into the tumor. Solid tumors wouldn't let the monoclonal in, and the patient's immune system kept chewing up all the monoclonals left floating around before
they could do their job. That's because monoclonals were made from
mouse cells, and the mouse protein simply screamed "foreign" to the
patient's immune system. Finding a way to make human monoclonals
was a tricky technical problem.

The manufacturing process was complex, making the cost of goods
too high for monoclonals to be commercially feasible in many cases.
Monoclonals have very complex three-dimensional shapes and are
composed of four different proteins chains that must be folded together properly to end up with a functional product. In fact, the early
1990s saw the spectacular failure of two monoclonal-based products.

Xoma Corp. (Berkeley, California) and Centocor Inc. (Malvern, Pennsylvania) took monoclonal products aimed at septic shock—the often-fatal result of systemic bacterial infection—all the way through Phase III clinical trials, only to have them fail to show sufficient therapeutic benefit to gain FDA approval.

What to do?

THERAPEUTIC BREAKTHROUGH

The key was to persevere and find solutions to these technical problems. Two companies, IDEC Pharmaceuticals and Centocor, hung in and solved the problems. Their reward was reaching the marketplace later in the 1990s with well-received products, which catapulted them into the top tier of biotech companies, with market capitalizations of over a billion dollars. In the case of Centocor, the promise of therapeutic monoclonals and resulting revenues led to an acquisition by Johnson & Johnson in July 1999 in a stock transaction valued at $4.9 billion.

IDEC was founded in 1986 and went public in 1991—just before the biotech stocks tanked in early 1992. As the company's stock price slowly sank into the sunset, along with all the other biotech stocks, IDEC's scientists ignored the naysayers and continued to slug away at the technical bugaboos holding back their products.

Their first strategic decision was to focus on a cancer where the tumor cells would all be accessible to the monoclonal antibody without having to come up with a new delivery method. IDEC chose a target protein found on the surface of lymphomas, in which the cancer cells are floating freely in the blood.

IDEC's real breakthroughs came in inventing a way to create monoclonals that would look like human proteins to the patient's immune system, and in developing a production process that brought the cost down to manageable levels. IDEC scientists replaced the mice with macaque monkeys, which make antibodies that are almost identical to the human version. The molecular biologists then found a way to convince Chinese hamster ovary cells (sounds kinky, but this is a well-established cell line for manufacture of human proteins) to churn out high levels of perfectly folded antibodies. The efficiency of the system got the cost of goods down to a level where patients could afford the treatment, and IDEC could still make a profit.

During the clinical trial process, IDEC got a vote of confidence from big brother Genentech in the form of a clinical and commercialization deal for the drug Rituxan. That deal, which included equity purchase by Genentech, began to focus some stock market attention on IDEC. IDEC signed up with Genentech to comarket Rituxan in North America and put big pharma player and Genentech parent Hoffmann-La Roche in charge of European sales and marketing. IDEC stock began a climb from down around $2/share into the $30s just before product approval in November 1997 and was still climbing toward $100/share when we went to press.

Best of all, IDEC had Rituxan revenues of $152 million in 1998—the very first year of product sales. Monoclonal-antibody-based products have become Wall Street's darlings, including Centocor's RheoPro and Remicade, which brought in sales revenues totaling $392 million for the year, and Genentech's Herceptin, aimed at metastatic breast cancer. Herceptin brought in $30.5 million in revenues between approval in September 1998 and year end. Biotech pipelines are crammed with monoclonal antibody products aimed at a broad range of clinical markets, including cancer, cardiovascular disease, inflammatory disorders, and transplant rejection.

part two

BIOTECH'S BUILDING BLOCKS

"Only those willing to risk going too far can possibly find out how far one can go."

T. S. Eliot

6

BIOTECH STAR WARS

When the biotech industry first began, its young companies were lambasted for trying to be all things to all markets. Industrial investors—nickel mining companies, big distilleries, oil companies—were hoping for a direct payoff from their investments in the new technology. Those nonbiomedical applications had to be shunted aside for a couple of decades, as the new industry got on its feet, proved the commercial and societal value of its technology, and showed its worth as a place for investment.

We watched the early companies strip away their industrial programs and focus almost exclusively on direct applications of biotechnology to protein products. Twenty years later, we now see the biotech industry spreading its wings and carrying its novel approach to product development far outside the biomedical realm once again. But this time, the trip may take us all the way to the stars.

The U.S. space program has made major contributions to understanding certain biochemical processes that affect biomedical research. Sending biotech into space via the space shuttle program has allowed scientists to learn about the effects of gravity (or lack thereof) on protein crystal formation and tissue culture. But it has also allowed researchers to study, for example, how nerves regenerate in high gravity versus microgravity. In one shuttle experiment, researchers found a 100-fold increase in the number of new nerves being grown under microgravity. These experiments suggest that forces we never dreamed of impact nerve regeneration and could be used to treat spinal cord injury and other nerve damage.

Another shuttle-based biotech experiment, designed by Tulane scientists, studied the effects of microgravity on more than 100,000 genes in kidney cells. The scientists found more than 1,600 changes in those genes, which included many transcription factors, such as the vitamin D receptor, which is important in bone strength. We still don't understand why these changes occur, but this information shows that there are dramatic changes that occur when organisms go into space. Hopefully, this discovery will lead in turn to helping astronauts better endure space exploration.

BIOTECH BEYOND THE SOLAR SYSTEM

But there are more ways of applying biotechnology than even the most fervent industry insider can imagine.

Dan Goldin, NASA Administrator, kept an entire ballroom of industry insiders on the edges of their seats as he shared his incredible vision of biotech in the 21st century at the May 1999 Biotechnology Industry Organization (BIO) International meeting in Seattle. This vision took the audience to the stars and back.

Goldin has been the NASA Administrator for the past 8 years—a record in such a politically volatile setting. He is described by his peers as a big-time visionary who has overseen the transformation of NASA from an organization hanging back from the forefront of technology into one dedicated to carrying out some amazingly innovative, productive programs "better, faster, and cheaper."

In 1998, Goldin had a better year than baseball star Mark McGwire. His team launched two shuttles to the Russian space station Mir, put John Glenn back in space, launched the first two components of the new international space station, carried out a wildly successful mission to Mars, and conducted several scientific missions.

Says Goldin, "The 21st century will be a time of biotech. Most people don't understand that we are entering a biological revolution. They don't see biotechnology as connected to things far beyond biology. Biotech has the potential to dramatically change electronics, computational devices via both hardware and software, and multifunctional materials."

He's counting on biotech to help NASA solve some of its toughest problems that are holding back space exploration—the cost of shoving heavy objects into outer space, the difficulty in controlling spacecraft and explorer modules from the Earth, and the need to develop incredibly energy- and time-efficient approaches to feeding astronauts and keeping them safe and healthy while light-years from home.

Goldin's vision of biotech in the 21st century looks like this: "It's the year 2030, and you still can't get good airline food. Today is the launch of NASA's interstellar probe, looking for clues about new life forms on planets in other solar systems. It took NASA using bioinformative technology and biomimetrics to build the spaceship. It doesn't look anything like any spaceship we're used to.

"The Coke-can-sized craft will reach and land on a passing asteroid 2 years from Earth launch. It will use its DNA-based biomimetic system as a blueprint to evolve, adapt, and grow into a more complex exploring and thinking system. It will ride the asteroid like a parasite, until it transforms into its next evolvable state—an intelligent interstellar probe. It will use the asteroid's native resources to accomplish the first phase of the mission. This may mean using the asteroid's iron, carbon, and other materials to build a nervous system and communications. This reconfigurable hybrid system can adapt its form and function to deal with changes in the environment and unanticipated problems. It will leave the host asteroid carrier and accelerate to a good fraction of the speed of light out to the stars and other solar systems."

Although this mission sounds light-years away from today's capabilities, here is the nearer-term reality from Goldin:

"NASA is already working toward building systems that mimic biology and are based on biological processes. Here are just two examples. NASA is working with a major automotive firm to embed adaptable neural network chips into your cars. They will react, adapt, and optimize engine performance to your car specifically as it ages and changes. And in the F15 fighter experimental plane are neural networks that can rapidly react to catastrophic failure of critical components—partial loss of a wing, total failure of the hydraulics. Through adaptive learning, the system will fly that plane safely to the ground.

"We hope that 5 to 10 years from now, systems will carry evolvable biologically inspired systems that operate closer to how our brains function, that assimilate and process info into knowledge and intelligence. No longer will systems be pure data collectors and processors. These new systems will process, think, react, and adapt.

"Think of the implications for transportation, manufacturing, entertainment, and the exploding information and communication sectors. What is the most highly compact, energy-efficient system to store and process information? Computers are binary, based on silicon semiconductors. As we push processing times faster and faster, power demands also escalate. The most powerful computer today is a teraflop—it can do 1 trillion floating-point operations per second and requires a megawatt to run.

"Your brain is a million times faster and operates on a few watts. We can't send a power cord to the international space station, and we certainly can't put a plug on an interstellar probe and carry a power cord light-years away.

"The future advancements in computational systems that we need can only be achieved with hybrid systems that mimic biological processes and that combine new concepts based not only on silicon and inanimate materials, but also on biochemical materials—DNA- and protein-based. A DNA-based hybrid system could be faster and a billion times more energy-efficient than a silicon-based system.

"How can we get there? By coupling NASA space- and ground-based research platforms with the best modeling systems and the biotech industry's vision and entrepreneurial spirit. Today, the biotech industry is being driven by improvements in information systems and communications. But the key is expansion of technology into other sectors."

"Today, agriculture and health care biotech are at the core of what the industry does. Lots of exciting things are happening in those areas that enhance life. But NASA is working on systems that attempt to mimic processes in the biological world. When we send probes to space, we will try to give them lifelike properties. We want them to be robust, self-reliant, adaptable, and evolvable, to heal when damaged, with complete self-awareness. They should be able to respond to conditions as they find them on those distant planets. They shouldn't walk off a cliff because someone in mission control told the robot to take 10 steps.

"We want to put colonies of robots on planets and have them thrive, not merely survive, to be as mobile as four-legged animals, to manipulate objects with the dexterity of a human hand, explore and have attributes, express emotions, have the ability to select and re-move leaders to perform tasks.

"We want to exploit biology to build life support systems to mini-mize the resupply problem on long trips—to create regenerative life support systems for astronauts. We want to convert materials we find on other planets to useful materials. The atmosphere on Mars is 95% carbon dioxide—the perfect raw material for plants to make oxygen. Could we introduce plantlike systems on Mars that will be able to create enough oxygen to sustain life? We are taking the first step in 2001, when we send a biochemical factory probe to Mars to do the first *in situ* testing to convert carbon dioxide to oxygen. This isn't science fiction any more. NASA will provide leadership in developing biotech as it relates to our missions in space and will ultimately bring back benefits to Earth.

"We have had great success with biotech experiments on the shuttle, but months or years of preparation leading to only 2 weeks in orbit is not enough to develop a new industry. The International Space Station represents an opportunity for unlimited major advances in available space and facilities."

Goldin says that 30% of the space on the space station is already allocated to commercial activities, with the potential to go to 50%. The station is expected to be fully functional in 5 years. The station will be size of the U.S. Capitol Building, with more pressurized volume than two jumbo jets.

NASA is pursuing three major research areas relevant to biotech in the space station. The first relates to the need for optimized food production in the small facilities available in space. To feed astronauts on the long voyages through interstellar space, we must be able to produce disease-resistant high-yield crops in small areas, with limited energy resources. Plant transgenics is the path to that goal.

The second project is driven by the reality that astronauts will be going into environments—such as Mars or under the ice of Europa—that potentially are highly dangerous and contain unknown toxins. To keep the astronauts alive long enough to explore and report back, the spacecraft crew will need to be able to analyze rapidly and develop countermeasures, then synthesize and tailor counteracting drugs that are immediately effective and can be manufactured in a very short time. Imagine what such efficient drug development processes would mean here on Earth when applied to the current decade-long drug development cycle.

The third project is based on the inability to take blood or tissue banks on trips where astronauts are gone for years. They will need access to regenerative and reparable blood and tissue supplies. Says Goldin, "NASA has already flown the first three-dimensional tissue culture reactor in the shuttle. It will operate on Earth, but the lack of gravity provides faster growth of larger, more complex cultures. Think of the potential for understanding tissue growth and the impact of drugs, especially for tumor research."

NASA is also leading the way in ground- and space-based astrobiology. In May 1999, NASA kicked off a new astrobiology institute at NASA Ames base in Santa Clara, California. Dr. Baruch Blumberg, developer of the hepatitis B vaccine and Nobel laureate, is the full-time director. According to Goldin, the primary goal of the institute is to answer those age-old questions: How did life begin and evolve, does it exist elsewhere in universe, and what is life's destiny on Earth and beyond?

"We will start by understanding life here on Earth. We know life exists in harsh, extreme environments on Earth, such as volcanic vents in the ocean floor. We may be able to capture and understand the universal fingerprints of the life process.

"At Ames, we have gathered the best minds in complexity theory, simulation models, all areas. We intend to look at life processes from chemical soup to biological reality. The biotech industry will play an important role in the institute by providing on-site researchers or through collaborations. It's time for NASA and biotech to expand their common goals.

"Biotech and biology will be the hallmarks of the 21st century. The rapid development of the silicon era led to rapid growth of companies such as Intel. The upcoming revolution in biotech will propel other companies as America starts populating other planets.

"It will be an exciting odyssey, and I am confident it will return benefits out of this world. Our grandchildren will be grateful for the work the biotech industry did today, creating biology-inspired products that will dramatically improve the quality of life on Earth."

PRODUCTS BEYOND PROTEINS

Goldin's vision of biotech taking us to the stars is invigorating, but very long-term. Nearer term, some pretty exciting new technologies are expanding biotech's arsenal of technologies far beyond the original science.

Biotech's early product development focus was driven by two key inventions: recombinant DNA techniques for engineering cells to make large amounts of important therapeutic proteins, and hybridoma technology used to create hybrids of immune system cells and immortal cancer cells to make very specific, selective antibody molecules termed *monoclonal antibodies*. The first-generation products emerging from biotech were all proteins, either recombinant versions of normal human proteins or monoclonal antibodies.

Almost as soon as the young companies and their partners started clinical development of the first biotech products—human growth hormone, insulin, interferon, and so on—the problem of drug delivery reared its ugly head.

Proteins are very large molecules. Their shape in three-dimensional space determines their function in the body. And therein lies the problem. Anything that mucks with protein shape can kill the therapeutic activity.

Drugs taken by mouth need to travel through the stomach and into the intestine to reach the blood vessels that will carry the drug throughout the body to do its job. The problem is that the stomach is specifically designed to take apart large proteins so that the body can use them as food. Think about those scrambled eggs you had Saturday morning. The stomach breaks them down into small pieces that can be absorbed by the intestinal tract. Good for food, bad for drugs.

This digestion problem has limited delivery of most proteins to administration directly into the blood by injection. This isn't a perfect solution, as there are enzymes in our blood that will take apart proteins. These enzymes, designed to protect us from proteins that don't belong in the blood, perhaps from invading microbes, limit the active life span of protein drugs in the body. Also, most people don't like injections. The thought of taking a drug by injection for extended periods of time can turn off the most fervent patient. So most protein drugs are limited to diseases where an injectable drug is acceptable, where the treatment time is short, or where the disease is so problematic to the patient that even an injection is acceptable if it helps.

For example, Amgen's two top-selling protein drugs—Epogen for red blood cell stimulation and Neupogen for immune cell stimulation—are widely used because the patients are already getting other treatments by injection, so adding one more is not a problem. And these patients need these drugs to survive, which makes the inconvenience easier to handle.

However, it's hard to imagine convincing patients to put up with an injection of an arthritis drug every day for the rest of their lives, if there is a pill alternative.

This protein problem stimulated the creation of several segments of the biotech industry. The search was on for novel, innovative drug delivery tools that would allow proteins easier access to patient tissues, and for a change in focus to small organic molecules, the choice of conventional pharmaceutical companies, as drugs. These small molecules—about one-10th to one-100th the size of a typical protein—can slip through the stomach and the bloodstream without digestion and can weasel their way into cells.

Biotech scientists also began using conventional biotechnology methods—genetic engineering, DNA and protein synthesis, biochemistry, novel separation and analysis methods—as tools to decipher just how our bodies work at the cell and molecule level. That information could then be used to design new drugs, including small molecules.

It was this inward investigation that began the journey on which we are still embarked—to understand exactly how and why we get sick and how to specifically and selectively aim new drugs at those disease mechanisms.

The end result of all this activity probably won't be protein drugs, in most cases. Some of the new products will be built out of other molecules found in our bodies—modeled on DNA and other genetic information carriers, on the complex carbohydrates that coat our cells and incoming pathogens, or maybe they will be actual cells engineered to carry out a specific task. In many cases, the end result will look a lot like the drugs that come out of big pharma research—small organic molecules built out of carbon, hydrogen, oxygen, and nitrogen molecules that stick to disease-related molecules in the body and stop the process.

And that's really what this all boils down to—lots of multisyllabic language that essentially means, "We make a drug that sticks to something in your body and makes it stop causing disease." It's only the details of the drug composition and how we figured out where to aim it that make for scary science.

Another new area emerging from biotechnology advances is tissue engineering—creating tissues and cells to replace missing or damaged parts of our bodies, or as long-term delivery devices for therapeutic proteins. And there is a growing group of companies using biotech for a new generation of chemical engineering—creating new chemical structures and improved ways of doing chemical reactions for industrial uses.

Chapters that follow present a glimpse of some of the most interesting areas being explored within the biotech industry and of the companies that have created their niche in each.

——— 7 ———

THE HUMAN GENOME
PROJECT

The Human Genome Project is an immense, international effort initiated in 1990 to create for the first time a road map of all of the genetic information contained in human cells. This is one of the most incredible scientific endeavors ever attempted, with somewhere in the ballpark of $3 billion being put to work in labs all over the world in a coordinated effort to reveal the secrets of our genes.

The results will take years to complete and decades to fully exploit. The Human Genome Project is moving along faster than expected, thanks to major advances in instrumentation and data analysis that have sped up the process of gathering and analyzing sequence information. Researchers are hoping to have a "working draft" representing about 90% of the genome by spring 2000.

Each of our cells contains 46 chromosomes—tightly wound bundles of genetic material carrying the codes for making all of the proteins in our bodies. Proteins in turn carry out many functions in the body, including building other kinds of molecules—carbohydrates, fats, and so on.

The code for an individual protein is called a *gene*. Genes are linear sequences of the building blocks of genes, termed *nucleotides*. Nucleotides are complex molecules containing a sugar (ribose), an organic ring structure called a *nucleic acid*, and a phosphate group hanging off one end that is used to hook to another nucleotide to build chains. The term for this molecule is *deoxyribonucleic acid*, or DNA (*deoxyribo-* means the ribose is missing an oxygen atom).

The nucleic acids come in four flavors—A, T, C, and G. The linear sequence of A, T, C, and G carries the code telling the cell how to build a specific protein, using the protein building blocks—the 20 amino acids. The sequence of amino acids in a protein determines that protein's shape and biochemical properties, and thus its function in the body.

Our chromosomes are composed of at least 100,000 different genes all strung together, separated by bits of sequence that regulate when, where in the body, and how much protein is made when an individual gene is turned on. The coordinated turning off and on of different genes creates different kinds of cells in the body, building different kinds of tissues and organs, all with slightly different functions. For example, the kidney cells make some of the same proteins as the lung, but they also make lots of different proteins throughout their life span. Most genes are turned off most of the time. When they are turned on, they usually cause some kind of change in a cell's behavior.

There are also vast stretches of what used to be termed *junk DNA*, sequences that don't appear to encode any proteins and that have no known function. However, researchers are beginning to learn more about this so-called junk DNA that suggests it may be important to the cell.

In fact, James Watson, one of the discoverers of the three-dimensional structure of DNA, liked to remind audiences at his talks that most of the Y chromosome, which imparts the male gender, is junk DNA.

Companies like PE Applied Biosystems (Foster City, California) invent machines and methods for rapidly reading the linear DNA sequence, putting together databases of the sequences, and using computer programs to guess where in all that sequence is the part encoding a protein. These programs can also provide some basic information about the potential shape of a protein and how it might be related to other proteins, based on its amino acid sequence.

There is a growing segment of the biotech industry focused on developing instrumentation, reagents, and software to support the exponentially expanding need for large-scale sequencing and data management. Many of the companies developing these products and services are still private, but look for them to start hitting the public stock market over the next decade.

These companies include Argonaut Technologies Inc. (San Carlos, California), Caliper Technologies Corp. (Mountain View, California), and Ciphergen Biosystems Inc. (Palo Alto, California).

There is also a growing number of companies focused on the software needed for the massive amount of data crunching needed to make sense of all the information being generated by different laboratories, and to look for correlations between different kinds of information to yield clues about gene function.

Researchers believe that the Human Genome Project is the first step toward creating an encyclopedia describing the entire human repertoire of protein synthesis, along with its regulation. Some labs are sequencing the genomes of other species, to compare and contrast with the human sequences. Related amino acid or nucleotide sequences may mean those genes have similar functions.

But the linear sequence of genes does not tell us what the protein does. If the protein being studied is not closely related to a protein that is already well understood, how do we figure out what it is?

SON OF GENOMICS

Part of the answer comes from a series of related experiments with related names, used to get hints about the potential role of genes and their encoded proteins.

Companies like Millennium Pharmaceuticals (Cambridge, Massachusetts) are using a technique termed *positional cloning genomics* to look for regions of chromosomes containing genes that seem to show up every time a patient has a certain disease. This mapping process gives the scientists clues about where in the human genome to focus if they want to find genes associated with certain types of cancers or diabetes, for example. Once a general location is found, the team sequences the genes in the area and looks for more evidence that one of those genes is directly involved in the disease under study. So basically, you start with a disease and work backward looking for gene sequences that seem to show up in patients and not in healthy people.

Sometimes, genomics turns up the code for an interesting gene with no known function, and the researchers need clues about what the gene does. In "functional genomics," scientists look at changes in animals or simple organisms like worms and flies when a gene with an unknown function is turned off and on. The changes give hints about how the gene works in the body. Sometimes animals are genetically engineered to remove a gene under study from their genetic material to study what the lack of that gene does to the animal. These experiments are known as *knockouts*, since the gene function is totally knocked out.

Research has shown that many organisms, even very simple ones such as the fruit fly, share related genes with humans. By studying gene function in these fruit flies, worms, and fish, we can get clues about gene function in humans. Most humans would object to participating directly in these experiments!

Where humans do participate directly is in investigation of changes in gene expression in healthy cells versus sick cells. *Gene expression* simply means that a particular gene is being read by the cell, and the encoded protein is being made. For example, studying changes in gene expression in healthy lung cells and those from lung cancer patients can identify which proteins might be involved in the shift from healthy to cancerous cells—and thus might be a target for drug design. Study of differences in gene expression and protein production is termed *proteomics*.

Pharmacogenomics goes one step further and looks for differences in gene sequence between individuals, in a search for gene mutations that might be used to predict increased susceptibility to disease or response to treatment. For example, once genomics identifies a group of genes that appear to play a role in lung cancer, scientists can compare those genes in healthy people and in cancer patients. This comparison might reveal differences in gene sequence between those two groups that *correlate* with getting cancer. These differences are termed *polymorphisms*.

In some cases, even a single nucleotide difference—a single "letter" in the genetic code—between people can signal a significant increase in risk of developing a disease. Remember—protein function is driven by the amino acid sequence, which in turn is driven by the gene sequence. A single nucleotide change in the gene could cause the cell to think that a different amino acid should be placed in the protein being made. The resulting protein would work differently from the "normal" protein, and that difference in function could lead to disease. Many of the cancer-related oncogenes are the result of a single amino acid change in proteins with important functions controlling cell division in normal cells.

In just one issue of the journal *Nature Genetics* in 1999, scientists reported using the gene sequence differences between healthy and ill people to identify nearly 200 genes that may play a role in heart disease, schizophrenia, and diabetes. The researchers found between 240,000

TABLE 7.1   Companies Using Genomics and Its Cousins

Company	Location	Stock Symbol
Axys Pharmaceuticals	South San Francisco, CA	AXPH
Celera Genomics	Rockville, MD	CRA
Hyseq Inc.	Sunnyvale, CA	HYSQ
Millennium Pharmaceuticals	Cambridge, MA	MLNM
Variagenics Inc.	Cambridge, MA	Private
Acacia Biosciences	Richmond, CA	Private
Affymetrix Inc.	Santa Clara, CA	AFFX
Human Genome Sciences	Rockville, MD	HGSI
Incyte Pharmaceuticals	Palo Alto, CA	INCY
Lynx	Hayward, CA	LYNX
Curagen	New Haven, CT	CRGN
Myriad	Salt Lake City, UT	MYGN
Gene Logic	Gaithersburg, MD	GLGC
Genome Therapeutics	Waltham, MA	GENE
Microcide-Iconix division	Mountain View, CA	MCDE
Ribozyme Pharmaceuticals	Boulder, CO	RZYM
Functional Genomics:		
Exelexis Pharmaceuticals	South San Francisco, CA	Private
Ontogeny Inc.	Cambridge, MA	Private
Lexicon Genetics Inc.	The Woodlands, TX	Private
Cell Path Inc.	Seattle, WA	Private

SOURCE: Biospace.com and BioVenture Consultants.

and 1 million small coding differences. Now comes the hard part—figuring out which of those are actually causing the problem, and not just a result of the disease, and then figuring out what to do about them.

Pharmacogenomics information can be useful in supporting diagnostic tests. Potentially, a diagnostic test that identified the presence of the cancer-associated mutation could help identify people at greater risk for developing lung cancer. As a result, the person at risk might be more motivated to quit smoking, adopt a healthier lifestyle, and get more frequent checkups.

Pharmacogenomics may also identify genetic differences that affect how people respond to various drugs. Some therapeutics need to be "digested" in the body to carry out their action. Patients lacking the protein that carries out that digestion will not be able to benefit from that drug. A diagnostic test would rapidly identify those patients and allow the doctor to use a different therapeutic approach.

The downside is the concern that this information might be misused—by insurance companies looking for ways to reduce the risk of big hospital bills among their clients, by employers looking for ways to deny promotions and raises, by the government for a variety of nefarious reasons. The companies working on this technology, joined by many bioethics and advocacy groups, are already in the midst of intense discussions about how to safeguard the use of this information.

The bottom line is that the Human Genome Project and all the related "-genomics" have the potential to vastly increase our understanding of how our bodies work, and how to help them work better. But most of the value will come only after we spend years figuring out the message in the code.

── 8 ──

TOOLS FOR
GENOME STUDIES

BioChips and Microarrays

In the past few years, people infected with HIV, the AIDS virus, have benefited from powerful new antiviral drugs that have changed the outlook for patients. With proper management, some patients can suppress their illness indefinitely, by taking a combination of medicines that keeps viral replication to a minimum. Unfortunately, the ability of HIV to mutate rapidly and repeatedly means that the wrong drug combination can allow a strain of the virus to grow unchecked, potentially becoming resistant to all existing therapies. With such high stakes and so many options, how do physicians know which drugs to prescribe and when to make the necessary changes?

Mutations, small changes in the DNA of HIV, can create variant versions of the virus that are not affected by the drugs used to treat the patient. Finding the specific variant, or *genotype*, of HIV in an infected patient is an important part of prescribing the right medicines.

Microarrays—also knows as *DNA chips*, or *biochips*—are a powerful tool for rapidly looking at small differences in genetic codes. They are becoming increasingly useful to both research scientists looking for clues about gene function and expression, and to doctors hoping to identify and head off serious infections before they kill patients.

DNA consists of four basic building blocks, termed *nucleotides*—A, C, G, and T. These building blocks are connected in long chains, and the order of the As, Cs, Ts, and Gs carries the code telling the cell how to build the encoded protein. The DNA in just one of our cells, if stretched out, is about two meters in length. It has been estimated that all the DNA in an individual's body could stretch to the sun and back.

In the cell, DNA usually is structured in two strands that twist together—the famous double helix—with complementary bases joined up in pairs. This pairing is based on chemical compatibility, which ensures that A always sticks to T, C to G, G to C, and T to A.

This predictable binding of bases joins complementary strands in a process called *hybridization*. Because hybridization is so predictable, it gives us a tool for reading and identifying DNA sequences, or genes. If an unknown sample of single-stranded DNA is exposed to a variety of short nucleotide chains, it will naturally want to link up with its complementary base pairs. Thus, a stretch of DNA reading GAT-TACA will want to find a strand that reads CTAATGT. When they find each other, the strands hook together, or hybridize.

Microarrays apply a production line approach to this basic concept. A collection of probes—short sequences of nucleotides synthesized to hybridize with the genes of interest—are placed in a grid on a glass slide or chip, where they can be exposed to samples of unknown DNA from patients or other test samples. A fluorescent "signaling" enzyme is attached to the end of the probe that glows only when the probe hybridizes with the gene of interest. This sends a colorful signal that the gene of interest is present in the sample being tested.

WHAT ARE BioChips USED FOR?

The Human Genome Project is all about determining the linear sequence of DNA bases in our chromosomes, the code for every protein made by our bodies. But this project can easily become a source of information overload. There are an estimated 100,000 genes in each human cell. Without a tool like microarrays, scientists would have no hope of finding the correct genes to study for any particular disease.

One of the most exciting uses for DNA arrays is gene expression profiling. That means looking for the genes that are turned on at a given moment and being used by a cell to make specific proteins. This type of profiling can tell a researcher which of our genes are active in a particular place, at a particular time.

Why do we care? Because this profiling gives us important clues about which genes play a role in cell functions or in disease. Researchers may find a rare gene that is active only in tumor cells and not in healthy cells, or one that is overactive in people with heart disease. This discovery gives scientists a way to choose which of the estimated 100,000 genes might be most important in causing heart attacks or in leading to tumor formation—and thus which should be studied for new ways to treat or prevent those diseases.

Microarrays allow researchers to effectively see the genome in motion, expressing genes over time. They have allowed researchers insights that would be very difficult to achieve with conventional experiments.

When the body needs to produce a protein, the gene encoding that protein unwinds at its location in the chromosome and is translated into a corresponding messenger RNA (mRNA) sequence. RNA is a chemical relative of DNA. This sequence travels out of the nucleus into the cell body and heads for the ribosome—a "factory" that reads the mRNA code and produces the encoded protein.

But at this intermediate stage—when the mRNA of interest is assembled and present in the cell—researchers can intercept the code and find out for themselves what kind of protein is going to be produced and which gene sequence was responsible for producing it. The biochip allows scientists to build a picture of genes turning on and off, by repeating this process over time. The researchers can also look at the differences in gene expression in different parts of the body, or in healthy versus diseased tissues, by comparing their biochip profiles.

Most microarrays are used to identify genes among a predetermined set of possibilities. Because the probes must be deliberately placed on an array, researchers need to have some idea of what genes they are looking for. Most companies sell a variety of chip products, each optimized to a different purpose. Some also sell customized arrays, made with probes chosen by the customer. PE Applied Biosystems recently began selling microarray probes that can be customized by the individual scientists in their own labs.

Microarrays are going to improve with the completion of the Human Genome Project. Although chips can now contain probes only for genes we know, the Genome Project and its private sector counterparts will soon give us a complete set of human genes.

Chip manufacturers plan to be ready for this huge increase in capacity. Affymetrix Inc. (Santa Clara, California), which pioneered the concept of DNA microarrays based on computer chip technology, can fit 250,000 probes in a matrix only 1 square centimeter in size. With an estimated 100,000 genes in the human body, a "universal" microarray is within reach. In fact, Incyte Pharmaceuticals Inc. (Palo Alto, California), which manufactures spotted microarrays through its Synteni division, has announced its intention to make a chip containing the entire human genome in the next few years.

Such a chip will allow researchers to look for the expression of any gene—even rare or unexpected genes—in samples. But even then, there will be room for a variety of products. A chip for the entire human genome may have probes representing some average version of every human gene (or every gene from some other organism), but genes vary in their sequence among individuals. Many researchers are looking only for a specific subset of genes and would like to know which important sequence variations are in a sample.

These pesky genetic variations that make us all different are the subject of great research and commercial interest. They determine who will have blue eyes and who will have brown; they also play an important role in determining who will develop Alzheimer's disease, who will react badly to certain medicines, and who will effectively resist viruses. Often referred to as *single nucleotide polymorphisms* (SNPs, pronounced "snips"), these gene variants can be quickly detected with arrays.

Once important SNPs are identified through pharmacogenomics research, arrays can be made that will detect which variation is present in a patient's sample. In the near term, that will offer researchers a powerful tool for linking genetic variation with disease and with observable phenotypic traits. Although many such chip products will make it to market sometime in the future, one version has just been introduced—Affymetrix's HuSNP GeneChip, an array that detects a variety of randomly chosen SNPs across the genome.

The HuSNP chip represents yet another application of microarrays—broad linkage analyses and genome mapping. Researchers will be able use the array to see general genetic similarities or differences among different groups of people, which can be correlated with diseases or other observable traits.

Down the road, a variety of SNP chips can be used for diagnostic purposes—determining in a health care setting the specific genotype of a patient to improve treatment and prescribing decisions, who will benefit from a medicine, who is at higher risk of developing cancer or cardiovascular disease, and so on.

Affymetrix's first commercial product was an HIV genotyping assay—a biochip that lets clinicians know which strain of HIV is present in a particular patient, and when that strain mutates following drug treatment. More diagnostic arrays will come as we learn more about the relation of sequence variation to disease outcome.

Motorola, better known for its communication devices, created a biochip division that has teamed up with researchers in Arizona and Alabama on a 3-year, $9-million project to create a small, inexpensive device for rapid diagnosis of life-threatening bacterial infections. This device, expected to carry all sample preparation and analysis on a single chip, may replace the time-consuming culturing tests (usually taking days!) currently used by hospitals and clinical labs.

COMPANIES PRODUCING MICROARRAYS

The table at the end of this chapter lists the leaders in the biochip world. These companies use a variety of technologies to create arrays. In addition, many researchers who don't need a high density of probes make their own arrays.

There are two basic ways of making arrays. One, used exclusively by Affymetrix, uses a photolithography process adapted from the silicon chip industry. This method has been likened to building a city by creating skyscrapers out of four individual floor plans. Affymetrix attaches these "floor plans" to a glass substrate. All of Floor Plan A is laid out, being attached to some areas of the array and not to others. Some of the spots left blank then get Floor Plan G, then C, and finally T. When it is time to build the second story, the process is repeated, with floors being laid down to methodically create desired sequences (e.g., AA, AG, CT, etc.). Affymetrix chips builds probes 20 to 25 stories high—20- to 25-nucleotide probes.

The second basic method uses complementary DNA (cDNA) probes prepared directly from samples, spotted onto a substrate. Companies use a variety of means to accomplish this method. Synteni, for example, uses pins to lay down tiny amounts of cDNA in an array. Protogene uses special glass surfaces so that its arrays create different surface tensions between probe locations and the surrounding glass surface. That way, probes stay isolated from one another in microdrops of liquid, and chemical reactions between probe and sample take place in the droplet. Others, like Rosetta Inpharmatics, use an ink-jet process to lay down probes.

Companies making microarrays will compete on several fronts:

Density and size: Not all microarray assays require a high density of probes, but those analyzing expression of a large number of genes do. Companies are continually striving to increase the density of arrays to support analysis of more and more genes on a single biochip. Affymetrix can put a quarter of a million probes in a square centimeter. Illumina Inc., a start-up company in San Diego, is developing a technology that it claims will allow it to put that many probes on the head of pin.

Probes: No chip could hold every possible variation of every human gene. Choosing the best probes for the best applications will continue to be a major competitive factor among chip manufacturers. Today, available probes depend to some extent on commercial agreements. Subscribers to Incyte's DNA sequence databases, for example, can get access to any Incyte sequence in a Synteni array. Affymetrix has an agreement that allows it access to proprietary sequences from the databases of Human Genome Sciences Inc. (Rockville, Maryland).

Speed: The DNA hybridization process takes hours and requires treatment with chemicals and heat. Some companies are trying to speed the process and increase the throughput of experiments. Nanogen Inc. (San Diego, California), for example, uses the natural electrical charge on DNA molecules to speed hybridization. By placing a controlled charge on individual probe sites, the company claims it can attract or repel molecules and complete the hybridization process in a matter of seconds. The faster the process, and the fewer steps required of the lab tech, the more likely it is that the test will be useful outside the specialized research environment.

Customization: Because arrays will always be optimized for specific applications, companies will compete on the ability to provide researchers with customized chips. Some companies like Nanogen are creating systems that will allow researchers to create their own chips in the lab without ordering a custom array that can take months to manufacture. PE Biosystems is developing the "zip chip," another platform that allows researchers to roll their own, quickly creating arrays that will answer their questions of the moment.

Accuracy: For genotyping in particular, where researchers want to detect variations as small as a single nucleotide, accuracy is vital. A

TABLE 8.1   Microarray Companies

Company/locations	Stock symbol	Array product technology
Affymetrix Inc. (Santa Clara, CA	AFFX	GeneChip and system for diagnostics, SNP identification and typing, disease management, expression profiling.
AlphaGene Inc. (Woburn, MA)	Private	Micromax spotted cDNA arrays.
Beckman Coulter Inc. (Fullerton, CA)	BEC	Non-photolithography-produced DNA arrays.
CipherGen Inc. (Palo Alto, CA)	Private	ProteinChip arrays for studying protein biology, based on surface-enhanced laser desorption/ionization (SELDI), a mass-spectrometry technology.
Clontech Laboraties Inc. (Palo Alto, CA)	Private	Atlas arrays for gene expression analysis and profiling, etc. Custom arrays available soon. Becton Dickinson plans to acquire.
Gene Logic Inc. (Gaithersburg, MD)	GLGC	Agreement with Affymetrix to build commercial gene expression database—uses GeneChips.
GeneTrace Systems Inc. (Menlo Park, CA)	Private	MALDI-TOF DNA analysis arrays.
Genometrix Inc. (The Woodlands, TX)	Private	Low- and medium-density oligo-nucleotide and cDNA microarrays with electrically charged surface films.
Genomic Solutions Inc. (Ann Arbor, MI)	Private	Customized DNA and RNA arrays and services, along with various instruments and genomics/ proteomics services
Genosys Biotechnologies Inc. (The Woodlands, TX)	Private	Panorama *E. Coli* hybridization arrays and custom arrays.
Human Genome Sciences, Inc. (Rockville, MD)	HGSI	Affymetrix to use proprietary HGS genes in its GeneChip arrays.
Hyseq Inc. (Sunnyvale, CA)	HYSQ	HyChip arrays and system for gene sequencing, SNP identification, and SNP typing. Working with PE Biosystems.

(continues)

TABLE 8.1   *(continued)*

Company/locations	Stock symbol	Array product technology
Illumina Inc. (San Diego, CA)	Private	Bead/substrate-based microarray system for SNP typing, expression profiling, disease management, diagnostics, immunoassays, drug screening.
Incyte Pharmaceuticals Inc. (Palo Alto, CA)	INCY	Spotted hybridization arrays through Synteni subsidiary, custom experiments done for customers.
Luminex Corp. (Austin, TX)	Private	LabMAP bead-liquid arrays for a variety of bioassays, including DNA hybridization assays.
Millennium Pharmaceuticals Inc. (Cambridge, MA)	MLMN	Five-year, $40-million program begun April 1997 to build functional genomics databases using GeneChips and Millennium technology.
Molecular Dynamics Inc./ Amersham Pharmacia Biotech (Sunnyvale, CA)	NVE	Spotted DNA arrays.
Motorola Inc. (Rolling Meadows, IL)	MOT	Biochip for DNA sequencing, gene mapping, and other assays in partnership with Argonne National Laboratory and Packard Instrument Co.
Nanogen Inc. (San Diego, CA)	NGEN	Electronic arrays for functional genomics, diagnostics, drug discovery, forensics, and other applications.
NEN Life Sciences Inc. (Boston, MA)	Private	Micromax spotted cDNA arrays for expression analysis in collaboration with AlphaGene Inc., contains 2,400 full-length human genes on a glass array.
Perkin-Elmer Corp. (Norwalk, CT)	PKN	HyChip array (see Hyseq), plus "universal" hybridization array technology licensed from Cornell University; MALDI-TOF array analysis.

(continues)

TABLE 8.1   *(continued)*

Company/locations	Stock symbol	Array product technology
Protogene Laboratories Inc. (Palo Alto, CA)	Private	DNA FlexChip arrays, micro-droplets on glass for hybridization.
Rapigene Inc. (Seattle, WA) (a subsidiary of Chiroscience plc)	CRO	High-throughput SNP genotyping.
Research Genetics Inc. (Huntsville, AL)	Private	Gene expression profiling using GeneChip arrays.
Rosetta Inpharmatics Inc. (Kirkland, WA)	Private	Ink-jet-manufactured arrays for SNP typing, expression analysis.
Sequenom Inc. (San Diego, CA)	Private	Spectro-Chip and MALDI-TOF analysis system for "industrial" SNP typing.
Tm Bioscience Corp. (Toronto, Ontario, Canada)	Private	Ligand "normalization" technology to make speed hybridization and make arrays more accurate, with Affymetrix.
Vysis Inc.	VVSI	Genosensor System and Ampli-Onc-1 array hybridization kit for gene amplification detection. Majority owned by Amoco Corp.

SOURCE: Biospace.com, BioVenture Consultants.

common strategy to increase accuracy is to make repetitive probes, so results are duplicated several times over for confirmation. Other companies are using different strategies that they hope will increase accuracy. Sequenom Inc. (San Diego, California), for example, uses arrays but detects sequence by a process using mass spectroscopy instead of hybridization.

Price: Concern about price goes beyond the direct price of the chip and supporting equipment. The cost of repeating experiments because of accuracy concerns, or of slowing throughput because of speed must also be considered. Also, the quantity of sample material required for an assay impacts price. This price again can hinge on chip size. Since a whole chip must be flooded with sample material, smaller chips means less reagent and cloned DNA required.

— 9 —

TREATING DISEASE
AT THE GENE

Antisense Drugs

In Chapter 8, the role of the gene in driving protein production in the cell is described, along with the search for disease-related genes in our chromosomes. In some cases, these disease-related genes are carried into our bodies by bacteria, viruses, and fungi.

One of the big problems with many existing drugs is the high level of adverse side effects. These side effects are caused by the drug molecule interacting with healthy cells in the patients, not just with the diseased cells. In the case of bacterial or viral infections, scientists try to aim the drug at targets found only on the bug and not on human cells. So far, these drugs are still having effects on healthy human cells.

In the late 1970s and early 1980s, scientists started thinking about how to put the growing pool of gene sequences to work for drug design. They realized that most organisms—bugs, humans, and so on—have unique gene sequences that are not found in any other organisms. Some of the genes in bacteria and viruses that cause infections, or that are unique to cancer cells, were identified and their sequence determined. The scientists decided to put that information to work, by creating drugs aimed directly at those unique gene sequences.

In 1989, Isis Pharmaceuticals (Carlsbad, California) was founded by Dr. Stanley Crooke, former president of R&D at SmithKline &

French, to exploit this new technology. Genta Inc., AVI Biopharma, and Gilead Sciences also were formed about the same time.

This approach is termed *antisense*, because it uses synthetic segments of genetic code to inhibit disease-related genes. Here's the basic idea: A mirror image of the target gene sequence is synthesized and delivered to the diseased cell or bug, where it sticks specifically to the target gene sequence and prevents it from working.

Sounds simple, right? But in fact it took almost a decade for the first antisense drug to make it into the marketplace. Antisense and related drug development approaches went through the same convoluted development phase faced by all exciting new technologies—how to convert a process that works in the lab into a commercial-scale, FDA-approvable process.

It took a while for scientists to figure out how to get the antisense compounds into the cells containing the target genes. People worried about safety, getting enough disease-fighting activity into the body, and the costly manufacturing processes. At an industry conference in 1995, Gilead Sciences Inc.'s founder and CEO announced that antisense didn't work and his company was shifting its focus. The group fell out of favor with Wall Street.

But finally, in 1998, the FDA gave Isis the okay to market Vitravene, the first antisense drug, to treat cytomegalovirus retinitis in AIDS patients who can't use other treatments. This infection causes blindness in patients. Isis has a pipeline of products coming hard and fast behind its trailblazer, aimed at cancer and inflammatory diseases. And other companies are hot on the trail also.

Antisense technology also has become an important tool for functional genomics research, because it allows researchers to turn selected genes off and on in test tube experiments or in animals. This ability lets the scientists see what changes in the animal or cell as the gene is manipulated.

Although antisense-based drugs and their relatives will probably never take over the pharmaceutical marketplace, they do address important niche markets where a targeted, highly selective drug is needed. If issues of drug delivery can be successfully addressed to allow use of oral drug formulations, the antisense marketplace may open up even further.

Dr. Stan Crooke, founder and CEO of Isis, says, "Antisense is one of very few platforms available for drug discovery. We had small molecules and proteins, and now antisense. We can make antisense aimed

TABLE 9.1   Biotech Companies Developing Antisense Drugs

Company	Location	Stock symbol
Isis Pharmaceuticals	Carlsbad, CA	ISIP
AVI Biopharma Inc.	Portland, OR	AVII
Genta Inc.	Lexington, MA	GNTA
Hybridon, Inc.	Milford, MA	HYBN

SOURCE: BioVenture Consultants.

at any gene, to treat serious diseases. Where the field is going next is greater patient convenience with oral and aerosol versions (the current antisense drugs require injection). Antisense is also of extraordinary value when used in dissecting biology.

"Antisense will probably not be useful where we have small-molecule drugs that work really well. For example, antisense won't be useful for CNS (central nervous system) disease, because the drugs can't get across the blood-brain barrier. Antisense probably won't be useful against most bacterial diseases, because the antisense molecules don't get into bacteria very well. Also, in bacterial infections you usually want a broad spectrum of activity (drugs that will act against many different strains of bacteria), so why go to the trouble to make a very specific drug aimed at a broad target?

"Finally, the cost to manufacture these drugs is still not low enough to replace cheap therapies like aspirin. But they will be crucial to treat diseases where exquisite selectivity is valuable. Overall, antisense truly is revolutionary as a tool and a therapeutic approach."

Crooke sees antisense as having made an important business contribution, as well. "This is the first time in the pharmaceutical industry where a new drug discovery and development platform is totally dominated by a single little company."

———10———

GENE THERAPY

Gene therapy goes one step beyond antisense in making use of our growing knowledge of the genes that control health and disease. In this case, the drug is not just a piece of synthetic DNA, but an entire gene encased in the paraphernalia needed to carry that gene through the body into the right cells and allow the gene to be read and expressed by the cell. Gene therapy in essence converts the treated cells into little factories, churning out the therapeutic protein.

Why in the world would you want to do this?

In the case of genetic diseases, like cystic fibrosis or Gaucher's disease, mutations in a single gene cause the loss of function in a protein that is very important for the health and life of the patient. Using the tools emerging from biotechnology research, scientists have been able to identify the responsible genes and to figure out what mutation was causing the disease. The next step is to use gene therapy to give the patient a replacement gene that encodes the functioning protein.

These patients need to be treated for their entire lives. Daily replacement of the missing protein via the usual drug therapy can work. But wouldn't it be better to have your own body pumping out the needed protein rather than stabbing yourself on a regular basis? And in the case of cystic fibrosis, the replacement protein really needs to be delivered into the cells having the most trouble—cells in the lungs. An injection simply would not be able to get enough of the protein where it's needed. And in many cases, the missing protein has such a complex structure that manufacturing enough to treat patients is so horrendously expensive that it is simply not feasible.

Scientists also are hoping to use gene therapy to treat more complex diseases, where the problem is not caused by a single mutated gene. For example, in coronary artery disease (CAD), blood vessels have become clogged up with atherosclerotic plaque, and blood flow is reduced. This process leads to pain and tissue damage. There are many factors—genetic, lifestyle, and environmental—that lead to CAD. Right now, the treatment is serious surgery to attempt to replace the damaged vessels or angioplasty to ream out the blockage. Wouldn't it be nice to be able to get the body to build its own new blood vessels to get around the blocked area, regardless of what caused the blockade?

Collateral Therapeutics (San Diego, California) and other private companies are working on a gene therapy product that delivers growth factor genes to the site of the blockade to stimulate production of new blood vessels. Studies in animals and early clinical studies suggest that this approach will in fact drive new blood vessel formation to restore blood flow to the surrounding tissues.

Gene therapy is another area of biotech development where early news left people very excited about the potential for treatment, only to be left hanging as scientists had to work out the inevitable details that made the technology tough to control reproducibly.

The very first gene therapy experiment in humans took place in September 1990. Dr. French Anderson of the National Institutes of Health treated a little girl born with adenosine deaminase deficiency, a genetic disease that causes a loss of adenosine deaminase function and thus cripples the immune system.

The good news? This approach allowed the patient's body to start making about 25% of the normal amount of adenosine deaminase. The bad news? Anderson ran into a problem that still haunts the field—he simply could not get the gene therapy to produce enough of the needed protein in the little girl to completely cure the disease.

Delivery of enough of the gene therapy, getting to enough cells in the patient's body, making enough of the therapeutic protein, over a long enough period of time to make a clinically significant different to the patient—today, a decade after the first gene therapy experiment, delivery, in all its permutations, is still the stumbling block.

Today, there are two major ways to get gene therapy into patients:

- remove some of the patient's cells, get the gene therapeutic into them, and put them back in the patient, or
- inject or otherwise deliver the gene therapeutic into the patient's body directly and let it makes its way to the right part of the body and do its thing.

TABLE 10.1   Gene Therapy Companies

Company	Location	Stock symbol
Ariad Pharmaceuticals	Cambridge, MA	ARIA
Avigen Inc.	Alameda, CA	AVGN
Cell Genesys	Foster City, CA	CEGE
Chiron Corp.	Emoryville, CA	CHIR
Collateral Therapeutics	San Diego, CA	CLTX
Targeted Genetics	Seattle, WA	TGEN
Valentis Inc.	Burlingame, CA	VLTS
Transkaryotic Therapies	Cambridge, MA	TKTX
Genetronics Inc.	San Diego, CA	GEB
Genvec Inc.	Rockville, MD	Private
Genzyme Molecular Oncology	Framingham, MA	GZMO
Onyx Pharmaceuticals Inc.	Richmond, CA	ONXX
Ribozyme Pharmaceuticals	Boulder, CO	RZYM
Vical Inc.	San Diego, CA	VICL

SOURCE: BioVenture Consultants.

There are two major ways to package the gene therapeutic for this trip:

- wrapped up in a genetically engineered virus, or
- "naked," with just a coating of fat to sneak it across the cell membrane

This virus idea is not as crazy as it sounds. Viruses have evolved over the eons to be experts at traveling through our bodies and entering specific cell types for the express purpose of using our cells' machinery to read their genes and make viral proteins. Researchers have found that certain viruses can be genetically engineered to remove the viral genes that cause human disease, rendering them reasonably innocuous carriers of the therapeutic payload.

Companies working on gene therapy approaches (see Table 10.1) are struggling to pull together many different pieces of technology— aimed at making the most effective viral carrier, able to carry a piece of DNA big enough to encode a useful protein along with all the extra coding that will tell the infected cell when and how much of that protein to make, able to efficiently carry the payload into a high percentage of the target cells, and able to hang around long enough to produce a sustained response.

Most of the ongoing gene therapy trials are aimed at cystic fibrosis, cancer, and cardiovascular diseases. And although there is still lots of tweaking to be done, gene therapy has certainly shown that it has the potential to be extremely useful in many important clinical settings. This is an area where strong corporate partnering will probably be crucial to bringing together all of the resources needed to effectively bring a commercial product to market.

Big pharma has shown its interest in this approach by partnering with many of the small biotech firms working on parts of the gene therapy puzzle and has acquired some of the more promising biotech companies (see Table 7.1). Schering-Plough bought Canji, Novartis bought Systemix and Genetic Therapy Inc., and Rhone-Poulenc Rorer bought Applied Immune Sciences as part of its gene therapy strategy.

Gene therapy has raised concerns in the public about the potential for changing human beings into something new, by tinkering with the very basis of life. There have been many discussions about the potential for misusing gene therapy to create "designer babies" with desirable traits—increased intelligence, less balding, better eyesight, resistance to disease, greater height, better personality, and so on. The flipside is a concern that a less-gifted class of people would also be engineered, to create a ready-made workforce.

Today, we really don't have the ability to create these "superbabies"—in part because we don't actually know how to control many of these traits. Genes play a role, but environment—our families, neighbors, schools, and so on—along with lifestyle choices make a big contribution also. On top of that knowledge gap is the fact that gene therapy aimed at one target for a finite period of time is not completely conquered—much less going after a range of traits for a person's lifetime.

But science has a way of moving forward continually, without waiting to see if society is catching up. Industry, academia, and the general public need to have some serious conversations about the use of this technology before it becomes a done deal.

─── 1 1 ───

FOLLOWING THE PATH
OF COMMUNICATION

Signal Transduction

One of the most exciting uses of biotech as a tool for drug discovery is to uncover the actual molecule-to-molecule interactions used by cells to carry information from the cell surface into the nucleus, where gene expression is modified, and the newly made proteins change cell behavior.

It all starts when something changes in a cell's outside environment. Imagine that you are a liver cell lounging around in the body of someone who just ate 14 chocolate chip cookies. Once those cookies are digested, an incredible amount of fat and sugar (in the form of glucose) is released into the bloodstream. Some of that sugar causes neighboring pancreas cells to dump out insulin into the blood.

As the insulin travels through the blood, some of it binds to your insulin receptors, big proteins sitting on your surface that specifically recognize and bind to some of that circulating insulin. Part of that receptor protein sticks right through the cell membrane into the inside of the cell.

When the insulin binds to the outside part of the receptor, it causes a shape change in the part of the insulin receptor sticking into your cell body. That shape change in turn causes a nearby protein inside your cell body to change, which in turn changes another protein— setting off a cascade of changes in proteins that lead all the way to the nucleus, where your genetic material is stored.

The cascade of changes leads to a change in gene expression, with genes associated with glucose transport, protein synthesis, fat deposition, and synthesis of glycogen (a storage molecule used to store up the energy from the sugar) all turned on. The net effect of this activity is to increase the amount of sugar sucked out of the blood, to increase the machinery needed to process that sugar into energy, and to store that energy in a useful form for later (when the cookies get put away).

This handoff of the message that "something stuck to the insulin receptor—quick, do something!" is called *signal transduction*. All communication between a cell and its environment is the result of some form of signal transduction. Anything that binds to a cell surface receptor—hormones, neurotransmitters, nutrients, and so on—exert an influence on cell behavior by using signal transduction pathways to cause changes.

Viruses, bacteria, and cancer cells, along with healthy cells, all use signal transduction to carry out important processes and respond to environmental changes.

Scientists have applied the tools of genomics (and its cousins), biochemistry, antisense, and monoclonal antibodies to discover the individual proteins that participate in these signal transduction pathways, and to identify what goes wrong with these pathways in disease. For example, many cancers have mutations that mess up the ability of the cell to tell itself to stop multiplying—the nucleus keeps getting the "divide now!" signal.

Once scientists identify the specific components of these signaling pathways that are not working properly in disease, they can design very selective drugs to correct the problem. For example, the new drugs aimed at Type II diabetes (essentially a signal transduction disease) appear to work by fixing a signaling problem somewhere between the insulin receptor and the cell's nucleus.

Some diseases are not caused by problems in the signaling pathway but could be treated with drugs that act on the pathway. For example, high cholesterol levels in the blood, known to be associated with an increased risk of heart disease and atherosclerosis, could be treated by turning on the signaling pathway that urges cells to make more cholesterol receptors. This process would allow more of the cholesterol to be removed from the circulation. In fact, some existing drugs such as lovistatin have been shown to work in just this way, by indirectly upregulating receptors on liver cells.

TABLE 11.1   Biotech Companies Focused on Signal Transduction

Company	Location	Stock symbol
Ariad Pharmaceuticals	Cambridge, MA	ARIA
Cephalon Inc.	West Chester, PA	CEPH
Idun Pharmaceuticals	San Diego, CA	Private
Immunex Corp.	Seattle, WA	IMNX
Ligand Pharmaceuticals	San Diego, CA	LGND
Mitotix	Cambridge, MA	Private
Myriad Genetics	Salt Lake City, UT	MYGN
OSI Pharmaceuticals	Uniondale, NY	OSIP
Onyx Pharmaceuticals	Richmond, CA	ONYX
Regeneron Pharmaceuticals	Tarrytown, NY	REGN
Signal Pharmaceuticals	San Diego, CA	Private
Scriptgen Pharmaceuticals	Waltham, MA	Private
Tularik Inc.	South San Francisco, CA	TLRK

SOURCE: BioVenture Consultants.

Drugs aimed at components of signal transduction pathways may be useful for treating neurological diseases, cardiovascular diseases, chronic inflammatory disorder, cancer, and Type II diabetes. Several of the companies active in this arena have been snapped up by other companies eager to expand their signal transduction programs, including Sugen (bought by Pharmacia & Upjohn) and ProScript (acquired by Leukosite).

There is a growing group of young biotech companies that are developing very snazzy technologies that allow researchers to figure out the individual proteins that participate in important signaling pathways, and then to use those proteins as drug discovery tools. These companies, which include Sangamo Biosciences Inc. (Richmond, California) and Rigel Inc. (South San Francisco, California), work hand in hand with other companies to figure out just what is going on inside cells and how to use that information to make innovative new drugs aimed at modulating pathways to affect disease processes.

——12——

BRAND-NEW KNEES

Tissue Engineering and Cell Replacement

So there you are, out on the mountain, new skis strapped on your feet, new goggles in place, new ski parka, looking pretty darned cool. Too bad your knees are already complaining about your plans for subjecting them to the damage of gravity and pounding moguls. If only there were a way to enjoy skiing without spending 50% of your vacation taking Advil and whining quietly in front of the ski lodge fireplace.

Biotech may have the answer for you—new knees!

As researchers have used biotech to understand the molecular messages used by cells and tissues to grow and prosper, they have begun using that information to figure out how to make those same tissue growth processes work in the lab.

Don't get all excited now—the technology is not yet at the point where it's okay to be reckless out there. But there is a bulging product pipeline heading toward advanced clinical trials and the marketplace that promises to provide or stimulate replacement parts for skin, bone, teeth, blood vessels, cartilage in the knee and other sites, liver, pancreas, bladder, and spinal cord nerves.

There are several components to this area of R&D—cell growth factors that stimulate proliferation of the needed cells, biodegradable three-dimensional matrices in which to grow the cells, the ability to grow the right cells in the lab and store them for when they are needed, devices for getting the new parts into the patient, and the ability to regenerate new parts that have the same characteristics as the originals. Genetic engineering also allows tissue replacement to be used as a sustained drug delivery device—getting the new liver to pump out missing enzymes, for example, instead of needing daily injections.

Part of the impetus behind this research activity is the lack of sufficient replacement organs and tissues for all the patients in need. Dr. Joseph Vacanti, at Children's Hospital in Boston, and Dr. Robert Langer, at MIT, have driven the tissue-engineering area forward for the past two decades through their research into how to make cells do what we need them to do and how to deliver them to patients. The two collaborators carried out a study in 1993 that showed that more than $400 billion is spent in the United States each year on patients with organ failure, including 8 million surgeries. Even so, 4,000 die while waiting for a new organ, and another 100,000 die before even reaching the waiting list.

Langer, Vacanti, and their growing roster of colleagues have developed biodegradable scaffolds to support the growth and development of cells into organs and have pioneered methods for implanting these devices in patients. Langer was awarded the Lemeulson-MIT Inventor of the Year Award in 1998 for his work in this area.

The first products in this category to reach the marketplace were the skin replacements, aimed at patients with severe burns or non-healing wounds. Previously, their only alternative was removal of skin from other parts of their body for grafting—or the use of cadaver skin as a temporary covering. Advanced Tissue Sciences (ATS) and Organogenesis are selling living skin replacements for burns and nonhealing wounds and continue to study other skin-healing applications. ATS is also extending its tissue replacement expertise into cartilage and cardiovascular applications.

Genzyme Tissue Repair's Carticel—in which a patient's own knee cartilage cells are removed, proliferated in the lab, and reimplanted—brought in $11 million in 1998, and its Epicel skin grafts contributed $6 million. Its parent company, Genzyme General, participates in a joint venture with Diacrin to develop NeuroCell cell implant therapies for Parkinson's and Huntington's diseases.

Companies including Osiris, Creative Biomolecules, and MorphoGen Pharmaceuticals Inc. are studying the growth factors and stem cells that drive creation of specialized tissues. And Acorda Ther-

TABLE 12.1 Tissue-Engineering/Cell Therapy Companies

Company	Location	Stock symbol	Tissue
Tissue Replacement:			
Acorda	Hawthorne, NY	Private	Growth factors, scar blockers, matrix for spinal cord
Advanced Tissue Sciences	La Jolla, CA	ATIS	Matrix and growth factors for skin, cartilage, connective tissues
Cell Based Delivery Inc.	Providence, RI	Private	Muscle cells engineered to deliver therapeutic genes
CellMart Inc.	Reno, NV	Private	Matrix and cell proliferation technology for pancreas
Circe Biomedical Inc.	Lexington, MA	Private	Cell replacement for liver
Creative Biomolecules	Cambridge, MA	CBMI	Growth factors for bone, cartilage, kidney, neurons
Cryolife Inc.	Atlanta, GA	CRY	Heart valves
CytoTherapeutics	Lincoln, RI	CTII	Cell therapy in brain tissue
Desmos Inc.	San Diego, CA	Private	Cell adhesion and proliferation for skin, connective tissues, pancreas
Diacrin, Inc.	Charlestown, MA	DCRN	Animal organs to replace pancreas and neurons, cell therapy
Encelle Inc.	Greenville, NC	Private	Animal organs to replace pancreas
Genzyme General Corp.	Cambridge, MA	GENZ	Brain cell implants
Genzyme Tissue Repair	Cambridge, MA	GZTR	Matrix and cell technology for cartilage, skin

(continued)

TABLE 12.1   *(continued)*

Company	Location	Stock symbol	Tissue
Integra LifeSciences Corp.	Plainsboro, NJ	IART	Matrix and cell technology for skin, tissue/bone/cartilage regeneration
Lifecell Inc.	Branchburg, NJ	LIFC	Engineering of animal tissues for heart, skin, connective tissue
Molecular Geodesics Inc.	Cambridge, MA	Private	Biomimetics for tissue engineering, bioimplants
MorphoGen Pharmaceuticals Inc.	New York, NY	Private	Stem cells, matrix, and growth factors for muscle
NeuralStem Bio-pharmaceuticals Ltd.	College Park, MD	Private	Brain stem cells
Organogenesis Inc.	Canton, MA	ORG	Matrix and cell technology for skin, liver, connective tissue, blood vessels
Orquest Inc.	Mountain View, CA	Private	Bone
Ortec International	New York, NY	ORTC	Skin engineering
Orthavita Inc.	Malvern, PA	Private	Spine tissue engineering, bone substitutes
Osiris Therapeutics Inc.	Baltimore, MD	Private	Stem cells and growth factors for mesencymal cells
Osteotech Inc.	Eatontown, NJ	OSTE	Bone graft matrix and factors
Progenitor Cell Therapy LLC	Hackensack, NJ	Private	Blood stem cells
Proneuron Biotechnologies Inc.	Kiryat, Israel	Private	Spinal cord repair
ReGen Biologics	Redwood City, CA	Private	Matrix and cell technology for cartilage

(continues)

TABLE 12.1   *(continued)*

Company	Location	Stock symbol	Tissue
Reprogenesis	Cambridge, MA	Private	Matrix and cell technology for connective tissue to rebuild organs
Spinal Concepts Inc./ Selective Genetics Inc.	Austin, TX, and San Diego, CA	Private	Growth factors for bone delivered in a spinal fusion device
Titan Pharmaceuticals	South San Francisco, CA	TTP	Matrix and cell technology for brain

SOURCE: BioVenture Consultants.

apeutics is taking a multiprong approach to enticing damaged spinal cord neurons to grow back across the traumatized area and reconnect the severed nervous system connections.

Spinal Concepts Inc. is collaborating with Selective Genetics Inc. to use its implantable device to deliver Selective's gene therapy product encoding a bone growth factor for spinal fusions. The device would encourage the growth of new bone into the region, getting rid of the need for the usual autograft procedure, in which bone is removed from another site on the patient and added into the spine. Orquest Inc. is part of a similar collaboration with Sulzer and Biopharm GmbH to deliver bone growth factors in a mineralized collagen matrix for spine repair.

We are still years away from being able to grow replacement organs in the lab for easy transplant, but the world of tissue engineering is rapidly approaching that day. In the meantime, the technology is making a big difference for a broad range of patients.

—————13—————

BUILDING NEW DRUGS
Combinatorial Chemistry

In 1969, a new painkiller called *ibuprofen* was introduced in the United States. Eventually licensed by American Home Products, it ultimately became the over-the-counter drug Advil, a pain reliever that has brought in billions of dollars in sales over the years.

In 1976, 7 years after the introduction of ibuprofen, Syntex (now Roche Bioscience) introduced a chemically related compound called naproxen sodium. Although similar to ibuprofen, it had some advantages that made it better for certain inflammatory conditions. It was sold as the drug Naprosyn and ultimately became the active ingredient in the over-the-counter medicine Aleve. Although this drug, too, fetched billions in revenues, its makers lost the benefit of the years that ibuprofen had all to itself in the marketplace. When Naprosyn lost its patent coverage in the mid-1990s, Syntex lost its cash cow product and became a takeover candidate for Roche.

Some modern chemists have asserted that if combinatorial chemistry techniques had been used in developing ibuprofen, naproxen sodium could have been discovered the very same day.

WHAT IS COMBICHEM?

Combinatorial chemistry (combichem) has gone in a few years from being a radical concept to a universally accepted tool for drug development. It is essentially a method for rapidly making a large number of related chemicals with as few steps as possible. The idea is to find the one compound with the best molecular shape and chemical characteristics for a given drug target.

To use combichem, you start with a drug target such as the insulin receptor or the enzyme responsible for letting HIV continue an infection. A good drug compound would bind specifically and selectively to that target and keep it from doing its job, thus stopping the disease. It would also be nice if the drug compound was water-soluble (since our bodies are about 80% water), had no toxic effects on healthy tissues, could be taken by mouth and make it intact through the stomach, and could retain its therapeutic benefit for several hours after making its way into the bloodstream.

The basic concept is to make an array of potential drug candidates with different chemical structures, look at their ability to interact with the drug target, and then go back and make lots of different versions (analogues) of the structures that had the most promising interactions with the target. This iterative process can be cycled through many times before finding the best drug lead to take into the development process.

Combinatorial chemistry is a numbers game. It involves using chemical and biological knowledge—and often specialized software—to reduce an astronomical number of potential compounds to a number that is merely very large and thus testable.

Years of chemists learning how to synthesize drugs in the labs have given us certain basic rules about chemical structures that make the best drugs—the infamous "druggable" structure. Although there is a virtually limitless number of chemical compounds that could conceivably turn out to be effective medicines, chemists have some idea of the kinds of structures they are looking for. One estimate holds that there are 10^{200} possible small organic molecules that a scientist could create in a laboratory. But if she synthesized just one molecule of each possible compound, their combined mass would exceed that of the universe by a factor of 10^{128}!* Obviously no chemist could hope to find a new drug through a comprehensive trial-and-error process.

Luckily, years of experience with the molecules that are already known to be effective drugs have given researchers some good ideas about the molecular structures they are looking for. Knowledge about the target or the disease it relates to gives chemists further structural guidelines. With enough knowledge and an intelligent, iterative process for refining compounds, researchers can make compound "li-

---

*A. W. Czarnik. (1995) *Chemtracts: Organic Chemistry*, No. 8, pp. 13–18.

braries" of a manageable size that still have a strong chance of fitting the target.

Even with a clear idea about the rough shape a drug should have, there is still room for a huge amount of variation. Just think of mixing together hundreds of thousands of jigsaw puzzles, with every piece similarly shaped but none identical. The chances of creating a library that has a perfect match for a target is small indeed. And that is where much of the competitive difference between combinatorial chemistry companies comes into play.

SYNTHESIS

In terms of actually creating libraries of diverse chemical structures, there is little to recommend one combinatorial chemistry company over another, or over the numerous private and public sector groups that synthesize compounds for their own research purposes. Various companies have specialized techniques or equipment that allows them to produce more compounds than their competitors, or larger volumes of each compound. But most people in the industry agree that pure contract synthesis of novel chemical libraries is essentially a commodity business.

That very fact proves how vital this approach has become to the drug industry. As a commercial endeavor, combinatorial chemistry didn't exist until 1990, when Dr. Richard Houghten at the Torrey Pines Institute for Molecular Studies in La Jolla, California, founded a company around a revolutionary new technology.

Although chemists traditionally took many steps to synthesize a single compound, Houghten developed a way to synthesize many compounds in relatively few steps. Building on earlier work that used a solid substrate to synthesize peptides, Houghten accelerated the process through the use of "tea bags"—porous membranes containing solid beads that could be exposed to a variety of chemical groups, thus adding them onto a core structure, or "scaffold."

The company he founded, eventually named Houghten Pharmaceuticals, now operates under the name Trega Biosciences Inc.

Trega has stiff competition, all of which uses a similar concept for creating chemical libraries. A core chemical scaffold is used as the root of the library, and a variety of chemical groups (known in the vernacular as *R groups*) are added onto it. Alternatively, chemists might combine several chemical groups to create a variety of scaffolds, then vary them by further modification. Choosing what to start with and what to vary requires knowledge of pharmacology, knowledge of structure-activity relationships, and ideally some knowledge about the drug target.

Libraries can have anywhere from hundreds to millions of compounds, and there is much debate over the relative advantages of bigger libraries with more possible candidates versus smaller batches that are presumably more focused on the target at hand.

CombiChem Inc., for example, starts with a library of *Universal Informers*—molecules with flexible three-dimensional structures that can bind to a variety of targets, kind of like a jigsaw puzzle piece made out of rubber. The advantage is that at least 1 from a library of 10,000 of these "floppy" structures is very likely to bind to a target. The disadvantage is that it probably won't bind very well, and you won't know exactly what shape it took when it bound. But by looking at overlaps in the compounds that do bind and using some computer modeling to look at "virtual" compounds and the target structure, the company says it can refine the initial lead into a targeted library of likely candidates.

Pharmacopeia, on the other hand, has a huge library of real compounds—over 5 million—and is synthesizing more at a rate of a million a year. The company targets parts of its library, based on modeling capabilities gained through the acquisition of Molecular Simulations Inc. and through pharmacological knowledge of certain target classes. But they also simply synthesize large numbers of druglike molecules in hopes that one of the structures will be useful for some target.

Combinatorial chemistry is not merely an invention of 20th-century science. There are a number of stunning examples of how nature uses a combinatorial process to adapt and evolve. Our own immune systems create antibodies to unknown invaders through an adaptive trial-and-error process, looking for compounds that bind to the invader and improving on them.

Scientists who isolate chemicals from animal and plant species often find a variety of related chemical structures, some created as the organisms adapt to new challenges in their environment. Various microorganisms use enzymes to engineer novel chemical structures, which in turn could be used as the basis for a new approach to drug design. Several combichem companies, including Diversa, Enzymed, Ixsys, and Kosan, are taking advantage of nature's clever metabolic pathways combined with genetic engineering to generate new chemical structures for combichem uses.

TABLE 13.1   Combinatorial Chemistry Companies

Company	Technology	Stock symbol
3-Dimensional Pharmaceuticals Inc. (Exton, PA)	"DirectedDiversity" compound arrays—automates synthesis and screening of compounds from a large "virtual" library of pharmacophores.	Private
Albany Molecular Research Inc. (Albany, NY)	Organic custom synthesis, along with other chemistry synthesis, optimization, analytical, and manufacturing services.	AMRI
Applied Molecular Evolution, Inc. (San Diego, CA)	Combinatorial biology ("directed evolution" protein optimization), combinatorial libraries.	Private
Argonaut Technologies Inc. (San Carlos, CA)	Instrumentation for solution- and solid-phase combinatorial synthesis.	Private
ArQule Inc. (Medford, MA)	Solution-phase synthesis of "Mapping Array" screening libraries and "Directed Array" optimization libraries.	ARQL
Array Biopharma Inc. (Boulder, CO)	Monomer pharmacophore arrays for sale by catalog, custom diversity libraries and optimization. Structure-based design capability, metabolism and toxicology assays.	Private
Axys Pharmaceuticals Inc. (South San Francisco, CA)	Combinatorial libraries in multi-milligram quantities, for both internal purposes and contract service.	AXPH
Charybdis Technologies Inc. (Carlsbad, CA)	Instrumentation for solution- and solid-phase combinatorial synthesis and cheminformatics.	Private
ChemBridge Corp. (San Diego, CA)	"PHARMACore" and other combinatorial libraries, licensed on a nonexclusive basis for screening.	Private
CombiChem Inc. (San Diego, CA)	Large "virtual" libraries of molecules designed on computer, with ability to synthesize targeted libraries.	CCHM (DuPont plans to acquire)

(continues)

TABLE 13.1   *(continued)*

Company	Technology	Stock symbol
ComGenex International Inc. (South San Francisco, CA)	"MeDiverse" maximum diversity library of 10,000 chemicals. Solution-phase synthesis in up to 100+-mg quantities.	Private
Discovery Partners International Inc. (La Jolla, CA)	Its subsidiaries IRORI and ChemRx Inc. make combinatorial chemistry libraries and offer optimization services. IRORI uses "AccuTag" solid-phase synthesis and radio-frequency tagging.	Private
Diversa Corp. (San Diego, CA)	"DirectEvolution" of enzymes, a combinatorial biology technique to optimize/diversify enzymes found in the environment.	DVSA
Gryphon Sciences Inc. (South San Francisco, CA)	Synthesis of proteins and protein family libraries.	Private
Kosan Biosciences Inc. (Burlingame, CA)	Combinatorial biosynthesis of polyketides	Private
Maxygen Inc. (Redwood City, CA)	"DNA shuffling," a combinatorial biology technique to create diversity in families of proteins, enzymes, viruses, etc.	Private spinout of Glaxo Wellcome/ Affymax Research Institute
Molecumetics Ltd. (Bellevue, WA)	SMART Libraries (solid- and solution-phase synthesis using scaffolds that mimic protein-binding sites) and structure-based drug design.	Private
Nanoscale Combinatorial Synthesis Inc. (Tucson, AZ)	Organic combinatorial library of almost 100,000 purified molecules, available in 96- and 384-well plates. Solid-phase synthesis on beads in nanogram quantities.	Private

(continues)

TABLE 13.1   *(continued)*

Company	Technology	Stock symbol
Ontogen Corp. (Carlsbad, CA)	OntoBLOCK solid-phase library synthesis with radiofrequency tagging.	Private
Orchid Biocomputer Inc. (Princeton, NJ)	Creates organic small-molecule and peptide libraries on "Chemtel" chips; uses "lab-on-a-chip" technology for rapid synthesis and screening.	Private
MDS Panlabs Inc. (Bothell, WA)	Large-scale synthesis and screening, plus natural products libraries.	Private
Pharmacopeia Inc. (Princeton, NJ)	Large libraries of small molecules, synthesized on beads. Total collection of over 5 million compounds.	PCOP
Phytera Inc. (Worcester, MA)	Natural compound libraries, expanded through combinatorial techniques (and altered culture conditions).	Private
ProtoGene Inc. (Palo Alto, CA)	Parallel array synthesis of organic small-molecule libraries.	Private
Sphere Biosystems Inc. (New Brunswick, NJ)	Solid-phase synthesis of libraries on "buckyballs," for radial display of compounds.	Private
Symyx Technologies Inc. (Santa Clara, CA)	Materials science program—combinatorial production of plastics, catalysts, polymers, electronics materials, etc. Does not make drug libraries.	SMMX
Systems Integration Drug Discovery Co. (SIDDCO) (Tucson, AZ)	A group of combinatorial and medicinal chemists who have formed a combinatorial chemistry consortium to share resources and knowledge to develop combichem capabilities at mid-size pharmaceutical and biotech companies.	Private

(continues)

TABLE 13.1   *(continued)*

Company	Technology	Stock symbol
Telik Inc. (South San Francisco, CA)	Large compound library, used for screening using the company's TRAP probability-based screening technology.	Private
Trega Biosciences Inc. (San Diego, CA)	Solid-phase chemical synthesis of peptide and small-molecule libraries. Pharmacokinetic screening and modeling from acquisition of NaviCyte Inc.	TRGA
Tripos Inc. (St. Louis, MO)	"LeadQuest" screening libraries (solid- and solution-phase synthesis) plus virtual compound modeling	Private
Versicor Inc. (Marlborough, MA)	Concentration on antibiotic discovery through combinatorial chemistry, high-throughput screening, and functional genomics.	Private spinout of Sepracor Inc. (SEPR)

SOURCE: Biospace.com, BioVenture Consultants.

This combinatorial approach to new compound creation is being applied outside the biomedical realm. Symyx Technologies (Santa Clara, California) is using combinatorial technologies to discover new materials—plastics, polymers, catalysts for chemical reactions, and electronic materials—for use in the electronics and chemical industries. Its list of corporate partners shows little overlap with those of its biotech brethren—Celanese, Ciba Specialty Chemicals, Dow Chemical Co., B. F. Goodrich, and Unilever. CombiChem (recently the target of an acquisition plan by DuPont) has added materials science combichem to its drug development capability.

—14—

AGRICULTURAL
BIOTECHNOLOGY

The earliest experiments in genetic engineering were done in the fields thousands of years ago. Much of the produce we eat today is significantly different from its long-ago ancestors. Oranges are bigger and sweeter; corn grows with a higher yield and softer kernels. Over the years, careful crossbreeding has accentuated desirable traits—like size, color, flavor, hardiness—and minimized unwanted characteristics. And much of this advancement took place long before the foundation of modern genetics, through slow, steady plant breeding.

Although the Czechoslovakian monk Gregor Mendel is credited with establishing the first principles of inheritance through his work with peas, breeders who worked before Mendel's day had already developed hybrid strains of many plants without understanding the principles through which their success was achieved. Luther Burbank, the 19th-century American breeder who developed hundreds of new strains of fruits, vegetables, and flowers in his career through careful cross-breeding and observation, believed that acquired traits could be inherited.

The tools of biotechnology allow plant breeders to improve on the traditional grafting and crossbreeding—techniques that rely on observation and intuition to alter the genomes of plants by hundreds of genes at a time. Today, genomics and genetic engineering allow breeders to home in quickly on the small number of genes that control commercially important traits such as improved tolerance to drought conditions, increased resistance to crop pests, and increased nutritional value.

Biotechnology allows us to engineer into crops traits that would never have occurred by traditional plant breeding, by introducing genes from one species into another. For instance, a gene from a soil microbe called *Bacillus thuringiensis* has been used to confer pest resistance on a wide variety of plants. This new trait allows the crops to prosper without the usual attack by insects and worms, without the need for excessive pesticides.

Given our long history with plant breeding, it's not surprising that some early biotech entrepreneurs thought agriculture was a natural starting point for proving the commercial value of biotechnology. The ag biotech supporters figured that because the research is conducted on plants, not humans, there is more flexibility in experimental design and quicker results (no clinical trials needed!). They also expected fewer regulatory hurdles and quicker approval times by going through the Environmental Protection Agency (EPA) rather than the Food and Drug Administration.

The good news is that the ag biotech sector generated many important scientific and product innovations. SunGene, based in the San Jose, California, area, was one of the first companies to develop RFLP (restriction fragment length polymorphism) gene-mapping techniques as a way to track genes and their mutations. Calgene did much of the early work using antisense to control gene expression, aimed at turning off a gene responsible for rotting in fruits and vegetables once they are harvested. Calgene and its brethren also investigated gene modification to change the metabolic pathways in plants. This allowed production of plant oils with improved nutritional value (lower in saturated fats, for example) or better industrial characteristics (better stability at high heat and temperature) that might allow them to replace petroleum-based oils.

Unfortunately, things didn't quite work out as planned. Many first-generation ag biotech companies have names that few remember, having either gone out of business or been acquired by the large agriculture companies—Monsanto, Rhone-Poulenc, Dow AgroSciences, BASF, and Hoechst. The benefits of early products weren't perceived as particularly desirable by consumers—tomatoes and carrots with longer shelf lives couldn't command a premium price, for example. In some cases, the buyers of the technology—the farmers—didn't see an advantage to the improved trait and weren't willing to pay a premium for it.

And the expected accelerated product development cycle never materialized—the wait for the right growing season, production of seed from the first-generation crops, and regulatory turmoil as EPA, FDA, and the U.S. Department of Agriculture argued over who was in charge all resulted in the public markets' losing interest in supporting the sector.

Calgene Inc. was eventually acquired by Monsanto Co., while BASF bought up SunGene, Dow bought Mycogen, and Hoechst acquired Plant Genetic Systems NV. Today, there are essentially no small ag biotech companies. However, there is a growing trend for the big ag companies to team up with biotech's genomics companies to speed up the search for commercially important genes.

Today, the products of biotechnology are used every day in agriculture. Monsanto estimates that nearly 40% of soybean acreage in the United States was planted with genetically modified crops in 1998. With the world's population predicted to rise dramatically in coming decades, new technologies that make efficient use of agricultural land are vital to our survival—and a rich potential business opportunity.

But there's also more trouble on the horizon. Many commercial ag biotech products, although successful, have concentrated on "agronomic" properties—that is, they offer economic benefit to the farmers who use them. Consumers benefit only indirectly, because fewer pesticides and herbicides are used in farming and thus the net result should be a cleaner environment. Most consumers don't see any real benefit in terms of food prices, however, and many fear that the use of biotechnology will be dangerous or will alter our environment in unexpected ways.

In Europe, public backlash against agricultural biotechnology has been widespread and vociferous, with the media giving acres of newsprint to discussions about so-called Frankenstein foods. Although U.S. consumers have generally shown less concern about genetically modified foods, protest over ag biotech has spread to U.S. shores, as well as to Canada, Japan, and elsewhere.

The industry has resisted labeling genetically modified foods in grocery stores for fear that such disclosure would frighten consumers. But more and more food processors—including, most recently, Archer Daniels Midland—are either demanding that farmers segregate genetically modified crops from other produce or refusing to buy genetically modified foods altogether. Gerber decided to make sure its baby foods are made with only nonengineered grains, to avoid protests.

Yet another obstacle to acceptance is the fact that many parts of the world where agricultural biotechnology would be most valuable—

where growing populations and poverty outstrip the land's ability to produce sufficient food—are also areas where understanding of the science behind genetic engineering is particularly limited. Finally, legitimate concerns about some applications of these new technologies have tainted many people's attitudes toward all genetically modified crops and have made them question the motives of the companies developing the new technologies.

Monsanto, for example, recently capitulated to widespread protest and decided not to engineer its "terminator" gene into seeds being sold in India. The terminator gene—named not by the company, but by an environmentalist opposed to the gene's use—would have stopped the plants from producing their own viable seeds, meaning that farmers who used to save seed from the previous harvest would have to purchase new seeds every season. . . from Monsanto. Of course, the flipside of this gene is that the lack of fertile seed would allow the company to quickly stop exposure of the environment should the genetically engineered trait show an unexpected problem.

Although a lot of public discussion lies ahead, the promise of agricultural biotechnology is enormous. Crops that help our environment by requiring fewer herbicides and pesticides are already a reality, but companies are focusing on the creation of plant strains with even more important properties. Crops of tomorrow may be able to thrive in areas now considered unsuitable for farming, because they will resist the ravages of drought and extreme temperatures. This would allow more people, particularly in arid Third World countries to support themselves by farming. Future crops may be far more nutritious than current food plants, making a fixed amount of land more efficient in terms of feeding human beings.

Tomorrow's crops may even produce medicines. The principles of recombinant protein production used today to make a number of important drugs are also being applied to plants. The cellular machinery of tobacco plants, for instance, is being used by a company called Biosource Technologies to produce a vaccine. And Monsanto is developing a plant that grows a form of biodegradable plastic! As we learn more about the genes that contain the code for desirable traits and products, plants may prove to be the most versatile biological factories we have.

part three

The Business of Biotech: Product Development and Financing

———15———

THE DRUG
DEVELOPMENT PROCESS

From Test Tubes to Patients

For investors in any biotechnology or pharmaceutical company, the driver of both opportunity and risk is product development. All the exciting science in the world won't generate long-term value unless it is used to create products that bring a significant revenue stream into the company. Most biotech investors are not able to judge the basic science of a company. However, a good understanding of the product development process can go a long way to giving you benchmarks for judging the relative risk of individual product candidates.

Keep in mind that this process—and the risk—is essentially identical for small biotech companies and for large pharmaceutical firms. The key difference is that big pharma has ongoing product revenues to cushion the inevitable product failure and often doesn't have to reveal when those failures occur. If the company is large enough, and the failure early enough, it is not a reportable event as defined by the SEC (Securities and Exchange Commission).

Unfortunately, most biotech firms don't have that luxury. Every product candidate is crucial to their success, and any speed bump usually must be reported. The bad news is that the business press and many investors tend to overreact to negative product development events. Hopefully, by the end of this chapter, you will have some tools to help you decide whether a news item is devastating or merely an expected hiccup in the road to FDA approval.

The Long and Winding Road

The discovery and development of a new pharmaceutical are long and arduous tasks. According to the Tufts Center for the Study of Drug Development, it takes an average of 15 years for a new drug to move from the discovery phase, into animal testing, through clinical trials, past the U.S. Food and Drug Administration, and into the marketplace. A January 1996 report from the Boston Consulting Group says that the average cost of generating a single new drug is $500 million—a frightening thought!

The scariest part of all this is the risk—estimates from the Pharmaceutical Research and Manufacturers of America say that for every 5,000 compounds that emerge from discovery and animal testing (termed *preclinical testing*), only about 5 compounds perform well enough to move on into human testing. And only 1 of those 5 makes it into the marketplace.

Just to keep the adrenaline rushing, getting a new product into the market doesn't guarantee long-term success. Abbott Labs had to pull an antibiotic (Omniflox) off the market when toxic side effects began to show up only a few months after marketing approval. Hoechst Marion Roussel removed its highly successful antihistamine Seldane from the U.S. market because it was found to cause abnormal heart rhythms when taken with the antibiotic erythromycin or with ketaconazole, an antifungal drug. Seldane also can cause abnormal heart rhythms in patients with liver disease. As soon as the FDA approved Hoechst's second-generation antihistamine containing the active metabolite of Seldane, Hoechst immediately stopped selling Seldane.

American Home Products Corp. (AHP), one of the top 10 pharmaceutical companies in the world based on product sales, opted to pull its new and incredibly successful obesity drug, Redux, off the market in September 1997 when reports began to circulate that the drug caused heart valve problems. Redux, licensed to AHP by Interneuron Pharmaceuticals Inc. (Lexington, Massachusetts), increases brain levels of serotonin, a neurotransmitter, by inducing its release from nerve cells and also inhibiting its uptake by nerve cells. The net result of this multisyllabic activity is loss of appetite, making it easier to stop overeating.

Redux was tested in more than 4,000 patients in 19 late-stage clinical studies. The product and its relative Pondimin (also sold by AHP) have both been sold in Europe for many years. The company and its advisers felt comfortable that any serious adverse effects would have surfaced in this time. There were some concerns about an increased risk of primary pulmonary hypertension, a dangerous lung disorder. The FDA advisory panel held two hearings to discuss Redux and narrowly voted to recommend that the FDA approve the drug. The bottom line was that the real health risks of obesity itself were felt to outweigh the potential risk from Redux.

The drug was approved in April 1996 for treatment of obesity, and had the fastest ramp-up of sales ever seen for a drug at that time. Interneuron Pharmaceuticals was enjoying its eighth position in the top tier of BioVenture Consultants' *Biotech Stock Report*, with a market capitalization of $1.4 billion. The sales of Redux reached an annualized sales rate of $220 million within its first 11 weeks on the market, according to David Crossen of Montgomery Securities. The drug brought in $132 million in revenues to AHP in its first year on the market and drove sales of AHP's existing complementary drug, Pondimin, to $172 million through combination use. Analysts predicted the drug would eventually produce sales of up to $1 billion.

But about 18 months after its rocket launch, Redux and Pondimin were voluntarily pulled off the market by AHP following reports from the Mayo Clinic in July 1997 that 24 healthy patients taking a combination (termed *fen-phen*) of Pondimin and another drug had developed heart valve disease. The FDA put out an advisory regarding potential heart valve problems and told AHP that the Redux and Pondimin packages would have to carry prominent warning labels discussing the risk of heart and lung problems.

As it became clear that both Redux and the fen-phen combo were being widely prescribed by diet centers and physicians, concerns arose that the drugs were being used by patients who were not really obese. In such patients, the need to lose a few pounds for essentially cosmetic reasons was not worth the risk of potential adverse effects from the drugs. The *New England Journal of Medicine* called for those patients not seriously overweight to stop taking these drugs, and the *Journal of the American Medical Association* published an article suggesting that the drugs had caused brain damage in monkeys and rats.

Patients who truly benefited from Redux treatment found themselves pitted against physicians and the FDA. AHP estimated that about 50 million people worldwide have taken drugs identical to Redux and Pondimin and suggested that surely any significant health problems would have surfaced by now. Nonetheless, AHP took the two drugs off the market in September 1997. Although AHP had revenues of $8.7 billion from other drugs to cushion the blow to shareholders, Interneuron stock dropped like a rock, dragging the company's market cap to around $477 million by October 1997.

The company decided to directly address the safety issue with follow-up studies. In March 1998, clinical investigators at Georgetown University reported at the American College of Cardiology that there were no statistically significant increases in heart valve problems in a placebo-controlled study of 1,072 patients treated over 77 days. These data are expected to support AHP and Interneuron as they deal with lawsuits from patients. But AHP has stated that it has no plans to reintroduce either drug, according to Dr. Steve Gerber, analyst at CIBC Oppenheimer.

As we went to press in late 1999, AHP was trying to structure a settlement that would award a proposed $4 billion, including coverage of medical checkups for those who have not yet shown signs of adverse effects. Plaintiff lawyers were accusing the company of not responding effectively to reports of adverse events in patients, the FBI was rumored to be investigating Redux's 1996 approval, and a judge rejected a proposed $100-million settlement on behalf of small player Interneuron.

Pfizer's Viagra is another good example of the problem. As prescriptions became easily available, use of the drug shifted to include men who were not really impotent and women—for whom the drug had not been approved or even tested. Reports of deaths began to come in as men on other medications had serious adverse effects from Viagra. Pilots have been warned to avoid taking the drug less than 18 hours before flying—the blue vision changes make it difficult to read the instruments! To date, neither the company nor the FDA has shown any desire to pull the drug, and both are relying on widespread warnings to raise patient awareness. Viagra continues to sell up a storm, and competitors are racing to bring their own products to market.

The lessons to be learned from these experiences? First, a drug can make it all the way through the clinical and regulatory maze, reap kudos from Wall Street analysts and high-profile physicians alike, and still hit unexpected roadblocks in the real world of the marketplace. If you're lucky, the product will be a survivor and earn back the $500 million+ the company spent to develop it.

Another key point to remember is that although drugs aimed at high-profile disorders can make a big difference to patients in real need and can make great profits for the company, the risk of overexposure is high. Redux and its brethren had an acceptable risk-benefit profile for many obese patients, but the ratio shifted significantly when usage appeared to spread into populations where the need for the drug was not as clear-cut.

Finally, coverage by the lay press can be a two-edged sword. Stories in the newspaper about new drugs or new technologies can drive stock prices up—unfortunately, this activity typically is based on overreaction to very early results and anticipation of rapid market entry. Entremed's experience in May 1998 is a classic example of press coverage gone awry.

A front-page story by Gina Kolata of the *New York Times* used quotes, exuberant adjectives, and an inflammatory headline to turn a story about early experiments in mice into a full-fledged run on Entremed stock. The stock price jumped from $12.06 to as high as $85 per share the day the story hit.

A year later, Entremed stock was around $23 per share, and the touted "cancer cure" is still in preclinical studies. Investors who got sucked into the stock may be disappointed—but keep in mind that the stock price does not reflect poor company performance. Rather, it reflects a return to a more realistic valuation based on the actual status of the project and the work that remains to be done before an anticancer drug reaches the marketplace.

Although the kind of experience AHP and Pfizer had would discourage most normal people, the biopharmaceutical industry knows that the right drug for the right patient population can bring the blockbuster payoff. Companies are avidly pursuing different therapeutic approaches to obesity and impotence, and Wall Street continues to reward them with rave reviews.

CHOOSING THE RIGHT MARKET

Although drugs aimed at newly discovered mechanisms of disease show the greatest promise of solving previously unsolved health problems, there often are unexpected toxic side effects that show up only in later stages of clinical testing—or even later.

Rezulin, Warner-Lambert's new treatment for adult-onset diabetes—affecting an estimated 16 million people in the United States—attacks the problem at a molecular level within the cell by cranking up cell response to insulin. Clinical studies in 2,510 patients showed that 1.8% of the test group had a significant increase in liver enzymes—signs of potential damage. The potential dangerous complications of diabetes far outweighed the risk of toxicity from the drug.

Unfortunately, once approved and used by a patient population that was larger and more diverse than the carefully chosen clinical trial participants, the drug caused serious liver problems. According to a *Wall Street Journal* report, Rezulin has been associated with 43 cases of acute liver failure, including 28 deaths and 7 liver transplants, between Rezulin's approval in 1997 and April 1999. The company revised the product's label in 1997 to recommend periodic monitoring of liver function and reported a subsequent drop in the rate of serious liver-related adverse effects.

These problems led the UK Medicines Control Agency to reject an application from Glaxo (the UK marketer) to reintroduce the product after Glaxo voluntarily pulled the product following concerns over reports from the United States and Japan. In the United States, these problems undoubtedly speeded approval of competing drugs and forced the company to include strong warnings about safety risks in its advertisements for the drug. In March 1999, the FDA's advisory panel recommended that the product's label restrict drug use to patients who have failed to respond to other available therapies and suggested removing the "monotherapy" label.

In spite of this restriction in usage, analysts, including Barbara Ryan at BT Alex Brown, continue to expect sales of $600 million in the year 2000—still a hefty sum. And the same FDA panel recommended SmithKline Beecham's Avandia and Eli Lilly's Actos, both for adult-onset diabetes and both acting through a mechanism similar to that of Rezulin. The FDA is expected to require warnings about monitoring liver function for these two products. In clinical studies, the rate of liver damage for Avandia and Actos was around 0.25% versus 1.8% for Rezulin.

So why get involved in this game at all? Two key reasons: (1) the opportunity to hit the jackpot—that drug that generates $1 billion or more each year in sales revenues, and (2) the chance to make a real difference to patients.

As you can see from the examples above, part of the trick to investing in this sector is understanding that no company—not even the big pharma pros—can accurately predict how a compound will do in development. Even once a product hits the market, unexpected issues can affect its performance. No drug is a completely innocuous entity—every drug has adverse effects of some kind. The trick of clinical development is to show that the benefits outweigh the perils. The trick of marketing is to grow the market as large as possible without recruiting patients who will suffer toxic side effects that may endanger the product for everyone.

Let's take a closer look at the stages of drug development—what happens at each step, where things can go awry, and what to consider as investors when trying to decipher a company's press releases about its clinical development program.

STAGES OF DRUG DEVELOPMENT

TABLE 15.1   The Drug Development Process: What Happens and When

		Clinical trials					
	Early research/ preclinical testing	Phase I	Phase II	Phase III	FDA review process/ approval	On market	Phase IV
Years	6.5	1.5	2	3.5	1.5	Took 15 years to get here	
Test population	Test tube and animal studies	20 to 80 healthy volunteers	100 to 300 patients	1,000 to 3,000 patients			Patients
Purpose	Look for safety, desired activity	Determine safety and dosage for the next phase	Evaluate effectiveness, look for potential toxic side effects	Confirm effectiveness, look for side effects from long-term use			Post-marketing surveillance of the patients to look for potential problems
Success rate	5,000 evaluated	5 compounds enter clinical trials			1 compound approved		

SOURCE: Pharmaceutical Research and Manufacturing Association.

DISCOVERY AND EARLY RESEARCH

The biotech industry has shown itself to be extremely adept at creating new ways to support the very front end of the process—discovery. In fact, the industry has become so successful at this stage that most large pharmaceutical companies devote a hefty share of their R&D

budget (up to 50%) to supporting research originating with their smaller biotech brethren.

The key to discovery is using the emerging new tools of molecular biology, cell biology, assay development, combinatorial chemistry, and high-throughput screening to probe the inner workings of cells and decipher just what is causing disease. Each new wave of technology advancement allows scientists to dive more deeply and specifically into the molecular and cellular interactions that cause the outer signs of diseases.

For example, in the case of adult-onset diabetes, it took the discovery of signal transduction pathways within cells (see Chapter 2) and tools to study those pathways before scientists were able to show that defects in the molecules within the insulin receptor signaling pathway led to diabetes. An important aspect of the research was to show that there are different defects within this pathway that can cause what looks like the same disease—diabetes. These defects have become targets for drug discovery programs, with the potential for treating different groups of patients with different drugs, depending on the specific cause of their diabetes.

In the past, researchers and physicians often did not know what was causing the symptoms they were trying to treat. The result? Most drugs were aimed at symptoms (for example, the pain, inflammation, and swelling of arthritis) without touching the basic cause of the disease (a chain of cell interactions that cause the chronic release of enzymes and other molecules that chew up joints and cause the symptoms). This meant that the disease often was never cured.

The new tools and technologies help researchers identify specific "targets" to go after with drugs. In the case of arthritis, the target might be the gene encoding an enzyme that destroys joint cartilage or the protein used by immune system cells in the joint to recruit other inflammatory cells to come join the party and cause more damage. Once a disease-specific target is found, scientists can look for chemical structures that can change the behavior of the target and stop the disease process.

Typically, hundreds or thousands (with combichem, maybe 100,000) chemical structures are tested for their ability to act on the disease target in a test tube or in individual cells (termed *tissue culture*)—in other words, whether they are "hits" or "misses."

These simple systems have fewer variables than a whole animal. The good news is that for this reason, it's easier to see if the compound works. The bad news is that a compound can work at this level but have properties that prevent it from working properly in a whole animal.

Sometimes compounds can act directly on a target in a test tube but can't make their way through the membrane that surrounds the cell containing the target. Sometimes, the compounds are chewed up by enzymes in the blood so quickly that they don't last long enough to act on the target. Often, a compound is simply not potent enough—patients would have to consume pounds of the stuff to get the therapeutic benefit. It is sometimes possible to tinker with a promising, but impotent, compound and crank up the potency or fix some of the other characteristics that otherwise would keep it in the "failure" bin. This is why animal testing is crucial—only in a whole, living animal can the compound's characteristics be further tested.

PRECLINICAL TESTING

Once a lead compound emerges from research, it's time to see if it works in whole animals—an exponential leap in complexity. Preclinical testing involves a series of tests in animals and lab tests to generate data that will convince the FDA that it is safe and worthwhile to try the drug candidate out on people. The tests also help determine how to give the drug to people so that it is most likely to work.

These tests are aimed at determining what happens when the drug is metabolized by a whole animal: Are toxic metabolites created? Does the drug lose its effectiveness? What doses generate the desired effects? What doses cause toxicity? How fast does the drug disappear from the blood, and where does it go? Can the drug be given as a pill without its losing its effectiveness through digestion in the stomach, or is injection required? Does the formulation need to be changed from intravenous injection to subcutaneous or to an inhaled version? Does the drug have any unexpected activities? Does it affect fetal development or pregnancy? There are studies that test what happens when an animal is treated for up to a year to look for effects from chronic exposure.

In some cases, when a drug will be used to treat a chronic disease—one that last for years rather than weeks—animal studies lasting up to 2 years may be required to study effects of chronic exposure and to look for potential cancer-causing effects.

An important issue is how selective a "hit" is. A compound that has the desired effect on the disease target but also affects the behavior of other molecules in the body is not a good drug candidate. The lack of selectivity can lead to nasty side effects by harming healthy cells in the body. A classic example of this lack of selectivity is seen in most cancer chemotherapy drugs. These drugs kill rapidly dividing cells—like cancer cells. Unfortunately, other cells that normally divide rapidly include the cells lining the gut, hair follicles, and the bone marrow cells that produce red and white blood cells. This is why cancer patients often lose their hair and become anemic during treatment.

Preclinical studies also are used to generate information about how to calculate the dose that should be used in the clinical studies. It is necessary to determine the largest dose that can be given to an animal before toxic side effects begin to show up. If that maximum tolerated dose is too close to the dose required to generate an effective therapeutic response (termed a *narrow therapeutic window*), the drug candidate may be dropped as too risky.

Some development programs are complicated by the lack of animal models for the human disease being studied. For example, animals can't be infected by the virus that causes AIDS. Therefore researchers have to work with related viruses—simian AIDS in monkeys and the version that infects cats.

Although it's possible to draw parallels between the human and animal systems, there are many differences (excluding, possibly, your ex-boyfriend). There are often slight differences in the proteins used by humans and animals to carry out the same activity. This can mean that a compound that works in animals might not work the same, or as well, in humans.

There has been great progress in developing tissue-based assay systems that resemble human organs—skin, corneas, kidneys—to use in testing, and perhaps to replace some of the animal testing required today. However, even though the cells being used are human, there is no replacement for testing in living patients. Other systems can only give us hints about how the drug might work, and how it should be given to increase the chance of success.

It can take 3 to 4 years of testing at this level to generate the information required by the FDA. Usually this same information is required by the other key regulatory agencies around the world before clinical studies can begin in other countries.

Along with the animal studies to understand how the drug works, the company needs to conduct studies of the drug compound itself:

how long it is stable at different temperatures (room temperature, refrigerated, frozen), what form (dry powder, ready-to-use injectable, pill or tablet) is best, and how to manufacture reproducible batches over time. Manufacturing and drug property issues could knock a drug contender out just as readily as efficacy issues. If the company can't make the drug at a cost that allows reasonable profit without pricing the product too high for the market, or if it needs to be injected and its competition is a once-daily pill, the product will have a tough time competing in the marketplace.

Good results in animals certainly make us more comfortable that the drug candidate will work in humans. But there is no guarantee. We still have to do the experiment in humans.

CLINICAL TRIALS: A WORK IN PROGRESS

Clinical trials are the studies done in humans—healthy volunteers and patients with the target disease—to test whether the drug candidate works in people. Actually, it's far more complicated than that. It's not just a question of whether the drug works or not. The data also must address:

- whether the drug works well enough to be worth giving to patients,
- whether the potential risk of toxic side effects outweighs the therapeutic benefit,
- which dose regimen (daily, two times daily, weekly, given for how long, given via which route—injection, orally, inhaled, sustained-release formulation, etc.) provides the best response and the least number of side effects, and
- whether the drug is better than, equivalent to, or worse than existing treatments for the disease.

In today's managed-health-care environment, where insurers essentially decide what drugs are used by controlling what drugs they will pay for, companies must build into their clinical trials a way to determine the cost-benefit ratio for a new treatment. In other words, even if the drug works, it must provide sufficient benefit to support the cost or else must make the total cost of care lower (perhaps through reducing the number of days a patient spends in the intensive care unit). This determination is termed *pharmacoeconomic analysis*.

Phase I: Phase I studies are designed primarily to look at safety in humans, and to study how the drug is metabolized and where it goes in the human body. Phase I will also provide important information to guide design of dosing for the later clinical phases, especially in terms of limiting nasty side effects. These trials usually involve 20 to 80 healthy volunteers or patients treated with increasingly high doses, covering doses all the way from no possible effect to potentially toxic. The number of volunteers used in these studies depends on how many doses are tested, and if the study design needs to examine issues such as the impact of taking the drug on an empty stomach or after a meal.

The goal of Phase I studies is not to assess the drug candidate's effectiveness, but to gain hints about the best way to use the product and whether it is safe to use in people. The information is used to design the Phase II studies.

Some companies may publish press releases that describe early "hints" of efficacy in Phase I studies. But remember—Phase I studies are neither designed to give nor capable of giving real information about effectiveness. The genetic variation and the wide differences in general health between individual patients in any disease population make it essentially impossible to see clearly whether the drug is effective in a small number of patients. The key is to make sure the drug is safe, and to design the study in a way that gives the most information possible about designing a dosing regimen for the trials to come.

Phase II: This phase of clinical development is designed to provide more information about how the drug behaves in people, and to begin providing information about effectiveness in patients. These studies typically include 100 to 500 patients, divided into several different subgroups. The subgroups are given the drug in different doses, by different routes (intravenous vs. subcutaneous, for example), and on different schedules (twice daily for 2 weeks vs. four times daily, for example).

Sometimes, parallel Phase II trials are run in different patient subpopulations. For example, in cancer trials, companies may run trials in patients with breast, ovarian, renal, and prostate cancer to see if the drug is broadly useful or if it seems to be more effective in certain cancers. This information allows design of Phase III trials that focus on those patients most likely to be able to respond well to the treatment.

In any case, more than one Phase II study is typically required to gather all the necessary information for optimal Phase III design. The Phase II results will allow companies to understand more thoroughly how their drug works in something more closely resembling the "real world," and to home in on the best combination of dose, treatment schedule, and patient subpopulation likely to respond to the drug. Safety issues continue to be important. Phase II trials will *not* provide definitive proof of effectiveness.

Phase III: The role of Phase III trials, sometimes called *pivotal trials*, is to generate data that will lead the FDA and the international regulatory agencies to give the company permission to market its new drug. Building on the hints about effectiveness, patient subpopulations, dosing regimens, and pharmacoeconomic issues, the company is hoping to end up with statistically significant proof that its product candidate is effective enough to warrant use and is safe enough.

The drug division of the FDA, in charge of small-molecule drugs, typically requires two Phase III trials before considering a New Drug Application (NDA). The exceptions are for drugs aimed at life-threatening diseases where no effective treatment exists, or where the candidate drug may reduce the death rate. However, in these cases, the FDA wants a more careful evaluation of the drug after approval and frequently asks for a number of postmarketing studies as a condition of approval.

The FDA's biologics division, which regulates protein-based or cell-based therapies, is regulated by slightly different rules. Several important biotechnology products, including Amgen's Epogen and Neupogen, were approved on the basis of a single well-done Phase III study. However, these were large studies, conducted at many different testing sites—in effect, they could be regarded as several studies combined into one.

—16—

SPEED BUMPS AND
BRICK WALLS

Clinical Trial Design

So how does the FDA define effectiveness? Now we get into the murky waters of statistical analysis and end points. Every patient is a little bit different from all other patients in ability to both metabolize and respond to the drug, in the ability of the drug to impact the specific disease, and in what is happening in the rest of the body. Not all heart attack patients are alike. The same drug given to different patients, all with the same disease from all outward appearances, may cause very different levels of response.

Add on top of all this the variation caused by differences in physician observation (how doctors decide if a patient belongs in the study, how they determine response to the drug), and we've got a tough assignment.

Phase II and the later Phase III studies have several design tricks that are aimed at evening out the variation so that the drug's effects (positive and negative) can be seen. These include the following:

- The presence of a placebo group, which does not receive the drug candidate, means that the study is *controlled*.
- The placebo group is most effective when neither the patients, the doctors, nor the company knows if any individual patient is in the placebo group or treatment group. Such a case is termed a *double-blind study*.

- Patients should be assigned to the treatment group or the placebo group randomly.
- The treating physicians and those involved in assessing patient response must use methods that are as consistent as possible—for the trial treatment and for any other standard care given to the patients. Otherwise, different medical centers may well come up with different trial results for the same drug candidate, simply based on differences in deciding which patients meet the entry criteria, in determining the level of the response, or in providing a different standard of care during the study.

The methods described are used to reduce bias in the trial by reducing the chance that those patients deemed less ill end up in the treatment group, for example. Any bias introduced in Phase II studies will have a serious negative impact on Phase III trial design, by potentially making the drug candidate appear to perform far better than it really can in a typical patient population.

Phase II studies should be designed to give the company information crucial to Phase III design. Some of the most important questions that should be addressed by Phase II studies and confirmed in Phase III are the following:

- Which patient subpopulation is most likely to respond most favorably to the drug candidate? There is great hope that pharmacogenomics will help companies more accurately predetermine which patient subgroups are able and likely to respond to treatment. But until we have all the information regarding which genetic variations correlate with the response to drugs, we are stuck with the old-fashioned approach of using Phase II to get hints. The FDA wants companies to designate their favored subgroups prior to beginning Phase III studies. Otherwise, the FDA will require another Phase III (read "expensive") trial based on the new subgroup.
- What is the primary end point—the clinically relevant benchmark that would indicate that the drug is having a positive effect? Are there secondary end points that might become primary end points in Phase III? It is important to choose an end point that occurs frequently enough that it will be possible to see a statistically significant difference between the treatment and placebo groups with a reasonable number of patients and in a

reasonable time. In other words, it's better to have a trial measuring increase in red blood cell numbers in anemic patients over a month than to be stuck with following patients for 10 years to look for a potential decrease in the incidence of Alzheimer's—for which there is no definitive diagnostic test as of press time.

The FDA has also changed its regulations to allow consideration of drug candidates where the trials measure surrogate end points in cases where the usual primary end point is tough to measure (such as in multiple sclerosis, a long-term chronic degenerative disease) or when the disease is fatal and no cure is available (AIDS). In these situations, the FDA is willing to consider end points that have some relevance to the underlying disease, while being faster and easier to detect. For example, the use of magnetic resonance imaging to detect brain plaques can be used to measure efficacy in multiple sclerosis trials, and the level of viral antigens in the blood is used in hepatitis and HIV infections.

In any case, the end point must be clinically relevant. For example, one reason Genentech's Activase for heart attacks got stalled in the FDA advisory committee was that the studies submitted the first time around focused on the ability of Activase to break up blood clots faster than the competition drugs. Unfortunately, the company forgot to show the panel data that the patients benefited from that rapid clot busting. Genentech was able to come back with the requested data, but it lost time and money in the process.

- The data from these trials are subjected to statistical analysis to determine if the treatment group responded in a manner that was sufficiently different from the placebo group that the difference was most likely caused by the treatment—not by chance. Companies must figure out how many patients are needed in each arm of the study to show a statistically significant impact on the primary end point—that is, there is less than a 5% chance that the benefit from the drug is not real.

This requires knowing what the expected incidence of the primary end point is in the placebo group, and having enough information to make a really good guess as to the expected improvement from the drug candidate. Statistical formulas are used to calculate the patient numbers required.

Guessing wrong on the placebo group incidence has trashed several biotech (and big pharma) product candidates. Studies aimed at treating chronic nonhealing wounds have been especially hard hit by this curve ball—just ask management at Magainin, Advanced Tissue Sciences, and Chiron. Historical data on these patients, who are often not given the best care under normal circumstances because they are poor, in nursing homes, and so on indicate a low rate of healing and a very long time required for wound closure when it does occur. Inclusion in a clinical study suddenly exposes them to a new level of wound care, and often the historical rate of nonhealing drops. This makes it much tougher to show an incremental improvement from a drug candidate.

- Define the control groups that must be included in the study. For diseases with no effective treatment, a new drug is most likely to be tested against the standard placebo group. However, in some diseases where an approved treatment exists, it would be unethical to include a "no treatment" arm. This means that the drug candidate has to go head-to-head against standard care—and has to work a little harder to show a significant benefit over and above the existing treatment.

Although most investors are not in any position to analyze data or the statistical structure of a trial, they certainly can ask management whether these methods are part of its company's trial design—the answer should be yes.

Some clinical settings are particularly tough for showing significant effectiveness. For example, head trauma patients have been a very tough population for clinical testing because every head trauma injury is different from all others—caused by something different, with a different level of severity—and the patients often have other chemicals in their bodies that may interfere with the drug candidate. Many head trauma patients fall into two broad categories—young males who ran their motorcycles into trees or other hard objects while driving under the influence of alcohol or drugs, and elderly patients taking multiple drugs for heart disease, high blood pressure, and so on, who fell and hit their head. The severity of damage and the site in the brain affected vary widely in this group. This makes showing a statistically significant effect of any one drug in this broad patient group very tough.

Well-designed Phase II studies allow companies to increase their chances of designing Phase III trials that will generate data that will convince the FDA to allow the product to be marketed. Meetings with the FDA to go over the Phase II data and to discuss Phase III trial design are very valuable. However, companies and investors alike need to remember that neither written nor verbal statements by the FDA are binding. The FDA is free to change its mind about what constitutes "approvable" data from a Phase III study at any time.

How should investors interpret press releases about Phase II or III data? The first and most important thing to remember is that clinical trials are experiments!

Phase II is the company's first opportunity to get real information about how its drug candidate works in the real world of patients, and to begin to refine which patient subpopulation and which dosing regimen are likely to show the most benefit. Don't drop a stock simply because one of the Phase II studies didn't pan out completely positively. No computer program or set of animal studies can provide definitive information on human responses. The only way to find out is to do the trial! The key is to ask whether management is planning the Phase II studies with all the points listed above in mind, and whether the company's strategic plan and budgeting process take into account the potential for speed bumps at this point.

It is important to keep in mind that even Phase III trials are risky. Well-designed Phase II studies should give the company and its investors some comfort that the Phase III trials will have a happy outcome—that is, drug approval. However, Phase III studies are conducted in a larger patient population than the Phase I and II trials. From a statistical perspective, this means that there is a greater chance that unexpected variables in the patients can impact the results.

The biopharmaceutical industry is full of examples of products that generated Phase II results that appeared promising, but that failed in Phase III trials. In many cases, there was no way to predict this outcome. However, there are some warning signs that investors can pick up before Phase III is completed that can indicate increased risk, including:

- Phase II studies with very small patient groups, which may miss important variables.

- Disease settings where the patient population will be widely variable in terms of severity, underlying biology, and range of other disorders present, making consistent therapeutic results difficult.
- Significantly different results from patient groups treated at different centers.
- Poor study design that may lead to FDA concerns about bias.
- An increase in patient enrollment goals for a trial in process.

A recent example of a promising product failing to gain FDA approval even after Phase III trials is Scios's Natrecor—a genetically engineered version of a naturally occurring cardiac hormone. During heart failure, the hormone dilates arteries and veins, suppresses hormones that raise blood pressure, and acts as a diuretic—all of which reduces the load on the heart. The company completed Phase II studies in more than 200 patients with congestive heart failure and designed a Phase III plan aimed at NDA filing by mid-1998.

The Phase III design had two components—a study in 120 patients testing two doses of the drug against placebo, and a 300-patient study that tested Natrecor head-to-head with the standard treatment usually given to these patients when they show up in the emergency room. Although the second, larger study would provide information on whether Natrecor had a clinical advantage, it was not designed to look at efficacy. That meant that potentially only 80 patients (one dose arm of the 120 patient study) might receiving the effective dose in a controlled Phase III.

In January 1999, the FDA advisory panel recommended approval of Natrecor. But in April 1999, the FDA turned the drug down. According to Scios CEO Richard Brewer, the FDA felt the drug had not been tested on enough patients to generate enough safety information. Scios stock dropped $5.88, closing at $3.81 on the news. The company will meet with the FDA to discuss what additional tests might be required. But the time, and money, needed to support these studies will definitely hurt.

Keep in mind that even if a Phase III trial does not produce data to support product approval, this may not mean that the product does not work or can't gain approval. Even Phase III trials are essentially experiments. If the first set of assumptions is disproved, the company hopefully will learn enough to decide whether a second set of Phase III trials with a different study design is likely to produce the needed

data. The key is whether management has been realistic about the potential for trial failure and has a strategic plan (and funding!) in place
to move forward.

Trial Design and Business Strategy

A great clinical development strategy is one that allows a company to
move quickly into a small market, then expand into related patient
populations with follow-up studies.

One recent example of this approach is the development of Enbrel
by Immunex and its marketing partner American Home Products.
Enbrel is one of the first drugs reaching the marketplace that works
by controlling the proteins involved with inflammation. The drug is a
genetically engineered version of the cell receptor for tumor necrosis
factor (TNF) and works by sopping up TNF released at the site of
chronic inflammation and thus stopping TNF from sending its tis-
sue-damaging signals to the immune system.

Immunex first aimed for, and got in late 1998, FDA approval to sell
Enbrel to treat patients with moderate to severe rheumatoid arthritis
whose disease is not affected significantly by existing treatments, and
to use in combination with methotrexate. This patient subgroup represents about one-third of the total 2 million patients with rheumatoid arthritis.

More than 1,000 patients participated in clinical studies, giving the
company a good sense of how the drug worked and what side effects
might show up. At this point, it wasn't clear that Enbrel was able to
directly affect the progression of the disease, but it was able to reduce
the symptoms of pain and swelling.

In May 1999, Immunex reported on Phase III studies in 633 patients showing that Enbrel was effective in patients with early stages
of rheumatoid arthritis who had never received methotrexate. Most
important, Enbrel slowed the progression of the disease by slowing
joint destruction. The company will use this information to ask the
FDA to expand the product labeling to include this broader patient
population.

The stock market responded to the good news by adding $35.31
per share, a 33% increase, in one day! (News of the original approval
moved the stock a mere $1.56, some of which peeled off by the next
day: November 2, 1998, $35.31; November 3, 1998, $34.65.)

─── 17 ───

BIOTECH BANKERS

How in the world do biotech companies raise the vast sums of money needed to fuel that decade-long product development cycle discussed in the previous chapter? Unlike high-tech start-ups, this is not something two guys in a garage can pull off. High-tech investors can count on those two guys to churn out a new application program in about 2 months with a $5,000 budget. Bring together 100 people, $25 million, and 2 years, and you've got a new operating system able to generate huge revenues on a pretty high gross margin.

Drug development requires a heftier infrastructure and investors willing to support the work for almost a decade before the company will know if the new drug even works in people, much less if it can generate profits. Even biotech companies working on agricultural applications or new technology tools (combinatorial chemistry, gene sequencing, etc.) require big bucks and lots of time to generate net income. Investors coming in at the start-up point have to hope that the company can raise the rest of the $250 million or so over the 10 years needed for product development.

The willingness of the venture capital community throughout the 1980s and early 1990s to invest broadly in new companies and technologies allowed the emerging biotechnology industry to reach a point where public market investors could participate. This enthusiasm was generated by the hefty profits those funds made investing in the beginning of Silicon Valley, and by the red-hot IPO markets in the mid-80s and early 1990s.

As we enter the new millennium, we've seen the public markets mutate from wildly enthusiastic about biotech stocks in the early 1990s, to snubbing the sector in the mid-1990s, to cautious toe dip-

ping in the late 1990s. The public markets turned against small cap
companies (including most of the biotech sector) during the late
1990s, and biotech was forced to turn to alternative sources of capital
to take up the slack. Luckily, biotech has always been agile at inventing novel financing vehicles to carry it through times when conventional financing was not possible. Private financings for public
companies raised 58% of the $2.4 billion raised by biotech companies
in the first 5 months of 1999, according to Jennifer Van Brunt, editor
of Recombinant Capital's *Signals Magazine*.

The composition of the investor group in biotech also has changed
over time. According to long-time biotech banker Lehman Brothers's
Fred Frank, the early biotech investors were primarily institutional
investors based in Europe and the United States. There were few analysts covering the new sector, and most of them were pharmaceutical
analysts who switched over to include biotech companies.

But when Genentech became the first biotech company to go public with great fanfare—hitting a high of $85/share that first day on the
market, "Biotech became an area where you had to be an investor,"
says Frank. "It also became fashionable for industrial companies like
W. R. Grace and Shell Oil to invest in biotech to give them a window
into the new technology. These industrial investors gave cachet and
validity to the biotech sector, and their interest implied the potential
for very broad applications of the science."

It was also a sector that engendered passionate investing. Most people have had a personal experience with serious diseases like cancer,
Alzheimer's disease, or heart attacks. Biotech holds the promise of
coming up for the first time with drugs that could vanquish these age-
old enemies that big pharma has been unable to conquer. Many investors saw, and still see, biotech investing as a way to "do good" and
maybe make money.

Let's take a look at where the money comes from and what factors
drive those investments.

THE VENTURE WORLD BEAUTY PAGEANTS

In biotech, most early money flows from the venture capitalists. This
means that every start-up must participate in the "beauty pageant,"
trotting its slide show around to the venture firms and hoping that
they will bite. For the first-generation scientist entrepreneur—heck,

even for the entrepreneur on her second or third company—this can be a frightening experience.

There's something about facing down a conference room packed with dour-faced men and women in dark suits that can turn the toughest technician into a vat of quivering Jell-O™. After all, these are the folks who can make or break your company before it has been around long enough to have its own Web site.

Dr. Ron Cohen has lived through this process as founder and CEO of Acorda Therapeutics Inc., created in 1995 to support development of innovative treatments for spinal cord injury and serious neurodegenerative diseases including multiple sclerosis. Acorda has raised about $28 million since 1995—$20 million of that in late 1998.

Cohen says, "Raising money from venture capitalists is hell on earth. It's like the old Woody Allen saying—90% of success is just showing up—again, and again, and again. Persistence is absolutely crucial, unless you have something that is hot enough to compete with the next Amazon.com. No matter how good your company looks, the VCs seem to be waiting to see if you stick around. When you visit this year, they're not interested. If you show up again, even though the story's about the same, just the fact you persevered and found a way to survive is a rite of passage."

Once you get the approval of a VC, you're still not home free. In the late 1990s' hot Internet market, most biotech venture partners found themselves having to argue fiercely with their high-tech partners to get their deals approved. With outrageously high returns coming so quickly from Internet IPOs, it was tough to convince the high-tech supporters to put some of the fund's money into the more expensive, slower biotech world. Many of the funds, including biotech champion Kleiner Perkins Caufield & Byers, backed out of biotech deals altogether in 1998–1999.

The good news is that nature abhors a vacuum—once the big funds started bailing out of the biotech sector, a new generation of smaller funds headed up by experienced biopharmaceutical cheerleaders started forming to take up the slack.

THE RIGHT STUFF

To have even a prayer of passing muster at this level, a company needs:

- Excellent management with relevant industry experience.
- A strong technology platform able to generate multiple product opportunities, not just a single product play.
- Access to financing alternatives when the public markets are closed.
- The ability to articulate the business opportunity, not just the sexy science.
- The right corporate location.

Dr. Michael Shepard, a long-time biotech entrepreneur, points out that there are so many really great ideas and talented people out there knocking on the doors of venture firms that the decision about whom to back is a lot like looking at all the straight-A students and deciding which ones to admit to medical school.

The go–no-go decision finally gets made primarily on a gut feel by the potential investors. An important factor affecting this gut response is the people who have associated themselves with the deal. Big bonus points are awarded to companies that align themselves with individuals who possess strong track records of involvement in quality companies. These supporters can be advisers and consultants to the company, members of the early board of directors, or part of the initial management team.

Shepard has lived through this process three times already, first as an early member of the science team at Genentech, next as cofounder and VP for research at gene therapy start-up Canji (now part of Schering-Plough), and currently as cofounder and chief scientific officer at NewBiotics Inc. (San Diego, California).

"Usually potential investors will look for three key people—an academic scientist, an experienced biopharma executive, and a business/finance person with a track record," says Shepard.

The quality of this initial team is crucial in making the venture investors comfortable with taking a big financial risk. Shepard points out that "one person with unusually strong skills and a great track record can allay the concerns of the potential investors enough to get the deal going. The litmus test for such an arrangement typically is whether this individual is willing to join the startup team and invest his or her own money in the new company. Later, when larger amounts of money are required, the company needs to recruit a CEO. This should be someone with lots of gray hair and a history of financial success. This person's primary job is to close deals—financings and corporate partnerships."

It sounds crazy, but the wrong location is another factor that can adversely affect a venture deal. VCs are pressed for time and don't want to spend days flying back and forth to visit a portfolio company. The venture firms that invest actively in biotech tend to have their home offices near San Francisco, Boston, or Princeton, which means a company in Texas or Florida has an uphill battle even getting on their "heads-up" list. This same location problem affects investment bankers and analysts.

Most venture capital funds invest only in a limited number of industries, such as retail, high-tech, biotech, and health care services. This limitation allows them to maintain a critical mass of experience in-house to make good investing decisions and to help their portfolio companies grow into successful public companies. Fund Web sites and *Pratt's Guide to Capital* provide information about the industries of interest—and the stage of company development—for the different venture funds. The number of funds actively investing in biotech deals is small and seems to be getting smaller daily.

BIOTECH FEEDING FRENZY

The venture funds that dove into biotech early on, like Kleiner Perkins, U.S. Venture Partners, Institutional Venture Partners, and their colleagues, were flush with cash from their computer hardware and software investments of the 1960s and 1970s and were drawn to biotech as the next exciting place to make a killing. Venture capitalists usually get their return on investment from initial public offerings or acquisitions of their portfolio companies. As their returns on investment climbed in the hot biotech IPO markets of 1983, 1986, and 1991–1991, other funds clamored to join the biotech investing frenzy.

Unfortunately, culture clash was almost instantaneous. Many of these newcomers to biotech venture investing were used to the two guys/2 months/$5,000 deals of Silicon Valley. Those software start-ups usually had a pretty good prototype of the product even before getting the venture backing, and the VCs could expect to ride their investment to an IPO in months, a year at most. Many of the VCs had come from some of the early software and hardware companies and had technical training in electrical engineering and physics that allowed them analyze directly the science behind the start-up.

Biotech deals are a completely different beast. The science often has not made it past the test tube stage when venture funding is sought. The cost of the research and the need for specialized facilities is so high that entrepreneurs simply cannot move the concept forward without outside sources of funding.

Many of the venture investors hoping to play in the biotech arena do not have training in the biological sciences and so are dependent on consultants (such as your wily author) to examine the scientific premise of the company and comment on whether it has a chance of succeeding. This is why many venture funds follow the lead of the top funds that specialize in biotech—co-investing in their deals or starting copycat companies.

This lemminglike activity means that it is important for any young company to enlist the support of the venture funds with the best reputations in their area. VCs with good track records have demonstrated competence at picking winners. Says Acorda's Cohen, "Investing is inherently risky. Nothing allays investors' nerves as well as the company of other investors." This same urge for reassurance is why investment bankers rely on that venture investor pedigree so much when deciding which biotech companies to take public.

Another reason for bringing in the top-tier VCs is the knowledge and networking they can bring to bear for their portfolio companies. Start-up companies can't afford to hire a full management team, and experienced managers often are not willing to take a chance with an unproven company. Strong venture investors can help young companies network with experienced management in other portfolio companies, can help provide recommendations to key service providers (accounting firms, lawyers, consultants, etc.), and can provide the clout to make the next tier of investors take note.

One of the real challenges of raising venture capital is the small number of truly visionary investors. If your technology is not in fashion, it's like pulling teeth to get them to look seriously at your plan—the same plan that might have been able to entice significant investment just a year earlier, when the area was hot. For the past few years, biotech VCs have been funding those deals that look as though they might be able to bring liquidity (go public or be acquired) at a much earlier time than has been seen in the biotech industry. In other words, they have been looking to reduce the risk and shorten the amount of time they and their limited partners have to wait for their return on investment.

This risk reduction approach has led to a spate of "tool" companies (developing single tools and services such as combinatorial chemistry or genomics) and the infamous "accelerated commercialization" in which research companies tried to in-license niche products rejected by other companies, in hopes of generating product revenues much earlier in their evolution. Unfortunately, as with many things in life, reducing risk usually reduced upside potential. And trying to force a "fad" business model on companies often led to general chaos and re-duced productivity as small management teams tried to do two mutu-ally exclusive things simultaneously—develop innovative research and run clinical trials effectively.

"External factors are probably the most important drivers of the level of investment in early-stage biotech companies. The people who invest in venture funds do so in order to make money. If they think biotech is not the best, most efficient way to make money, if there is a better sector, they have to go with it. Investors have children, spouses, and dogs to support, too," says Shepard.

The flipside of this is that hot biotech markets tend to bring the fringe investors out of the woodwork. These groups, blinded by the potential earnings of blockbuster drugs and awesome IPOs, often don't understand the realities of biopharmaceutical product develop-ment cycles or the risk of drug development. This lack of understand-ing tends to make them impatient investors, ready to bail at the slightest sign of danger.

THE CHANGING VENTURE PICTURE

One of the scariest aspects of the slowdown in the public market in-terest in biotech has been the apparent loss of venture capital support for private biotech companies. The key player in the early days of biotech, Kleiner Perkins Caufield & Byers (former home of Genen-tech cofounder Bob Swanson), has almost completely bowed out of biotherapeutic investing, as have many of the other long-time indus-try supporters, including Weiss Peck & Greer, Sierra Ventures, and Accel Partners.

In spite of this shift in loyalties, biomedical venture investing still contributed a hefty $2.7 billion to private companies in recent history. The most active U.S.-based health care venture investors in 1998

TABLE 17.1   Venture Capital Invested in U.S. Life Sciences Companies (millions)

	1998	% change from 1997	# 1998 deals	Average deal size
Biotechnology/ biopharmaceuticals	$963.2	22	191	$5.5
Medical devices/diagnostics	$686.6	11.5	173	$4.0
Health care information and services	$1,100.9	6.6	256	$4.3
Totals	$2,750.7	9.1	620	$4.4

SOURCE: Information from Wilson Sonsini Goodrich & Rosati Spring 1999 *Life Sciences Bulletin*, VentureOne Corp.

were at The Sprout Group, New Enterprise Associates, Alta Partners/Burr Egan Deleage, MedVentures Associates, Delphi Management, InterWest Partners, Mayfield Fund, Piper Jaffray Ventures, Oxford Bioscience Partners, Institutional Venture Partners, Highland Capital Partners, Domain Associates, Oak Investment Partners, S. R. One (the venture arm of big pharma SmithKline Beecham), Bretwood Venture Capital, and Three Arch Partners.

Although these firms remain actively engaged in biotech, many of their investments are not in therapeutics companies but in companies focused on diagnostics, services, or devices. The hope is that these companies will reach net income in less than the infamous decade required for biotherapeutics firms.

As you can see from Table 17.1, biotech-pharmaceutical deals represent only 35% of the total amount of venture investment in the life sciences arena. Nonetheless, the dollars invested in biotech deals are still on the rise.

The amount of venture money flowing into biotech companies is still in an upward trend. Every time the public markets frowned on biotech, the venture funds pulled back, and vice versa. The good news is that although you can see the increase in venture dollars flowing into non-U.S. biotech firms, there is also an increasing flow of dollars into U.S. companies from European venture funds, including BB Bioventures, Atlas Ventures, and Apax Partners.

Some of this activity has been generated, ironically, by the massive layoffs of experienced pharmaceutical executives and managers be-

TABLE 17.2   1998's Largest Biotech Venture Deals

Company	Amount raised (millions)	Round	Company description
Praecis Pharmaceuticals (Cambridge, MA)	$37.8	Third	Developing peptide-derived drugs
The Medicines Co. (Cambridge, MA)	$36	Fourth	In-licenses late-stage drugs to develop and commercialize
Dyax Corp. (Cambridge, MA)	$31.4	Mezzanine	Novel approach to combichem, compound libraries
Lexicon Genetics Inc. (The Woodlands, TX)	$31	Mezzanine	Functional genomics with special mice
Ontogeny Inc. (Cambridge, MA)	$28	Fourth	Function genomics/ developmental biology models for target discovery
Orchid Biocomputer (Princeton, NJ)	$27.5	Third	Rapid identification of genetic mutations correlating with disease
Cell Pathways, Inc. (Horsham, PA)	$21.6	Fourth	New drugs for cancer and pre-cancerous cells
Acorda Therapeutics (Hawthorne, NY)	$20	Second	Novel treatments for spinal cord injury and MS

SOURCE: Information from Wilson Sonsini Goodrich & Rosati Spring 1999 *Life Sciences Bulletin*, VentureOne Corp.

cause of the big pharma mergers of the past few years (Glaxo and Wellcome, Pharmacia & Upjohn, SmithKline and Beecham, Ciba-Geigy and Sandoz to form Novartis, Roche's acquisition of Syntex). These execs are enamored of the life sciences and see entrepreneurial biotech firms as the key to pumping life into the languishing big pharma pipelines.

And in the United States, some folks remain hardy supporters of the biomedical world of venture investing. Craig Taylor, longtime life science venture investor with Asset Management (renamed Alloy Ventures, Palo Alto, California), has no intention of abandoning this arena. "Why do we hang in there? Our fund was in Amgen, IDEC Pharmaceuticals, Pharmacyclics—the technology works, it just takes time to reach the products. There is so much great technology, so much interesting science coming out of labs every day. The rate of technical innovation is ramping up, and there is real economic benefit to products based on new biological information. The question is how to best extract that value. I believe that the market will cycle out of Internet, just as it has cycled out of every other technology sector. But more important the science will bust through the logjam, and money will flow again into biotech."

Taylor also raises the point that the venture investors and other in-dustry supporters are in biotech for more than making a buck—or a million of them. There are certainly easier sectors for get-rich-quick schemes. The key driver for most is the strong desire to do good, to make a difference in the world through your brains and hard work. "The investors who in the hot markets took two guys and a mouse public—those guys are gone now; they've moved on to Internet deals. What remains are the dedicated true believers, who know what they are doing and have done it successfully before."

Filling the Venture Vacuum

Local activism is taking place around the country, as local govern-ments and pension funds see biotech as a great economic develop-ment ploy and have given up on coercing out-of-town VCs to invest locally. For example, in mid-1999, the state of Wisconsin pension trustees approved the formation of a $50-million venture fund to sup-port life science entrepreneurs in that state.

The sudden availability of managers fleeing the Glaxo Wellcome merger also helped stimulate the accelerated growth of local venture capital investment in Raleigh-Durham, North Carolina, home of ma-jor R&D groups for both companies as well as Duke University and its medical center and the University of North Carolina at Chapel Hill. In 1998, the state of North Carolina, in conjunction with the North Carolina Biotech Center, created the North Carolina Bio-science Investment Fund. This $20-million-plus venture fund will be devoted to investing in local biotech start-ups. The hope is that local investment will get these firms up and running to a point where larger, non-local venture funds will step up and invest.

Another growing source of early biotech financing is composed of "angel funds" and other seed-stage funds formed by investors who made their fortunes (or at least enough capital to play) in the first-generation biotech companies. These biotech cheerleaders are eager to support the newest generation of companies, and they have the ability to understand the technology as well as the trials and tribulations of developing biotherapeutics.

For example, George Rathmann, the first CEO of top biotech firm Amgen Corp. and founding CEO of Icos Corp. (Bothell, Washington), started up Falcon Technology Partners with his children. Genentech cofounder Robert Swanson founded K & E Management Ltd. to pursue his interest in supporting innovative biotech start-ups like Cytokinetics Inc. and AGY Therapeutics Inc., both in south San Francisco.

Robert Blum, VP of business development at Cytokinetics and former Genentech employee, says that Swanson's entrepreneurial flare was what brought him into biotech in the first place. And his willingness to help grow the next generation of companies—with money and advice—made Swanson a great angel investor.

"When I was a high school student in the late 1970s, lots of my friends had posters of sports heroes on their walls. I had the *Business Week* cover of Bob Swanson as the biotech guru. I saw biotech as an opportunity to blend my enthusiasm for science with my interest in building businesses. That's why I moved to California to go to Stanford—I was truly inspired by this new sector. Now, I am part of the founding team at a start-up biotech company, and Bob Swanson is one our early investors. He is very actively involved, always makes time when we need him even though we are probably one of his smaller investments. He is exactly what a newly minted entrepreneur wants—someone who has proven it can be done in a way that transforms an entire industry."

Constance McKee is a great example of this new breed of eclectic biotech angel. A former opera singer turned venture capitalist, McKee put in time at Yale and Stanford before heading up Cambridge Quantum Fund (CQF). This fund was the very first set up to extract start-up companies from Cambridge University (UK).

McKee helped found six companies with CQF and currently is CEO of start-up neuro drug delivery company Xavos Corp. (Woodside, California) while also helping other biotech entrepreneurs get the basics in place. She prefers "the thrill and heartburn of start-ups to the more staid life of a venture capitalist. There are two kinds of equity you can bring to a start-up—sweat and cash. And they each need both."

Her experience working with Philips Electronics (U.S. division of Royal Dutch Philips NV) on its high-tech acquisition streak in the late 1990s convinced McKee that life sciences angels are different from technology angels.

"In the life sciences, it's not enough just to understand the markets; you must know the technology and what it takes to get products to market. With pharmaceuticals, there are no new business models, no shortcuts to the market, no new value-added models, and very few ways to shortcut risk without severely infringing on the upside potential. Those of us who play in this sector have to accept the realities of drug development and must be open to other ways of generating return than only IPOs. The world has changed—the demand is for products, not IPOs. Most VCs are locked into building corporate assets and creating public companies. Angel investors can afford to build products and sell those products to big pharma."

McKee is a member of Tenex Medical, an angel fund (www.tenexmedical.com) formed in the late 1990s to fill the growing gap in early-stage investment funds available for life science entrepreneurs as the venture funds began to back away from biotech and into the Internet. Tenex was founded by Paul Quadros, a former general partner with the venture fund Technology Funding; Frank Ruderman, who was CEO or a senior executive at several Bay area biotech companies; Mitch Stevko, a senior investment banker with Piper Jaffray who worked with many life science clients; and Alfred Mandel, a former marketing executive with Apple Computer and founder of Redgate Communications.

The Tenex process starts with a presentation by carefully screened companies at one of Tenex's bimonthly dinner meetings. Companies are selected for their ability to achieve meaningful business benchmarks (read: the ability to reach the next milestone to support a significant kickup in valuation) with an infusion of $250,000 to $750,000 from Tenex.

Many of the members of Tenex have made money as biotech entrepreneurs in northern California and really know how to start companies and roll up their sleeves to build teams, intellectual property

TABLE 17.3   Money Raised by Private Biotech Companies (millions)

Year	Total venture capital investments (millions) (% growth)	Venture capital invested in U.S. companies (millions)	Venture capital invested in non-U.S. companies (millions)
1987	$216	$216	NA
1988	$318 (47%)	$318	NA
1989	$442 (39%)	$442	NA
1990	$427 (–3%)	$427	NA
1991	$675 (58%)	$675	NA
1992	$530 (–22%)	$530	NA
1993	$644 (21%)	$568	$76
1994	$449 (–30%)	$423	$26
1995	$452 (0%)	$398	$54
1996	$697 (54%)	$594.5	$102.5
1997	$790 (13%)	$673	$116
1998	$1099 (39%)	$778	$321
1999 1Q	$1,082	$982	$100

SOURCE: Information prior to 1993 from Recombinant Capital (www.recap.com, San Francisco, CA). All other information from BioWorld Publishing (www.bioworld. com, Atlanta, GA).

portfolios, and clinical development strategies right from the start. Others, who were brought into companies as professional managers, wouldn't know how to start the company—but know how to recognize a good investment. Ironically, McKee's biotech investing stake came from an Internet start-up she helped out with sweat equity.

THE DOLLARS AND SENSE OF VENTURE ROUNDS

Traditional biotech venture financing begins with a seed round of $250,000 up to $5 million (see Table 17.4; keep in mind these numbers don't reflect the vast majority of unreported seed rounds of $250,000 or less). Often, this start-up money comes from the founders, their friends and family, and private investors who are convinced that the business idea is worth supporting.

The seed round typically is used to set up the formal corporation, to begin the process of setting up agreements between the new company and the source of its technology and intellectual property (usually academic scientists), and to begin pulling together a written business plan that will generate interest and support from other in-

TABLE 17.4   Typical Capital Raised by Biotech Firms

	Seed round* ($millions)	1st round* ($millions)	2nd round* ($millions)	3rd round* ($millions)	4th round/ mezzanine* ($millions)	IPO** ($millions)
Range	$2.5–$7	$1.4–$17	$4.5–$13.6	$8.6–$17	$5–$37	$10–$65.7
Average	$5	$7.5	$8.6	$13.4	$18.5	$29.3
Total raised (average)					$53 prior to IPO	$82.3 through IPO

SOURCE: Information courtesy of *BioWorld Financial Watch*.
*Based on January–April 1999 financings.
**Based on 1998–1999 IPOs.

vestors and industry supporters. This means, not surprisingly, that lawyers get much of this initial capital.

Another key ingredient of the new company is people—the right people. Company founders are often scientists or young business types. They usually don't have the skills and experience needed to handle all of the business and finance issues crucial to getting New Co. off on the right foot. They also usually need to import additional technology and scientific expertise to keep an eye on the company's research progress.

This lack of experience means the founding team must recruit a scientific advisory board and board of directors to supply that expertise. Together, the founders and these advisers can begin the task of forging a meaningful business plan and a research plan that will generate "proof of concept" data—(explained in Chapter 2). The advisers usually get stock and some cash for their participation.

The next round or two usually bring in $2 million to $10 million from experienced venture investors based on initial data supporting the technology idea. The money is used to find a home for the company, build an R&D team, recruit key management executives (usually a CEO/president, a head of research, and a head of business development), and start the task of product development.

The last round of private financing, sometimes termed *mezzanine*, can come from investors or corporate partners willing to buy equity or provide large up-front payments in exchange for access to New Co.'s technology. These rounds, intended to drive the company into position for an IPO, usually bring in more money than earlier rounds.

The mezzanine rounds reported for the first quarter of 1999 averaged $18.5 million but reached as high as $37 million.

This funding should be used to get ready for preclinical or even clinical testing of the lead product candidates, hiring downstream development staff, and designing a strategy for corporate partnering.

——18——

INITIAL PUBLIC
OFFERINGS

The initial public offering is a major milestone for any company. But for biotech firms, it is absolutely required to raise the kind of capital needed for the final push to bring product candidates close to market launch. In this industry, creating a sustainable, growing biotech business that will provide a strong return for all participants demands entering the public markets.

This milestone also provides an exit strategy for early investors—which is important to keep the flow of venture investment into start-ups. When the venture capitalists are worried that their holdings in private companies won't be converted into shares in public companies that can be sold and converted into profit, they pull back from investing in new companies. VCs and institutional investors fund the new companies that grow up and go public, generating profits that the VCs and other investors can plow back into new companies.

A crucial ingredient for a successful biotech IPO is a reputable investment banker, preferably with a track record in the biotech arena. The right banker not only supports IPOs in tough markets but also can provide a strong base of institutional investors and ongoing support in the form of active analyst coverage and secondary financings. For the biotech sector, the support of institutional investors is needed to balance out the short-term trading of hedge funds, Internet-based day traders, and the general public.

Who are those top-tier bankers? The names have changed significantly as merger mania struck the banking industry in the late 1990s. As of June 1999, the top names were Lehman Brothers, Hambrecht & Quist, BancBoston Robertson Stephens, J. P. Morgan, CIBC Oppenheimer, NationsBanc Montgomery Securities, BT Alex Brown, Cowen & Co., SBC Warburg Dillon Read, ING Baring Furman Selz LLC, Prudential Vector Healthcare, and Morgan Stanley Dean Witter.

According to Dr. Carol Hall of *BioVenture Consultants Stock Report* (Chestnut Hill, Massachusetts), the ability of a biotech company to attract the attention and active help of a strong banker will vary significantly with overall stock market conditions. "In a hot market, investors are excited by new offerings, and bankers may be willing to help less mature companies complete IPOs. During the red-hot market of 1991–1992, many biotech firms went public while still far from moving product candidates into clinical trials," says Hall. This prompted cranky journalists, including yours truly, to describe the market as "public venture capital."

In "down markets," the bar is raised substantially, and only more mature companies are attractive to investors, says Hall. Investors want to see much more than sexy science—they want to see product candidates in Phase II and Phase III clinical trials (see Chapter 17 for an explanation of clinical trials). "In the late 1990s, investors were not interested in biotech IPOs and in fact shied away from most small cap companies in all technology sectors. Only 12 biotech firms successfully made it into the public markets from January 1998 to April 1999, of the two dozen or so biotech companies that tried," says Hall.

Market timing—raising money when your area is hot—is almost impossible. In 1999, biotech was still struggling to be heard above the Internet roar in spite of having a fabulous pipeline of near-term product candidates and a growing war chest of corporate partner dollars. Those companies running out of cash while still a year or more from product launch had to bite the bullet and raise capital at a truly terrible market valuation. The alternative was a slow, lingering death.

In 1998, the nine biotech IPOs brought in between $12 million up to $65.7 million for their companies, with an average of $27 million. In the first quarter of 1999, only three IPOs made it through the tough market for small cap companies. These offerings brought in a total of $105 million, averaging $35 million per company. Not surprisingly, the two smallest IPOs were managed by less prestigious banks. It took the marketing muscle of the big boys to bring in significant funding during this tight market (see Table 18.1).

TABLE 18.1 U.S. Biotech IPOs January 1998–December 1999

Company (ticker)	Date completed	Gross (millions)	Bankers
Transgene (TRGNY)	3/98	$65.7	Lehman Brothers, Credit Suisse First Boston, BancAmerica Robertson Stephens
CuraGen (CRGN)	3/98	$37.7	Morgan Stanley Dean Witter, Lehman Brothers, Bear Sterns
LJL Biosystems (LJLB)	3/98	$14.6	NationsBank Montgomery Securities, Hambrecht & Quist, Volpe Brown Whelan
Nanogen (NGEN)	4/98	$42.9	Morgan Stanley Dean Witter, Lehman Brothers, SBC Warburg Dillon Read
RiboGene (RBO)	5/98	$16.1	Gruntal & Co.
CombiChem (CCHM)	5/98	$18.9	BancAmerica Robertson Stephens, Donaldson Lufkin & Jenrette, Salomon Smith Barney
Ophidian (OPHD)	5/98	$11.8	Dirks & Co., Security Capital Trading
Collateral Therapeutics (CLTX)	7/98	$16	Bear Sterns, Raymond James, Vector Securities
Abgenix (ABGX)	7/98	$23	BancAmerica Robertson Stephens, Lehman Brothers
Invitrogen (IVGN)	2/99	$45	Donaldson Lufkin & Jenrette, Warburg Dillon Read, Piper Jaffray
Albany Molecular Research (AMRI)	2/99	$50	ING Baring Furman Selz, Hambrecht & Quist
ImmTech (IMMT)	4/99	$10	New China Hong Kong Securities, China Everbright Securities
VaxGen (VXGN)	6/99	$40	Prudential Securities, Punk Ziegel & Co.
BioMarin Pharma (BMRN)	7/99	$58.5	U.S. Bancorp Piper Jaffray, Vontobel Securities, Schroders Securities, Leerink Swann & Co.
BioPure (BPUR)	7/99	$42	J. P. Morgan, Adams Harkness & Hill, Robert W. Baird & Co.

(continues)

TABLE 18.1   *(continued)*

Company (ticker)	Date completed	Gross (millions)	Bankers
Genentech (DNA)	7/99	$1940	J. P. Morgan, Goldman Sachs, Merrill Lynch & Co., Warburg Dillon Read, BancBoston Robertson Stephens
Symyx Technologies (SMMX)	11/99	$77	Credit Suisse First Boston, Donaldson Lufkin & Jenrette, Invemed Associates, Schroder & Co.
Maxygen (MAXY)	12/99	$110	Goldman Sachs, Robertson Stephens, Invemed Associates
Tularik (TLRK)	12/99	$112	Golman Sachs, Robertson Stephens, Invemed Associates

SOURCE: Information courtesy of *BioWorld Financial Watch*.

IPOs are an important goal for biotech companies, opening up a whole new world of potential investors and bringing in enough cash to fuel product development for at least a year or two.

Dr. Louis Lange, CEO of the cardiovascular company CV Therapeutics (CVTX), is a big fan of the IPO transformation process. "We went public in November 1996, and it's been much easier for our company hands down since then. We have more credibility with investors, our valuation is clear, and we can use the stock to make deals with other companies. It's the next step in the company evolution continuum."

But there is a dark side to going public. Says Lange, "The process was arduous—like pulling teeth without ether. We were on the road for 3 weeks, with 42 meetings in front of lots of folks who were generically smart but had little personal experience with drug development. The public market for biotech had peaked in May 1996, and too many really early-stage companies went out. Our roadshow was in the autumn and was an uphill battle, even though the meetings went well for the most part."

Dr. Ron Cohen was part of the founding team at Advanced Tissue Sciences (ATS) before founding Acorda. ATS was working on a new area—tissue engineering—to provide skin grafts for patients with serious burns and nonhealing wounds. Prior to its IPO, the company had raised only $1.5 million from an angel investor and friends of the family. The company managed to go public during the hot IPO window in 1988 at a development stage that otherwise would been more suitable for true venture investing.

Says Cohen, "It was the first real money we had in the company, around $5.5 million net, giving us our first real chance to do some significant work. We had to make our way through a remarkable thicket of SEC regulations, legal work, and watching each line in the offering document be scrutinized. Nothing prepared us for the change—constant public scrutiny, the need to report constantly, the deluge of investor inquiries."

Dr. Tina Nova, president and CEO of Nanogen Inc. (San Diego, California), knows the value of being able to tell the story to investors. Nanogen is part of the most recent generation of biotech companies, combining molecular biology and computer sciences to create "organic computers" that can identify specific gene sequences and correlate those sequences with diseases in patients. Dr. Nova has been around the biotech industry since the early 1980s, starting out as a scientist at Hybritech, San Diego's very first biotech company, before migrating to the senior management side.

Nanogen's technology was tough to explain because Nanogen was so different from existing companies in the mid-1990s, with its combination of electronics and molecular biology. At the same time, this made the selling job easier because the science *was* so novel and exciting. Says Nova, "VCs (venture capitalists) love sexy science that is cutting edge, and there wasn't much competition at the time. All investors like what is fashionable at the time—I could not have sold an antibody-based company like Hybritech to save my life then, no matter how good the fundamentals! For public and private companies, the trick is to somehow be part of the current investing fad."

The flip side? Good companies often go begging in tough markets because they don't fit the current "sexy" profile or don't have the current buzzwords in their business plan. Nova helped take her company public in the brief financing window that opened in the spring of 1998. "We were criticized for going public so early in our evolution as a company. But we didn't have enough cash to get to product commercialization, and we felt that it was important to raise capital while the market would let us. We turned out to be right! The window slammed shut right after our IPO raised $62 million in April 1998. Even before it shut, we had a hard sell. People wanted to see revenue before they would invest. We sold them on the rationale that the cash would be used to complete the product launch."

Once Nanogen management decided to take the company public, the big question was which bankers to use. This is an incredibly time-consuming process, much like romancing many suitors prior to a big dance. "We were lucky in that several banks wanted to take us out. That was great, because it gave us some choice. Even so, we had to sell the company to them, in a process very similar to wooing the venture investors. First, you meet with a couple of scouts, who report back to the office. If you pass that test, they come back with the analysts. Only after the analysts sign off on the deal do you finally meet with the firm's top bankers. Take this process and repeat it with another 10 banks."

How does a biotech company decide which banks are desirable? Says Nova, "We selected Morgan Stanley, Dillon Read, and Lehman Brothers primarily because at the time they had analysts who really understood our story. It was very important that they understood what differentiated us from other competing investments, and that they could sell the deal to their internal sales force and to investors. Because they understood our story, we knew they would put us in front of the right potential investors. The top banks know what their investors would like, what they have invested in already. The big questions every biotech company has to answer for potential investors: How are you different from other companies, and why should I buy your stock?"

As Nanogen's Nova says, "Today, e-commerce is in, and you can't sell biotech to save your life. At some point, the market will realize most Internet companies lack the basic fundamentals of a sustainable business. Biotech supporters need to hang tough until then."

The work is still not over even once the IPO is completed. Investors absolutely *hate* to buy stocks that promptly plummet. This means management must actively support the aftermarket—the performance of its stock once that IPO is done and investors have put their hard-earned dollars into the company coffers. "To support your investors' investment, you must constantly stay in touch with your new group of investors. Your company's stated milestones and financial projections must be met," says Nova.

Even when you do everything right, events outside your control can cause your stock to dive. In the case of Nanogen, the biotech market (and most of the small cap stocks in all industries) crashed soon after its public offering. The stock price went from $11 at the IPO, up briefly to $12, and down to $3 by year end—still during the lockup for the private round investors and employees. None of this downward activity was based on Nanogen's actions; rather, it was based on the broader market.

Nova says the key is to keep doing the right things, even when the market seems to be ignoring your progress. "We continued to meet our milestones and did exactly what we said we would do, but the stock was still in the tank. In markets like this, there is nothing you can do—it's very frustrating. Management has to spend time with employees telling them what is happening to keep them from panicking. But when the biotech market started turning up in the beginning of 1999, our share price crept back to $9 per share. Our staff stuck with us—we've had less than 10% turnover since inception."

Ironically, Nova sees bad markets as having a good side—if you are lucky enough to have sufficient cash in the bank. "Our investors weren't about to sell into a down market. They basically put us on their back burner. This quiet period allowed us to focus on getting the job done. We've got about $50 million in the bank, which lets us ignore this market and focus on building the business."

DISCLOSURE: THE GOOD, THE BAD, AND THE UGLY

The most important difference between public and private companies is that public companies have an obligation (and SEC regulations to back that up) to report on any events that might have a significant effect on their business—and thus their stock price. Here's where it gets sticky for biotech companies. They now have to reveal absolutely every speed bump in every project to an audience of investors who don't really understand the drug development process and who thus tend to overreact to almost all news—good and bad.

Big pharma companies also have to reveal "material events." But they have the advantage of numerous marketed products bringing in lots of revenue. An event that would be a stock price disaster for a biotech stock—a problem in Phase II clinical studies, for example—is barely a blip on a big pharma stock performance chart.

The Immune Response Corp. (Carlsbad, California) had a bad run-in with this phenomenon in May 1999 when an interim analysis of a Phase III clinical trial for its AIDS vaccine revealed a "good news/bad news" problem. It turns out that the new "triple drug" treatments for HIV-infected patients drastically reduce the rate of disease progression to full-blown AIDS and eventually death—which is good news, unless you are trying to show that your vaccine also slows AIDS progression.

The bad news—the drugs were doing such a good job that the monitoring board couldn't detect a difference between the patients treated with the vaccine (along with regular "triple drug" treatment) and those treated with "triple drug" treatment alone. The clinical study was halted, because it would never be able to show a statistically significant benefit from the vaccine.

The Immune Response Corp. and its partner, Agouron Pharmaceuticals Inc., instead did see a significant reduction in the level of AIDS virus in the blood of a subgroup of the patients randomly tested for this so-called surrogate marker. This is termed a *surrogate marker* because it is assumed, not yet proven, that reduction in virus levels equals a better prognosis for the patient. The partners are hoping to convince the FDA to focus on this new marker of vaccine effectiveness.

So—the bottom line is that the vaccine probably worked. You just couldn't see it above the effect of the drug therapy. A combination of new studies and reanalysis of existing studies may win the day. This would be a valuable addition to HIV treatment because a monthly vaccine injection would certainly be easier for patients than the complex, multidose per day regimen of the three drugs.

How did the stock market react? It dropped Immune Response Corp. stock 36% by the close of the day, to $7.56/share.

This overreaction can work in the opposite direction, too. In May 1998, a breathless piece of reporting on the front page of the *New York Times* made it sound as though EntreMed Inc. (Rockville, Maryland) was just about to cure cancer. In fact, the reporter had overblown an earlier experiment in mice. But new investors had no way to judge the news, other than its front-page position in a top-tier newspaper—and drove the stock up about 330%. It plummeted again as investors realized the truth of the situation and a year later was trading closer to its 12-month low of $11/share than to its 12-month high of $85/share.

Meanwhile, Pfizer was forced to revise the warning label on its Trovan antibiotic in mid-1999 to include a warning about the potential for serious liver damage after 140 cases had been reported since February 1998—and its stock dropped a mere 1% on the news to $101/share. If the problem had arisen in early clinical testing, we might not ever have heard about it. Pfizer's revenues are so big that a single product blip in the pipeline might not have a significant effect on its business and thus might not be reportable according to SEC regulations.

SHAREHOLDER IDENTITY CRISIS

The composition of investors usually changes when a biotech firm goes public, with many of the venture investors and early institutional investors taking their profits once the lockup period expires. *Lockup* refers to a period of time, typically 18 months, that folks holding stock from a company's private venture days must wait post-IPO before selling their stock on the public market. This restriction prevents a sudden sell-off of shares in a newly public company and helps support the after-market for the new investors.

The IPO offering memorandum will give you a sense of how many shares are in the hands of private round investors, and how long they are required to hold the stock before selling. In recent years, venture investors have been holding onto their stock—in part because investing in public biotech stocks was a much less risky approach than investing in private start-ups and hoping the stock market would let them go public!

Biotech CEOs also have to grapple with a sudden influx of individual investors, who can be very enthusiastic about the company's technology and product prospects. But these same investors usually do not have technical backgrounds and often are not able to fully understand what the company is up to.

In the case of more established industries, it's not that important to understand how the technology behind products actually works. You don't need to know how personal computers or cell phones work to invest intelligently in Nokia or Dell Computers. But it can be very tricky making investment decisions in biotech stocks when the science is still driving events.

We will talk about ways to reduce the risk of biotech investment decisions in Chapter 22.

———19———

CREATIVE FINANCING

The biotech industry has shown itself to be extremely creative at designing new and innovative financing vehicles to power this long and risky product development cycle. In tough times, when the usual suspects are just not interested in plain vanilla secondary stock offerings, biotech execs and their bankers have been able to generate cash with a series of alternative approaches that target subsets of investors.

In 1998, public biotech firms raised just over $3 billion using private placements, rights offerings, loans, debt offerings, warrant exercises, and PIPE financings, according to *BioWorld Financial Watch*. Each of these transactions has a different structure, and investors may find themselves desperately trying to decipher when a creative deal is a good investment and when it is a really bad idea.

The common theme to all of these investment vehicles is that they are very effective for strong companies that have the ability to weather an unexpected negative result in product development programs. But any transaction that is not "plain vanilla" should be carefully considered if the company has a low market capitalization (below $250 million) and has been struggling along. Any adverse event is likely to kick its feet right out from under that company, and investors are taking an even bigger risk than usual.

Let's take a look at some of the investment vehicles used to date.

Tracking stock and other off-balance-sheet financings: Genzyme Corp. (Framingham, Massachusetts) perfected the art of using tracking stocks to raise capital for technology without having to brave the general public markets. Genzyme distributed stock in Genzyme Molecular Oncology (GMO) as a tax-free dividend to its shareholders in late 1998. Genzyme also spun out its surgical division as a tracking stock in 1999.

155

According to Dr. Gail Maderis, president of GMO, this spinning out of a tracking stock focused attention on a new technology that might get lost in the larger Genzyme business and allowed investors to decide whether they want to hold the more conservative parent company or the young, feisty (and riskier) GMO, while allowing the parent to continue to benefit from the tax advantages of an R&D organization burning cash. This structure also allows the parent company to create a "small company" environment and stock incentives for employees involved in the innovative programs.

This tracking-stock approach removed the drag of the low profit margins of the surgical division and the long wait for product revenues of the molecular oncology group from Genzyme General's highly profitable base business in replacement protein therapies.

Perkin Elmer Corp. (PE) used the same approach in creating its Celera Genomics business unit—a joint venture created with genomics superstar Dr. Craig Venter. PE's longtime institutional investors were not convinced they wanted to support this high-tech stuff, but there is a universe of new investors eager to support Celera.

Farah Champsi, managing director at BancBoston Robertson Stephens, points to a slightly different approach used by Ligand Pharmaceuticals and a group of private investors to extricate a risky research program from its more developed product programs. They agreed to pony up $25 million by the third quarter of 1999 to fund a new private corporation called X-Ceptor Therapeutics. This company will investigate orphan nuclear receptors—proteins found in the nucleus of the cell, clearly important but with an as-yet-unknown function. The research may yield very important new drugs—but we won't see anything reach the clinic for many years.

A new management team will run X-Ceptor, and Ligand has the right to acquire the company for any combination of cash or Ligand common stock for $61.4 million in 3 years or up to $79.8 million in 4 years.

This spinout approach allows the parent company, Ligand, to stay focused on its more near-term programs and to use someone else's money to pay for research that remains accessible to Ligand while not abusing the Ligand balance sheet.

Convertible preferred-stock offerings: Convertible offerings became quite chic in 1998, according to BioWorld's 1999 State of the Industry Report. The basic aim is to let the company and its investors benefit from future increases in stock price driven by positive events,

TABLE 19.1   Money Raised by Biotech 1994–1998 (in millions)

Type of financing	1994	1995	1996	1997	1998
IPOs	$468.2	$493.7	$1,610	$780.6	$246.7
Follow-on Public	$556.2	$1,665.2	$2,884	$1572.6	$778.7
PIPE/ Reg. S	$180.6	$147.6	$148.4	$68.7	$117.9
Public/ other	$575	$1,099.5	$2,214.5	$2,129.5	$2,946.9
Corporate partner payments	NA	$106.8	$257.8	$188.5	$256.8
Venture rounds	$449.5	$452.3	$697	$789.6	$1,098.8
Total ($M)	$2,230	$3,965.1	$7,554.1	$5,529.5	$5,445.8

SOURCE: Courtesy of *BioWorld Financial Watch*.

while protecting them from unexpected negative stock performance. You buy preferred stock, which can't trade but which converts into common stock upon reaching some benchmark time or stock price.

The price of the preferred stock is set at some discount to the price of the equivalent amount of common stock at the time of the offering. Many offerings are set up to entice investors to hold off on conversion as long as possible, by offering an increasing conversion discount the longer the investors wait. This approach is designed to keep investors from selling off the stock as soon as it converts, which could counteract any good news and drive down the stock price.

Companies try to structure these deals to take advantage of upcoming milestones—completion of clinical studies, corporate partnerships, and so on—that are expected to raise the stock price. As long as the milestones are met, and the stock price responds, everyone is happy. If the news is bad, the stock will drop and the converted stock can't be sold for a profit. Some convertible offerings have a reset option on the conversion price, which protects investors from precipitous drops in common stock price. But if the stock drop is serious, and the company was already in trouble, this reset option can be a final death blow.

Why take the risk of doing a convertible offering? The company does it to raise needed cash in a resistant market, when investors must be enticed with a discount of the current stock price. As Robertson's Champsi points out, converts have a more favorable impact on the earnings per share (EPS) than a plain vanilla public offering, because the net earnings get divided by fewer outstanding shares to calculate the EPS. These deals can also bring in a new set of investors to the company that might not be interested in a common-stock deal. Also, because converts do not need to follow SEC registration regulations, the deal typically gets done more quickly (and thus costs the company less).

The trick for investors is to discern the difference between converts offered by quality companies—where the chances are good that the stock price will rise on future good news—and those designed to bail out desperate companies, which stand a good chance of dying if there is more bad news.

In the latter case, the converted stock is probably not worth much even with the preferred discount. A current version of converts done for troubled companies has been termed *death spiral converts* by cynical bankers, who see those offering these deals as driven by transaction fees.

The eight public biotech convertible debt (or preferred) deals sold to institutional investors in 1998–1999 raised $1.6 billion. The market capitalization of the companies involved ranged from $750 million to $2.0 billion. IDEC Pharmaceuticals ($1.7-billion market cap at time of deal) and Human Genome Sciences ($940 million) raised $215 million in 1999 with such deals.

Thirty private biotech convertible deals were completed in 1998–1999, raising nearly $700 million. The typical deal size was $10 million to $20 million, and the companies involved had market caps ranging from $50 million to $200 million. Investors included hedge funds and smaller institutional players. The terms can be expensive to the company, because of the smaller size of the deal and the liquidity issues.

Sometimes, convertible deals are done between corporate partners to further strengthen the bond between the two companies and to raise more cash for the smaller company. In April 1998, Affymetrix sold $50 million worth of Series AA Convertible Preferred Stock to Glaxo Wellcome. Affymetrix pays a 6 1/2% dividend on these shares until they convert into common shares. The convert price is about

$40 per share. Glaxo ownership in Affymetrix increased from 33.8% prior to the offering to 35.3% on a fully diluted basis.

Revenue-based transactions: In 1997, Xoma Corp. (Berkeley, California) and its bankers carried out a financing transaction usually seen in the entertainment and gold-mining industries, according to BioWorld. The basic idea is to trade uncertain future product royalties for immediate cash. Xoma had been struggling for a decade or more to bring its late-stage product candidates into the marketplace to generate some revenue. Meanwhile, the company had burned through most of its cash, and impatient investors were not interested in giving Xoma any more.

The royalty interest deal allowed Xoma to exchange royalty rights for the anticancer monoclonal antibody Rituxan for $17 million from Pharmaceutical Partners. Xoma licensed key patents to Genentech, which in turn sublicensed them to its Rituxan development partner, IDEC Pharmaceuticals (San Diego, California), which used those rights in the process of commercializing this new lymphoma drug. Pharmaceutical Partners takes on the risk of future product royalties being generated by IDEC and Genentech, and Xoma gets the operating cash needed to keep its own product candidates moving forward. Between the upfront licensing fee from Genentech and this innovative transaction, Xoma raised $20 million to fuel further development of its own products.

Champsi points out that Cephalon used a similar approach to raise funds, based on future sales of its Provigil for narcolepsy. This debt offering raised $30 million through the private sale of revenue-sharing notes that are repayable by the company in cash in February 2002. The deal carries an annual interest rate of 11% and is secured by the U.S. rights to Provigil. Additionally, investors receive a 6% royalty on U.S. sales of Provigil for up to 5 years. Cephalon has the right to redeem the debt at a premium prior to maturity, which would reduce the royalty period to 4 years.

The deal includes 5-year warrants to purchase shares of common stock at a 25% premium, and investors forfeit 480,000 of the 1.92 million warrants if Cephalon reaches certain sales levels—a nice incentive for performance.

Private investment in a public entity transactions (PIPEs) and Regulation S deals: In this scenario, private investors buy newly issued shares of a public company's common stock at a discount of the public market share price. Once the registration statement is effective, the shares can be freely traded and the company gets the cash. Regulation S deals are very similar, except that the shares are sold to overseas investors and don't have to be registered. Investors can sell the shares after a short holding period, usually 30 to 60 days. In the 1990s, Regulation S offerings took advantage of the sudden increase in European investors interested in biotech deals.

—— 2 0 ——

CORPORATE PARTNERS AND
THE URGE TO MERGE

IF YOU'VE GOT THE MONEY, HONEY. . .

Most biotech companies have to wait almost a decade for product revenues to begin flowing. In the meantime, there is an eager market anxious to tap into biotech's innovative products and technologies—the well-established pharmaceutical companies.

Why would biotech companies share the fruits of their labor with potential competitors?

- Survival: The biggest challenge for most biotech firms is to survive long enough to bring products to market. When capital markets are in love with biotech, almost any company can raise cash. But in tough markets, that burn rate keeps chugging. Biotech execs know that the greatest science in the world counts for nothing if you can't stay alive long enough to develop it. In 1998, corporate alliances brought in more capital than did equity deals ($4.5 billion vs. $3.5 billion, according to Recombinant Capital).
- A corporate partner provides validation: Most public stock investors—retail or institutional—are well aware that they don't have the technical backgrounds to independently analyze science-based companies and their product development efforts. These folks look for outside verification that a biotech company's science is top-notch. The willingness of a pharma partner to invest tens of millions of dollars for product rights can be the biotech equivalent of the Good Housekeeping Seal of Approval.

161

Bayer AG made its faith in Millennium Pharmaceuticals' (Cambridge, Massachusetts) technology and team extremely clear when the German pharma company popped for a $33-million up-front fee, $97 million in equity purchase, $219 million in research support and licensing over the next 5 years, plus another potential $116 million in milestone payments. This incredible deal, which won the Breakthrough Alliance Award at the 1999 Recombinant Capital ALLICENCE Conference, gives Bayer access to 225 drug targets—Bayer still has to do all of the drug discovery and development!

Neurogen got a boost in June 1999 when Pfizer agreed to pay $27 million over 3 years for nonexclusive access to Neurogen's rapid-drug-discovery technology aimed at neurological disorders. Neurogen's stock responded by rising 16% on the news to $14.63/share.

- Freedom from Wall Street: The biotech stocks have taken shareholders for roller coaster rides ever since the industry began—often for reasons having little to do with the fundamentals of the individual companies. Most CEOs are anxious to have alternative sources of capital to smooth out the bumpy capital markets. Long-term corporate partnering deals can provide a nice cushion. Some companies, such as Tularik Inc. (South San Francisco, California) and Millennium Pharmaceuticals Inc. (Cambridge, Massachusetts) have actually used alliances to bring their companies to "breakeven" or even profitability, well in advance of any product revenues. Tularik avoided the public markets altogether until December 1999, relying solely on partners and private investors to bring in sufficient cash to keep a wide range of impressive research programs racing forward.
- Global business strategy: It's clear that the biopharmaceutical business has gone global, just like all the other market sectors. Most biotech firms can't afford, and don't have the in-house expertise, to build an international presence in time for their first product launches. And some markets, such as Japan and the Far East, are almost impossible to crack without some local help. Many biotech execs, and a growing number of big pharma folks, use geographically defined alliances to ensure that their products will make it into worldwide markets.

Gary Lyons, CEO of San Diego–based neurology company Neurocrine, learned this geography lesson well during his time at Genentech. His company's corporate partnerships with Janssen (compounds aimed at anxiety, depression, substance abuse) and Novartis (multiple sclerosis) retained copromotion rights for Neurocrine in North America, while giving "rest-of-world" rights to the partners in exchange for royalties. This approach to partnering gives Neurocrine a chance to build an in-house sales and marketing capability in a manageable manner, while relying on an experienced partner to carry the ball in foreign territories.

- Balancing the need for near-term cash with long-term value growth: Well-designed corporate deals provide more than upfront cash. They also provide the biotech partner with access to a team with decades of experience pushing drugs through the clinical and regulatory process and into the marketplace. These relationships can provide "on-the-job" training for the biotech managers, as well as access to a network of service providers to help with the next project. That experience can then be applied to the next internal project, and the reliance on outsiders is thus reduced.

BIG PHARMA'S TICKING TIME BOMB

Okay, we can see why biotech companies are anxious to deal. But why are the pharmaceutical companies willing to part with their hard-earned cash?

There are two compelling reasons. The first is the hard reality that big pharma's research departments simply have not been as productive as the smaller biotech firms when it comes to rapidly developing innovative new technologies. According to *IMS Health*, the pace of new product approvals is slowing, dropping from a peak of 53 in 1996, to 39 in 1997, to 29 in 1998. The wonderful world of managed health care dictates that new drugs must provide a real benefit over existing drugs, and in a cost-effective way. This means no more third-generation versions of old drugs—a time-honored tradition in the pharma industry. If the big boys want to stay in the stream of new technologies and novel approaches to drug discovery, they *must* collaborate with biotech teams.

Ironically, investors are the other reason companies like Merck, Glaxo Wellcome, Eli Lilly, and their brethren have to partner with biotech. Big pharma must feed the "earnings growth" beast, that dou-

TABLE 20.1   Big Pharma Products Losing Patent Protection

Year 2000			Year 2001		
Product/ company	*Expiration Date*	*U.S. sales (millions)*	*Product/ company*	*Expiration Date*	*U.S. Sales (millions)*
Estraderm/ Novartis	Jan.	$26	Mevacor/ Merck	June	$420
Neurontin/ Warner-Lambert	Jan.	$429	Plendil/	June	$125
Cytotec/ Monsanto	Jan.	$64	Ceftin/ Glaxo	July	$365
Vasotec/ Merck	Feb.	$872	Stadol NS/ Bristol-Myers	Aug.	$98
Glucophage/ Bristol-Myers	March	$727	Elecon/ Schering-Plough	Sep.	$41
Ultram/J&J	March	$384	Eulexin/ Schering-Plough	Sep.	$64
Ziac/AHP	March	$150	Alphagan/ Allergan	Sep.	$82
Buspar/ Bristol-Myers	May	$464	Prilosec/ Astra	April	$2,933
Hytrin/ Abbott	June	$482	Vantin/ Pharmacia & Upjohn	Dec.	$74
Soronox/ J&J	June	$244	Prinivil/ Merck	Dec.	$368
Cardura/ Pfizer	Oct.	$280	Topamax/ J&J	Dec.	$57
Lotrisone/ Schering-Plough	Oct.	$175			
Pepcid/ Merck	Oct.	$747			
Total		$5,044	Total		$4,627

(continues)

TABLE 20.1   *(continued)*

Year 2002			Year 2003		
Product/ company	*Expiration Date*	*U.S. sales (millions)*	*Product/ company*	*Expiration Date*	*U.S. Sales (millions)*
Accurpil/ Warner-Lambert	Oct.	$318	Serzone/ Bristol-Myers	March	$214
Relafen/ SmithKline	Dec.	$449	Ticlid/ Rohm & Haas	May	$231
Monopril/ Bristol-Myers	Dec.	$171	Lotensin/ Novartis	Aug.	$304
Augmentin/ SmithKline	Dec.	$926	Floxin/ J&J	Sept.	$147
			Ortho Novum/ J&J	Sept.	$151
Total		$1,864	Total		$1,047

SOURCE: From CIBC World Markets, May 26, 1999 Pharmaceuticals Report

ble-digit earnings growth that their investors have come to expect. More and more of the sector's blockbuster drugs are losing their patent protection, driving revenues down (see Table 20.1). Big pharma has spent the years since 1994 grappling with the stark reality that their new product pipelines are pretty empty. Where to find new products to keep the growth going? Biotech.

BUY VERSUS MAKE

Big pharma is making increasing use of its purchasing power to buy access to products, product candidates, and early-stage technology from biotech partners. According to *BioWorld Financial Watch*, the total precommercialization (before royalties) value of biotech/big pharma deals is on the rise, growing from less than $1 billion in 1991 to $1.4 billion in 1993, and reaching $3.7 billion in 1998. The number of deals between biotech and big pharma tracked by *BioWorld* grew from 69 in 1993 to 221 in 1998.

The typical biotech/big pharma deal includes:

- An up-front licensing fee that gives the big pharma partner rights to use the technology;
- R&D funding for the life of the agreement (typically 3 to 5 years initially) that covers the people and supplies used by the biotech partner to carry out the work;
- Milestone payments that give the biotech partner rewards for moving the project forward and reaching benchmarks that are significant for product commercialization (for example, filing for FDA permission to start clinical testing, starting Phase I/II/III trials, filing for marketing permission, product launch);
- A purchase of equity in the biotech partner by the big pharma partner. This last point is not always included. The big pharma companies don't always see stock as a useful commodity and usually buy the shares because the biotech firm wants them to.

The amount of money a biotech company can command for each of these points is very dependent on the perceived quality of the company and its technology, whether the technology is seen as "cutting edge" or the third runner-up in an area, how crucial the technology is to the big pharma partner's internal strategy, and how hungry the big pharma partner is for new product candidates to fill its pipeline.

Recombinant Capital's study of the alliances completed in 1997–1998 by the top 20 big pharma companies shows that the average financial commitment ranged from $41 million to $59 million, depending on the stage of program development. Average up-front payment ranges from $1.4 million for early-stage technology deals to $10 million for more developed programs. The average R&D funding ranges from $16 million to $6.5 million (later-stage programs require less R&D work), and milestone payments range from $18 million for early-stage deals up to $37 million for late-stage deals. The more risk is reduced by having more developed product candidates, the more the partner is willing to pay for the privilege of taking that risk.

Average equity investments for all of these deals are around $4 million. There was a huge uptick to $8.5 million to $16.5 million in the 1994–1996 time frame, when the public markets were truly atrocious and biotech firms were desperate to raise capital.

There were some huge big-ticket biotech deals in 1998 that surpassed any previous alliance price tags. The hands-down winner was Millennium Pharmaceuticals (Cambridge, Massachusetts). In October 1997, this genomics company signed an agreement worth up to $218 million with Monsanto—the richest biotech deal—then more than doubled the stakes with its $465-million target discovery whopper in September 1998 with Bayer AG.

Other big-ticket items illustrating big pharma's keen interest in cancer and vaccines include Corixa Corp.'s (Seattle, Washington) $111-million vaccine deal with SmithKline Beecham, Cell Genesys's (Foster City, California) $153-million gene therapy cancer vaccine program with Japan Tobacco, Epimmune's (San Diego, California) $100-million cancer vaccine agreement with G. S. Searle, a $132 million alliance between Coulter Pharmaceuticals (Palo Alto, California) and SmithKline Beecham for Coulter's anticancer monoclonal antibody Bexxar, and finally Glaxo Wellcome's $321 million deal with PowderJect Pharmaceuticals to develop needle-free delivery systems for DNA vaccines for infectious diseases.

One thing to keep in mind—these big numbers include almost 50% of the total in milestone payments, which must be earned! The press releases touting huge deals are describing what industry insiders term *biobucks,* the total possible amount of money if everything goes perfectly. Because Wall Street has focused so much attention on corporate deals as a source of cash and validation, the press releases tend to go for the biggest number possible, even though only a small fraction of that amount will actually hit the company coffers in any given year of the deal.

It is often tough to get management to cough up the details of how much money comes in the door upon signing, how much is committed on an annual basis, and how much is dependent on hitting benchmarks. But be on the lookout for deal announcements that mention up-front fees and committed research funding of at least $20 million. That is the lower limit for a deal to be seen as significant by Wall Street. The unmeasureable upside, of course, is product royalty income, which is paid to the biotech company once the product makes it onto the market and sales revenues start coming in. Every product and every deal has a different royalty structure—analyst reports on the biotech company can give you some ballpark ideas of the probable range of royalty rates for specific deals.

The most active partner with biotech to date is Hoffmann-La Roche, with more than 120 alliances accumulated since 1988, according to Recombinant Capital (see Figure 20.1). Following close behind are SmithKline and American Home Products with about 90 deals

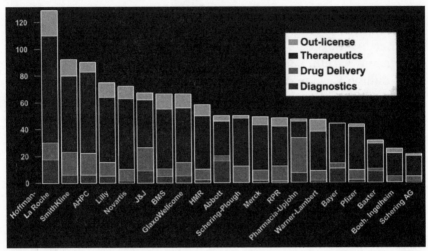

FIGURE 20.1 Biotechnology Alliances of Top 20 Pharmas Ranking by Cumulative Number of Alliances
SOURCE: Recombinant Capital.

each, with another 17 companies trailing from about 80 cumulative deals down to 30 for Schering AG. An overwhelming majority of these deals involve therapeutic products or technologies aimed at generating therapeutics (see Figure 20.2). Most of the alliances in-

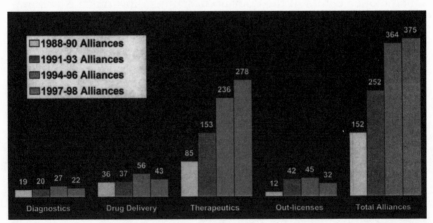

FIGURE 20.2 Biotech Alliances of Top 20 Pharmas, Alliance Type by Year of Signing (N=1,143)
SOURCE: Recombinant Capital.

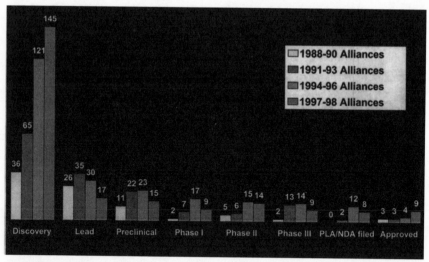

FIGURE 20.3 Biotech Alliances of Top 20 Pharmas by stage at Signing
(*N*=700)
SOURCE: Recombinant Capital

volved technology still in the discovery phase when the deal was signed, though deals around product candidates in clinical testing are starting to rise now that the biotech companies have been around long enough to *have* product candidates (see Figure 20.3).

These deals have evolved from simple R&D contracts with straightforward "cash for technology rights," into more complex deals that last for years and can include hefty equity purchases by the partner, up-front technology access fees, R&D funding for the life of the deal, milestone payments triggered by the biotech firm's reaching important product development benchmarks, and royalty payments once any resulting products reach the marketplace.

Increasingly, biotech companies are negotiating to retain more of the downstream rights, including manufacturing, co-marketing, and co-promotion rights. Often, separate deals are struck with different partners for different parts of the world, sometimes with the hope that the biotech company can retain the U.S. market for itself.

In the 1999 *Bioworld Annual Report,* Jennifer Van Brunt points out that the alliance between Cell Genesys Inc. and Japan Tobacco Inc. was structured to share the costs, and hopefully the profits, of world-wide product development equally between the partners. In addition, Cell Genesys retained all North American marketing rights.

These cost-sharing components usually are set up as options to be exercised by the biotech company, with the big pharma partner as the default supporter of all costs. That way, if the biotech company is struggling for cash, it doesn't have to exercise the option until it is back on its feet and can simply stick with a royalty stream of income.

ACQUISITION AS AN ENDGAME

Ever since the nasty down market in the late 1980s, industry analysts have been calling for consolidation in the biotech sector—starting with Steve Burrill, Ernst & Young's first biotech business unit chief, and growing to include every venture investor with more than two biotech portfolio companies and many of Wall Street's analysts.

The reason for this "urge to merge" talk is the incredible growth in the number of companies, from 360 biotech companies in 1988 to 1,386 in 1999 (the 1989 numbers come from M. Dibner, *Biotechnology Guide USA*, London, 1988, Macmillan; the 1999 numbers from M. Dibner, Institute for Biotechnology Information, www.biotechn-info.com). The universe of public biotech companies has exploded, leaving investors and analysts alike boggled by the number of companies to sift through looking for gems.

The reality that everyone grapples with is pure mathematics. If it takes an average of 10 years and $250 million to develop a new drug, and you have 1,386 companies, you're talking $346,500 billion—just a tad more than the VCs and public investors had planned on. Although biotech has shown itself to be incredibly adept at raising funds, this might be asking a bit too much of the system.

Until recently, there hasn't been as much merger and acquisition (M&A) activity as you might expect, given the pressures on these companies to raise money in resistant stock markets. But 1998 saw a surge in M&A deals. Big pharma went shopping for deals, and larger biotechs saw a chance to add critical mass to increase their own odds for survival.

Craig Taylor, a partner at Alloy Ventures, sees this shopping spree as an important part of the biotech industry's evolution and potentially as a way to get VCs interested in the sector again.

"The big problem with funding start-ups is the time and money needed to get to product launch. We need a financing model that requires less capital to get there, which means we also need management teams that can do more with less. And therein lies the rub—there aren't enough great folks who can run these companies efficiently enough. Maybe this drives consolidation. But although everyone thinks this has to happen, the folks in the companies are fighting consolidation tooth and nail."

Taylor has hit on the key point—the same passion, determination, and entrepreneurial spirit required to create and grow biotech companies makes it really tough to walk away from the dream of independence and turn the technology over to another management team. Not to mention the incredible fights over relative valuation of private companies that ensue at the board of directors level.

A few industry insiders are trying to help make consolidation happen by using money to force the issue. Several are raising funds that will be used, at least in part, as an outside mechanism to force consolidation. To date, none of these have made much headway. The bankers and consultants, with that big transaction fee waiting at the end of the deal, seem to have the most interest in forcing the issue.

Alloy's Taylor points out that the spate of biotech mergers and acquisitions in the late 1990s (see Table 20.2) may actually help kick-start the venture investing engine once again by providing an exit strategy alternative to IPOs.

Says Taylor, "The large pharmaceutical and medical device companies are still no better at innovation than they used to be. Their internal R&D groups can't support their huge sales and distribution engines. In order to fill this ravenous monster, they continue to show willingness to in-license product candidates and buy companies. If a few more mid-tier biotech firms with interesting product pipelines—but lacking the clinical development oomph needed—get bought, more of the big pharma companies may get concerned about all the good biotechs with product candidates getting snapped up. Right now, the buyers are concentrating on biotechs with late-stage clinical trials or significant technology platforms, which they can just plug into their existing infrastructure."

The potential kicker? Says Taylor, "The seed corn is not being planted now. The lack of venture funds willing to invest in biotech is good for big pharma now because the tight funding means they are getting great deals on acquiring or collaborating with the biotech companies. But once they are done with the mid-tier company acquisitions, what happens? As potentially the last standing medical investor in Silicon Valley, if Alloy is smarter about financing new biotechs—creating fewer companies and spending less to get pro-

TABLE 20.2   Big Pharma Acquisitions of Biotech Companies

Biotech co.	Big pharma buyer	Date	Deal (millions)
DNAZ Research Institute*	Schering-Plough	1982	$30
Agrigenetics*	Lubrizol	1983	N/A
Hybritech	Eli Lilly & Co.	1985	$375
Genetic Systems	Bristol-Myers	1985	$294
Zymogenetics*	Novo Nordisk	1988	$NA
Sungene*	Lubrizol	1989	$ND
Damon Biotech	Abbott Labs	1989	$9
Praxis Biologics	American Cyanamid (now part of AHP)	1989	$237
Gen-Probe	Chugai Pharmaceutical	1989	$110
Triton Biosciences*	Schering AG	1990	N/A
Codon*	Schering AG	1990	N/A
Genentech	Roche Holding	1990 6/99	$2.1B for 60% Full acquisition
Immunex	American Home Products	3/93	$600 for 54.6% stake
Genetics Institute	American Home Products	1/92	60% stake for $666
Systemix Inc.	Novartis AG	2/92 2/97	60% for $392 40% for $75.6
Applied Biosystems	Perkin-Elmer Corp.	2/93	$330
Sphinx Pharma*	Eli Lilly & Co.	9/94	$75
Selectide Corp.*	Marion Merrell Dow (now Hoechst Marion Roussel)	1/95	$58
Chiron Corp.	Ciba-Geigy (now Novartis)	1/95	$2,100 for 49.9% stake
Affymax NV	Glaxo	3/95	$539
Genetic Therapy Inc.	Novartis AG (Sandoz)	8/95	$295
Applied Immune Sciences Inc.	Rhône-Poulenc Rorer	12/95	$84.9
Mycogen Corp.	DowElanco	2/96, 12/96	$239 for 52% stake
Canji Corp.*	Schering-Plough Corp.	2/96	$54.5
Calgene Inc.	Monsanto Co.	3/96, 11/96	$250 for 55% stake

(continues)

TABLE 20.2   *(continued)*

Biotech co.	Big pharma buyer	Date	Deal (millions)
Trophix Inc.*	Perkin-Elmer Co.	5/96	N/A
Agracetus Inc.	Monsanto Co.	5/96	$150
Athena Neurosciences	Elan Corp. plc	6/96	$635
Genetics Institute Inc.	American Home Products	12/96	$1,000 for remaining 40%
GenScope Inc.*	Perkin-Elmer Corp.	2/97	NA
Calgene Inc.	Monsanto Co.	5/97	$240 for rest of co.
Perceptive Biosystems Inc.	Perkin-Elmer Corp.	1/98	$360
Sano Corp.	Elan Corp. plc	3/98	$392.8
Apollon Inc.*	American Home Products	5/98	N/A
Gene/Networks*	Warner-Lambert	5/98	N/A
Somatogen Inc.	Baxter International Inc.	5/98	$189
Neurex	Elan Corp. plc	8/98	$740
Penederm Inc.	Mylan Labs	10/98	$205
Sequus Pharma. Inc.	Alza Corp.	10/98	$580
Nanosystems	Elan Corp. plc	10/98	$150
Mycogen Corp.	Dow AgroSciences	11/98	$411.6
DeKalb Genetics Corp.	Monsanto Co.	12/98	$3,700
TheraTech Inc.	Watson Pharma. Inc.	1/99	$300
Depotech Corp.	Skyepharma plc	3/99	$55.7
Agouron	Warner-Lambert	5/99	$2,100
Sugen	Pharmacia & Upjohn	6/99	$728
Sibia Neurosciences	Merck & Co.	9/99	$57 for 69% stake
CoCensys	Purdue Pharma	9/99	$7
Diatide Inc.	Schering AG	9/99**	$128
CombiChem	DuPont Pharma	10/99**	$95
Centocor Inc.	Johnson & Johnson	10/99	$4,900

*Private company at time of transaction.
**Not finalized.
SOURCE: Information from BioVenture Consultants, BioWorld.

ducts to the market—those companies should be worth more. It's supply and demand. Demand from big pharma should remain steady for new products, so if the supply drops . . . "

THE PROBLEM WITH SUCCESS

Given the big kickup in valuation awarded by the public markets to biotech stocks that finally make it into the top tier of companies with products in the marketplace, why are these companies willing to be acquired just as they reach that lofty peak?

Roger Longman, editor and managing partner at Windhover Information Inc. and long-time biotech analyst, says that the real issue goes back to that numbers game mentioned above. Getting that first product through the entire process costs big-time—and then investors want you to keep doing it so that revenues continue to climb at a hefty double-digit rate. Once a biotech firm gets products on the market, investors start to compare it to the big pharma companies.

But biotech companies can't spend at the extraordinary rate required to keep churning out new products. It's not just a question of having the bucks. Longman points out that analysts and investors look carefully at the amount spent on R&D as a percentage of sales. "If that percentage tops 15% to 25%, Wall Street thinks you are a bad investment because the analysts want earnings to hit a certain mark. From their perspective, every percentage point over 25% of sales that you spend on R&D, you're really spending shareholders' money."

Big pharma has oodles of products already on the market that can provide a profit cushion to spend on R&D without hurting net earnings. But biotechs don't have that cushion. This is why Agouron Pharmaceuticals agreed to get bought by Warner-Lambert in early 1999, soon after it's great new AIDS drug started generating revenue. One product does not a pipeline make, and Wall Street won't let Agouron spend more than 25% of sales on research—but it *has* to spend that money on research to build a pipeline. Wall Street liked Agouron's AIDS drug but worried about upcoming competition in that marketplace and the lack of near-term products in the pipeline. What to do?

Get bought out by Warner-Lambert for $2.1 billion—just a tad over Agouron's market cap of $1.76 billion (based on outstanding shares) when the deal was announced at the end of January, 1999, and about five times the current revenues for the sale of Agouron's products.

Why not just ignore Wall Street? Because biotech companies need Wall Street's support to do more financings, and they need their stock price to go up—for investors, but also for employees. Longman points out that "biotech firms are in competition with big pharma for that small pool of really smart scientists and executives. These folks can go to work for Roche at its campus in Palo Alto—the heart of biotech land—can get good benefits, and the price on Roche's stock options keep going up. Agouron's options for employees were under water. Without the support of investors and Wall Street, you lose those golden handcuffs."

Start-Up Fratricide

One of the unanswered questions is whether we will all learn anything lasting from this last industry cycle of massive company buildup based on hot market returns, followed by an inability to finance or even track all of the new companies. Brook Byers, of Kleiner Perkins Caufield & Byers, once termed this "start-up fratricide"—the lemminglike drive of the venture community to create many copies of a "hit" company. If one genomics company is good, surely fifteen are even better!

Unfortunately, fifteen really aren't better. And usually forcing investors to choose between fifteen companies with differences that are not discernible to nontechnical folks means that there will never be enough cash—or excellent management—for more than a couple of these companies.

The problem, of course, is that nobody knows in advance which start-ups will make it and which will not. Science is based on unexpected results, serendipity. After all, Amgen's original business plan called for programs in chicken and pig growth hormone—its fabulously successful products Epogen and Neupogen weren't even imagined in the old days. There is a real concern that the more risk is reduced, the more the upside potential is reduced as well.

Is hypergrowth inevitable? Alloy's Taylor points out that start-up fratricide isn't exclusive to biotech. "The same thing happened in the late 1970s around the disk drive company successes. Venture investors saw the incredible return on the first disk drive companies and used that enthusiasm to invest in disk drives, and in all of the suppliers to the disk drive companies, and consequently each step in the chain got overdone." The ensuing crash in this sector certainly did a

TABLE 20.3   Biotech Acquiring Biotech

Company bought	Company buying	Date	Price (millions)
Cytotech*	Quidel*	1989	N/A
Ingene	Xoma Corp.	1989	$40
Integrated Genetics	Genzyme Corp.	1989	$29
BioGrowth*	Celtrix	1991	$14
GlycoGen*	Cytel (now Epimmune)	1991	$6
Applied bioTechnology*	Oncogene Science (now OSI)	1991	$10
Genex	Enzon	1991	$13
Somatix*	Hana Biologics	1991	$10
Invitron	Centocor	1991	$6
Cetus	Chiron Corp.	1991	$650
Monoclonal Antibodies Inc.	Quidel*	1991	$64
Biosurface Technology*	Genzyme Corp.	12/94	$56
Synergen	Amgen Corp.	12/94	$262
Genica Pharma.*	Athena Neurosciences (now part of Elan)	2/95	$25.9
Vestar Inc.	NeXagen Inc.	2/95	$76.9
Glycomed	Ligand Pharma.	5/95	$57
Telios Pharma.	Integra LifeSciences Corp.	8/95	$35
Triplex Pharma. and Oncologix Inc.	Argus Pharma.	9/95	N/A
Viagen Inc.	Chiron Corp.	9/95	$95
Cellcor Inc.	Cytogen Corp.	10/95	$19.5
Univax Biologics Inc.	North American Biologicals Inc.	11/95	$150
Khepri Pharma*	Arris Pharma. (now Axys)	12/95	$21
Osteo Sciences Corp.*	Metra Biosystems Inc.	2/96	$10
Lexin Pharma.	Sparta Pharma.	3/96	$9.4
MYCOSearch Inc.*	Oncogene Sciences Inc.	4/96	$5
Genetrix Inc.*	Genzyme Corp.	5/96	$36.5
Rgene Therapeutics Inc.*	Targeted Genetics Inc.	6/96	$14.8
Genome Systems Inc.*	Incyte Pharmaceuticals Inc.	7/96	$7.7

(continues)

TABLE 20.3 *(continued)*

Company bought	Company buying	Date	Price (millions)
ChromaXome Corp.*	Houghten Pharma.	8/96	$5.4
Combion Inc.*	Incyte Pharma.	8/96	$3
Aston Molecules Ltd.*	Oncogene Sciences	9/96	$2.6
NemaPharm Inc.*	Sequana Therapeutics Inc.	10.96	N/A
Innovir Labs Inc.	VIMRx Pharmaceuticals Inc.	12/96	$9 for 66%
Darwin Molecular Corp.*	Chiroscience Group plc	12/96	$120
Chemgenics*	Millennium Pharma.	2/97	$103.2
Houston Biotechnology Inc.	Medarex Inc.	2/97	$9.1
Somatix Therapy Corp.*	Cell Genesys Inc.	5/97	$85.8
Alanex Corp.*	Agouron Pharma.	5/97	$74.5
MycoTox Inc.*	Alpha-Beta Technology Inc.	6/97	$3
PharmaGenics Inc.*	Genzyme Corp.	6/97	$28
Trophix Pharmaceuticals Inc.*	Allelix Biopharmaceuticals	7/97	$23
Mercator Genetics Inc.*	Progenitor Inc.	8/97	$30
Avid Corp.*	Triangle Pharma.	8/97	$9.6
CellGenEx Inc.*	CDR Therapeutics* (became Xcyte Therapies)	9/97	ND
StemCells Inc.*	Cytotherapeutics Inc.	9/97	$7.9
GenPharm International Inc.*	Medarex Inc.	10/97	$65
Amplicon Corp.*	Tularik Inc.*	11/97	$19
Synteni Inc.*	Incyte Pharma.	1/98	$95.7
Sequana Therapeutics Inc.	Arris Pharma. (now Axys)	1/98	$118.5
VacTex Inc.*	Aquila Biopharma.	4/98	$8.2
Aptein Inc.*	Cambridge Antibody Technology Group plc	5/98	$11
Northwest Neurologic Inc.*	Neurocrine	6/98	$4.2
Virus Research Institute Inc.	T Cell Sciences Inc. (now Avant)	8/98	$150
Seragen Inc.	Ligand Pharma.	8/98	$67

(continues)

TABLE 20.3 *(continued)*

Company bought	Company buying	Date	Price (millions)
Matrigen Inc.*	Prizm Pharma. (now Selective Genetics)	9/98	N/A
Hexagen plc	Incyte Pharma.	9/98	$27.7
ImmunoTherapy Corp.*	AVI BioPharma	9/98	$5.8
Oncormed Inc.	Gene Logic Inc.	9/98	$39
CytoMed Inc.*	UCB Pharma and Leukosite	10/98 and 1/99	$18
GeneMedicine Inc.	Megabios Corp. (now Valentis)	3/99	$38
NaviCyte Inc.*	Trega Biosciences	11/98	$6.6
ImmuLogic	Cantab Pharmaceuticals plc	2/99	$20
CellPro Inc.	Nexell Therapeutics Inc.	2/99	$3
Anergen Inc.	Corixa Corp.	2/99	$8.5
ChromaXome division of Trega	TerraGen	3/99	$6.5
polyMASC	Megabios Corp. (now Valentis)	8/99	$19.8
Roslin Bio-Med*	Geron Corp.	5/99	$26
OraVax Inc.	Peptide Therapeutics plc	5/99	$20
Prostagen Inc.*	Cytogen Corp.	6/99	$2.5
Ribi Immunochem	Corixa Corp.	6/99	$56.3
Chiroscience Group plc	Celltech plc	6/99	$528
Metra Biosystems	Quidel Corp.	6/99	$22.9
ProScript Inc.	LeukoSite Inc.	6/99	$2.73
Peptimmune Inc.*	Genzyme General	7/99	N/A
V. I. Technologies	Pentose Pharmaceuticals*	7/99	$45
RiboGene Inc.	Cypros Corp.	8/99	$13.7
Quidel Corp.	Metra Biosystems	8/99	$23
Allelix Biopharm.	NPS Pharma.	9/99*	$80
Genetic MicroSystems*	Affymetrix	9/99	$88
U.S. Bioscience	MedImmune	10/99*	$440
Enzymed	Albany Molecular	10/99	$20.6

(continues)

TABLE 20.3   *(continued)*

Company bought	Company buying	Date	Price (millions)
Leukosite	Millennium	11/99	$635
Cadus	OSI Pharma.	11/99	$2.2
Celtrix	Insmed	12/99	$140

*Private company at time of transaction.
SOURCE: Information from BioVenture Consultants, BioWorld.

good job of cutting down on the number of companies—unfortunately, investors got burned along the way.

This same build-die cycle happens in all successful new sectors—it struck with a vengeance in the late 1990s with Internet companies. The first few companies made a huge impact by providing a truly novel way to do business. But they were quickly followed by "me-too" companies that didn't offer that same exponential growth in value. "How many companies does it take to supply you with pet food?" says Taylor. "Then all of a sudden, nobody is interested in any Internet companies because they have lost their edge and the real concerns about revenue growth become more obvious."

part four

BIOTECH STOCKS

————21————

THE BIOTECH STOCK
LANDSCAPE

Biotechnology is poised to explode over the next decade, in products and in profits. In its first two decades of existence, the industry has created more than 75 FDA-approved drugs, vaccines, and diagnostic tests that have completely changed the practice of medicine and generated billions in sales revenues. Much of the impact of biotechnology outside medicine has yet to be revealed, or even imagined. Participating in this exploding industry as an investor is both wildly exciting and absolutely terrifying, thanks to the unpredictable nature of stock performance.

Much attention has been focused on the risk of investing in biotech stocks. Although individual companies certainly are risky investments, because of the risk inherent in drug development, individual and institutional investors have found a way to make significant returns on biotech portfolios. In a mixed portfolio of 24 biotech stocks, one that contained both companies that had positive product news and those that took bad news hits along the way, Hambrecht & Quist's biotech team found that investors would have realized a return of 749% in the period from December 30, 1994, to June 30, 1999! This outperforms the NASDAQ index (250%), the Russell 2000 index (80%), the AMEX Drug Index (269%) and the PSE Semiconductor Index (241%) during that same time.

Some individual stocks did even better during that time. IDEC Pharmaceuticals rewarded patience with a 3,526% increase, thanks to its launch of the anticancer drug Rituxan; MedImmune delivered a 3,771% pop as it drove two anti-infective products home.

It's impossible to predict which individual companies will be successful in the long run and which will die a painful death even before reaching positive earnings growth. This uncertainty points to strategically investing in a portfolio of biotech stocks, not just banking on a single play. But there is absolutely no doubt that health care will continue to be a growing necessity in our society.

The demographic realities of our society mean that a growing percentage of the population is entering a time of life when the diseases and disorders of aging occur. As a sector that is contributing significant products to the health care of the aging population, biotech should continue to prosper. Or as Craig Taylor, long-time biotech investor and General Partner with Alloy Ventures, puts it, "Soon everyone will be communicating all the time, anywhere, with beautiful color monitors, but parts of their bodies will need fixing." And that's where biotech comes in.

Why invest in biotech stocks instead of sticking with big pharma stocks? It's probably not a bad idea to have both types of companies in your portfolio. But the tough public markets of the late 1990s meant that biotech offered a significant price advantage (though biotech CEOs may not see it that way). Because biotech companies usually are significantly lower in market capitalization than their big pharma cousins, and their stock prices tend to be lower, you can generate a diverse portfolio and capture significant product upside potential without investing huge sums.

Analysts and investors like to complain that that biotech stocks are overvalued. Although there are definitely times when individual stocks seem pricey, I would argue that biotech stocks are in fact un-

TABLE 21.1   BioVenture's Merck Index: Biotech's Top 100 Versus Merck 1999

	100 top biotechs*	Merck & Co.
Sales	$6.6 billion	$26.9 billion
Market cap	$100 billion	$168 billion
Market cap to sales	15-fold	6-fold
R&D spending	$4.55 billion	$1.8 billion
Number of employees	36,100	57,300
Drugs in Phase III or before FDA	140	5
**Drugs on the market	65	35

*Based on *BioVenture Consultants Stock Report* data 6/25/99, rolling four quarters.
**Significant prescription drugs only.

dervalued. Let's compare Merck, one of the most successful big pharma companies in the world, with the entire top 100 biotech companies (see Table 21.1).

Given the risk that any given product will fail before reaching the marketplace, it seems like a good idea to place your investment bets where you get the most product opportunity bang for your buck. The Merck/Biotech Index in Table 21.1 shows that you could buy into the entire top 100 public biotherapeutic companies—and their product candidate pipelines—for less than the price of one big pharma company. This supports the idea that the biotech industry is still undervalued, at least as of 12/99 given the product opportunities it holds.

Let's take a look at how the sector has performed historically and what the stock market has traditionally rewarded with increasing stock price.

WHAT DRIVES STOCK PRICE?

Dr. Carol Hall, my business partner and a principal of BioVenture Consultants, has followed the biotech public stocks since the 1980s as one of the first biotech stock analysts and as a corporate financier. In 1992, she began formally tracking the top 100 stocks and looking for patterns in their performance. This database of information on stock performance and balance sheet behavior forms the basis of BioVenture Consultants' *Stock Report*.

It used to be fairly straightforward to predict the benchmarks that would drive a biotech company's stock—or at least so it seemed in the 1980s and early 1990s. During the red-hot biotech markets of 1983, 1986–1987, and 1991–1992, any new biotech company with a sexy science story could raise oodles of cash. But the rest of the time, companies were rewarded with market cap increases as they moved product candidates through the development benchmarks of animal studies that showed the drug worked, then into Phase I, II, and III of clinical trials.

Although product launch was always the ultimate stock stimulator during biotech bull markets, each of these earlier milestones was rewarded with stock price increases in return for reducing the risk of eventual product success. Biotech execs and their bankers were pretty confident about taking their companies public in the absence of product revenues, as long as they could show progress in moving candidates through this well-defined pipeline.

This nice, simple scheme began to fall apart in 1992–1993, when well-publicized product failures made it clear that biotechnology was not going to improve the odds of product development. The biggest disappointment, and the most damaging to the entire biotech sector, involved a trio of companies working on drugs to treat sepsis—a systemic bacterial infection usually affecting trauma and surgery patients.

Centocor Inc., Xoma Corp., and Synergen Inc. all came to the FDA with products designed to prevent the high death rate in sepsis patients. In each case, Wall Street analysts raved about the fabulous data backing up each company's hopes for FDA approval and the potential for annual sales of up to a whopping $1 billion. Sepsis represented a huge market opportunity— an estimated 500,000 patients, of whom one-fifth die—with no existing product competition.

But in each case, the products failed the final regulatory hurdle. Centocor had built up a big sales force in anticipation of market launch, and both Synergen and Xoma spent the bucks to build manufacturing facilities. The bad news almost killed Centocor and Xoma, and Synergen languished until Amgen Corp. acquired it in 1994.

Thanks primarily to the bad sepsis product news in 1992, the AMEX Biotech Index performance dropped from over 240 points to under 140 points against a relatively flat S&P 500 performance. The combination in March 1993 of Clinton's press conference on health care reform stoking fear and trembling in the sector and the final sepsis failure dragged the AMEX Biotech Index below the S&P 500 performance and even pulled the NASDAQ index down 8.5 points.

The public markets soon started turning away from biotech and other speculative high-technology upstarts in favor of large-cap, lower-risk stocks. Investors also seemed to lose what little faith they had in the ability of Wall Street biotech analysts to use good judgment when it came to writing about banking clients.

Biotech execs were forced to face some unpleasant facts: (1) Sexy science would carry them only so far. At some point, a path to products aimed at meaningful markets had to become clear to investors. (2) Meeting early product development milestones would not guarantee investor interest. Investors had been made painfully aware that product risk remained all the way through Phase III clinical trials. Consequently, they were less likely to reward success in earlier stages of product development—animal studies, Phase I and II clinical trials—with significant stock price movement.

In response, biotech execs—egged on by their venture investors, who were desperate for an IPO, or by their dwindling bank accounts—went through several fads in a desperate attempt to find the magic combination of buzz words that would lure investors back.

A particularly deadly fad was termed *accelerated commercialization*. The basic idea was to take a young company with early research programs and try to make it look like a more mature company by "in-licensing" product candidates that were further down the development path—preferably in Phase II or Phase III clinical trials. These candidates were usually sitting on the shelf at a big pharma company because the market opportunity was not sufficiently large (over $500 million in potential annual revenues) to make it worthwhile spending the time and money to take the product all the way to market. Of course, the warts on these abandoned products were like those on used cars—not always obvious.

The problem was that most young companies did not have the experienced staff able to identify and develop top-notch product candidates, nor the financial resources to acquire those they did find. The result? Mediocre products brought in-house that took management time and energy (not to mention funding) away from the company's proprietary research, and that failed to fire up investor imagination. Somehow, a company developing hair products for scalp psoriasis is just not as inspirational as a company working on drugs to combat deadly fibrosis diseases such as kidney failure and scleroderma.

Some companies were able to identify and acquire products with true revenue-producing capability that allowed them to survive the Wall Street drought. But survival might require mutation from a biotech company into a company selling generic versions of off-patent products, as happened to Gensia—now called Sicor and selling generic versions of hospital care products. The company is alive, but boring—and not likely to produce that blockbuster drug we all dream about.

It's very tempting to think of biotech as a "special, unique" industry that should be performing independently of the rest of the stock market. But in fact, as was pointed out by the infamous Michael Milken at an Oxford Partners venture conference in 1994, biotech is responding to the same pressures and business cycles as the communications, hardware, and software industries. Start-up fratricide, that irresistible drive to create 500 companies where there is business for only 4 to prosper, was first seen clearly in the disk drive sector—and nearly killed that sector off completely.

FIGURE 21.1   AMEX Biotech Index Versus S&P 500 Performance
(1991–1999)

Biotech's Three Tiers of Stock

As you can see from Figure 21.1, the biotech stocks took a big hit in 1992 with the bad product news and have been slowly recovering ever since. The sector, which had been outperforming the S&P 500, moved downward even as the rest of the stock market was rising. Things have been looking up—literally and figuratively—since mid-1995, with biotech regaining lost ground and mirroring the same basic upward pattern of the broader stock market. In fact, the biotech sector was so hot in the last few months of 1999 that the AMEX Biotech Stock Index essentially caught up with the S&P 500 Index by year end, and surpassed it in January.

It's important to realize that the entire biotech sector does not behave in the same manner. The stocks fall into three basic tiers, according to market capitalization. These three tiers show very different patterns of stock performance (see Figure 21.2).

BioVenture Consultants' stock report follows those companies using biotechnology tools—recombinant DNA, protein/gene analysis and synthesis, monoclonal antibodies, genomics, antisense, and other molecular manipulations—to create novel drugs for human therapy.

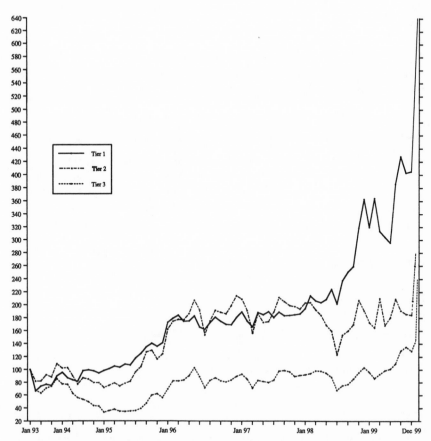

FIGURE 21.2   1st, 2nd, and 3rd Tier Performance over Time

The focus is on human health care because that is where the biggest impact on society and the largest profits are made. Once companies drop below $10 million in fully diluted market capitalization (including warrants), they are dropped from the report.

(See Appendix D, which shows the most recent version of BVCSR, with companies/stock and earnings performance, various graphics.)

These numbers provide a pretty clear message that the stock market is continuing its 1990s trend of rewarding those companies that get products through clinical trials, through FDA approval, and into the marketplace. Many of these approved products are being sold with the help of a big pharma partner. The marketplace also likes to see backup compounds in the development pipeline to support future revenue growth. The Tier 1 companies fulfill these requirements and get investors' seal of approval in the form of strong market performance.

TABLE 21.2   Tier Summary

The stocks are divided into three tiers:
• Tier 1: Market capitalizations greater than $800 million
• Tier 2: Market capitalizations between $800 million and $125 million
• Tier 3: Market capitalizations less than $125 million

	Tier 1	*Tier 2*	*Tier 3*
Total market cap	$182 billion	$20 billion	$2 billion
Average market cap per company	$7.6 billion $61 billion– $807 million	$351 million $739 million– $130 million	$69 million $124 million– $13 million
Average price performance year to date	+261%	+132%	+49%
Products on market*	14 co's + 5 tool/service co's	14 co's + 6 tool/service co's	1 tool/ service co's
Products in Phase III of FDA submission*	4 co's	22 co's	4 co's
Total number of companies in tier	24 co's	57 co's	23 co's

SOURCE: December 1999 *BioVenture Consultants Stock Report.*
*Most advanced product status.

In other words, investors in biotech stocks reward real revenue—just the way investors in other sectors do. Fancy technology can also fire up the imaginations of investors, as demonstrated by the presence of tool/service companies Millennium Pharmaceuticals, Affymetrix, and Human Genome Sciences in the top tier. Although these companies do not have approved drugs on the market, they have created broad technology platforms in genomics and related areas and have been able to convince corporate partners and investors that products will result from these programs. In addition, their CEOs have successfully outlined for investors their plans for developing proprietary products—drugs and diagnostic devices—to generate revenue.

For long-term price performance, there needs to be a clear path to product revenue resulting from technology coupled with steady progress down that path toward market launch.

The presence of product revenues drops off significantly when we move to the Tier 2 companies—only around one-third have real sales revenue; instead, the others depend on payments from corporate partners for revenue. The missing revenue is the primary reason for the more than 20-fold drop in market cap and almost 50% lower year-to-date price performance for this group of 58 companies, versus the top tier stocks.

But don't write these stocks off! Tier 2 companies are well worth watching. Figure 21.2 shows that this group tracked right along with the top-tier stocks right until early 1998, when the larger cap stocks took off and left their second-tier brethren in the dust. All it takes for a stock to make the move from Tier 2 to Tier 1 is a significant product approval, and several of these companies have promising product candidates working their way through development and aimed at the marketplace. But even for those companies remaining in Tier 2 for the foreseeable future, the tier has provided nice returns on average to its investors.

Tier 3 companies have been languishing since 1993, with almost no net change in market valuation for the group since 1993. These stocks have an average market cap five times lower than the average Tier 2 company ($69 million vs. $351 million).

None of the current Tier 3 companies has an approved drug on the market, though most have product candidates in Phase II or Phase III clinical trials. This means that a chunk of the product risk has been removed—the compound has successfully made its way through initial clinical development. The major business risk for most of these companies is that they will run out of money, and not be able to raise more, before their products make it to market.

Seven of the Tier 2 and 3 companies fall into a group termed the *tool companies*. This was another 1990s venture capital fad that attempted to reduce product risk and the time it took to generate revenue, in this case by planning to sell access to technology rather than actual drugs. These companies offered corporate partners access to combinatorial chemistry, genomics, or novel drug target identification methods and left it up to the partners to create the drugs. Unfortunately, this approach left investors cold, for the most part. As more companies were formed around the same basic tools, their technology and services were viewed as commodities rather than rare and valuable assets.

Because so many companies got started around similar technologies, potential corporate partners could strike lots of small deals with a whole bunch of these biotech firms. Thus, the partners spent minimal dollars to test out lots of different approaches to the same problem but left the biotech companies without enough cash to move forward. For the most part, only the first company created in each category, or the one with a clear technical or intellectual property advantage, made it into the upper stock tiers.

Many of the Tier 2 and Tier 3 companies have technology and products in development that could catapult them into the upper realms of the sector. The key is whether they have the management team and ability to access capital to push that first product into the marketplace—the ultimate milestone.

After making a slow start in early 1999 with price performance running between a net drop of around 10% and a 10% average increase, all three tiers showed a positive trend throughout the rest of the last year of the millennium. The accelerating rate of good product news and a trend of investors shifting attention to small cap stocks helped fuel stronger performance.

The first group to respond, not surprisingly, was Tier 1. This group of companies jumped to a 63% average year-to-date increase in market cap after lingering around the 10% to 20% mark for most of the second quarter. By the end of December 1999, Tier 1 was showing an awesome 261% price performance for the year, followed by Tier 2 with a 132% increase and Tier 3 with a respectable 49% increase. During that time, the S&P 500 index produced about a 30% increase.

WHAT MAKES STOCKS ACT THIS WAY?

One of the big reasons for the huge discrepancy in current price performance between Tier 1 and Tier 2 has little to do with the fundamentals of these companies and a lot to do with basic math. There is simply too much money trying to invest in Wall Street. Why is this a problem?

Imagine that you run an investment fund that has ballooned up to $1 billion in the past year, not at all unheard of thanks to the huge influx of people looking to participate in the wild Wall Street performance of the late 1990s. You need to find quality stocks in which to park those dollars, which means you need to do in-depth homework on the potential investments and continue to monitor those companies to ensure that your investment is performing well.

A money manager or stock analyst can cover only about 10 to 15 companies in any real detail. This means that such investors prefer to place big chunks of their funds in a small number of stocks. Most funds have rules that forbid owning more than 5% of any given company, because of SEC reporting regulations that kick in at that level of investment.

These numbers add up to a focus on large cap stocks—stocks with market capitalizations well over $1 billion. Some funds are willing to consider companies with market caps as low as $800 million. But very few are configured to invest in the vast majority of biotech public stocks, even if the investment manager likes the company and believes it will be successful. They simply can't invest, under the rules of their funds, because they will end up owning too much of the company or else will have to invest in 100 different stocks to put all of their fund to work.

Contributing to this problem is the continued contraction of Wall Street firms as the banks merge with each other. Even in the heyday of early biotech investing in the 1980s, only a small number of banks had competent biotech analysts. Among these were Lehman Brothers and PaineWebber—the big banks in biotech—and the smaller "boutiques" known for their focus on technology-based stocks, including Hambrecht & Quist, Montgomery Securities, Robertson Stephens, Alex. Brown, and Cowen.

As of late 1999, Hambrecht & Quist, the last independent boutique, was in the process of being acquired by Chase Bank. Montgomery Securities, Robertson Stephens, Alex. Brown, Cowen, UBS (which had absconded with several of H&Q's biotech analysts), and other key biotech teams got merged into behemoths that often saw no reason to keep all of the analysts.

This merger mania means that fewer experienced analysts are following the biotech industry, and those analysts remaining have to choose a small number of companies to follow from the 300+ potential public biotech firms. Not surprisingly, the analysts focus on those biotech stocks likely to appeal to their institutional investors—which means large cap stocks.

Another reason for the relative lack of Wall Street participation in many biotech stocks in the late 1990s was concern over perceived risk. Now that the biotech industry has been around for a couple of decades, institutional investors have had the chance to see that the risk of drug development in biotech companies is essentially the same as the risk in big pharma—but without the existing product revenues of big pharma to cushion the blow of product failures.

TABLE 21.3   Consolidation in Investment Banking: Biotech Loses Coverage

- Alex. Brown/Bankers Trust/Deutsche Bank
- Cowen/Societé Generale
- Dollon Read/UBS/SBC Warburg
- Furman Selz/ING Group
- Montgomery/NationsBanc/BancAmerica
- Oppenheimer/CIBC
- Robertson Stephens/Bank of America/Fleet Financial
- Salomon/Smith Barney/Citigroup
- Vector Securities/Prudential
- Hambrecht & Quist/Chase Bank

There have been some product failures in the final stages of clinical development over the past decade that have stoked the cynicism of investors and analysts and reminded us all of the risk of drug development—the previously mentioned sepsis drugs of Centocor, Xoma, and Synergen; some eagerly awaited neurobiology products including Cephalon's Myotrophin and Regeneron's BDNF for Lou Gehrig's disease; and Scios's Natrecor for congestive heart failure and renal disorder and its Fiblast for stroke.

In most of these cases, the failure was not absolute—the product seemed to be effective for some of the patients, but in an unpredictable manner as far as the FDA was concerned. But the money and time required to redesign and carry out new Phase III trials may be more than a biotech company is willing to spend.

This has convinced many investors to wait for product candidates to jump over more development hurdles—sometimes waiting until Phase III clinical trials are completed—before investing. There is still significant opportunity for stock price growth, and the risk is much lower than jumping in when a product candidate is in the earlier stages of development. (More on this approach below.)

A third huge factor behind the late 1990s lack of interest in most biotech stocks is the latest hot fad on Wall Street—Internet stocks. In 1998, the ISDEX, an Internet stock index, rose 187%. Just as Genentech's incredible IPO performance triggered a massive influx of public investor dollars into biotech, Netscape's August 1995 IPO generated palpitations in the hearts of venture capitalists and investors everywhere. Netscape's IPO price was driven up to $28 a share by intense investor interest, giving the young—and profit-free—company an initial market cap of $1 billion. The price jumped to a high of $74.75 in its first day of trading.

The message—that the Internet was the hot new thing—was not lost on investors, nor on the banking and venture communities. One of Netscape's underwriters, Hambrecht & Quist, has been a long-time supporter of the biotech industry. And Kleiner Perkins Caufield & Byers, one of Netscape's venture investors, and an important biotech supporter, turned a $5-million investment in Netscape into a stake worth $256 million at the end of the company's first public day.

And therein lies the rub. The traditional supporters of biotech find themselves in the unenviable position of supporting yesterday's news. The fact that most Internet companies have yet to demonstrate an ability to generate sustainable, meaningful revenues is irrelevant. There is money to be made—hundreds of millions of dollars, and none of this waiting around for a decade to get a product approved! Many of the long-time biotech venture investors walked away from biotech start-ups in 1998 and 1999, though all signs are that funding is still flowing.

There is another market force that is affecting all stocks, not just biotech—stock churning. This term describes the constant turnover of stock by investors. Stock churning has hit an all-time high, driven in part by the flood of individual investors into the frothy stock market. According to a report in the September 3, 1999, issue of *Business Week*, 76% of the shares of an average U.S. company listed on the New York Stock Exchange changed hands during the past year versus only 46% in 1990. And stocks on NASDAQ had shareholder turnover that was nearly three times that seen on the NYSE in the same period.

This incredible volatility in shareholders means that negative news or general market mishaps could have an exaggerated impact on stock price. And that in turn makes it tough for companies to retain top employees, do deals based on stock, or plan financings in any rational manner.

It also changes the dynamic between management and shareholders. If your shares are held an average of 7 days by any given shareholder, as is the case for Amazon.com *(Business Week)*, it's unlikely that those shareholders are paying any real attention to the company's long-term strategic plan or noticing if the firm is making its milestones.

CEOs can't make strategic decisions aimed at moving the stock price; they have to make decisions that aim for a growing, successful operating business. This means ignoring the siren calls of Wall Street analysts sometimes—an issue not confined to biotech.

So Why Invest in Biotech?

So why should you, as an investor, even consider biotech investments? Why not simply run to the Internet stocks?

- Because folks who bought IDEC Pharmaceuticals at the end of 1994 and sold in mid-1999 got a whopping 3,526% increase in stock price. Not bad, and certainly better than the S&P index or NASDAQ.
- Because wildly hot new areas usually stay hot just long enough for the early investors to get out. This rule has been proven over and over since the Dutch tulip bulb investing craze of the 1630s. By the time the average investors gets in there, the sector will start to respond to the concerns of Wall Street over net earnings, and the roller coaster ride of stock price will be beginning. Your chances of bad timing—buying high and selling low—increase with every day post-IPO. Just as biotech lost its initial luster and had to begin responding to investors' calls to build sustainable businesses with revenues, so, too, will Internet stocks.
- Because there is a huge groundswell of important biotech products reaching the final stages of development, just as the market for those products is growing thanks to our aging population. The top 100 public biotech companies have an incredible 140 product opportunities in final stages of clinical testing or waiting for the FDA to make its go–no-go decision. The upside potential for these products and their companies is huge, even given the risk of late-stage failure, and biotech companies are the unchallenged champions at creating these new drugs.
- Because even current market conditions have left a vast sea of undervalued stocks out there, just waiting for investors to ride them back up. The trick, of course, is to make the best guess as to which will succeed.
- Because in the end, it's important to put your investment dollars to work helping to build something of value. And let's face it— supporting research to create the first real treatment for

Alzheimer's disease has got to be more meaningful than creating on-line sites for having dog food delivered to your home.

Assuming that you buy the concept that it's worth putting some investment dollars into the biotech sector, how can you make an educated guess about which companies are your best bet?

22

PICKING THE
RIGHT STOCKS

As we have already seen, new drug development is unpredictable. Companies need to spend millions of dollars and about a decade waiting before they know if their new products will be sufficiently safe and effective to reach the marketplace.

With hundreds of public companies out there claiming to be biotech firms, how can investors hope to pick the winners?

The key to biotech investing, as with any technology-based sector, is to focus on a few key characteristics of top-flight firms and invest in a basket of stocks that share those characteristics. This approach increases your chances that at least one of those will hit, and hit big. We'll look at these characteristics in the next section.

A diversified portfolio approach is not unique to biotech. Most advisers recommend buying several stocks in any given sector to increase the probability that your portfolio will produce a good return.

Willingness to hold onto your stock for long periods of time is very important. Remember—Amgen stock languished below $5 a share before blasting out to become the Number One biotech company, with a market capitalization exceeding General Motors by the fall of 1999! Although not all biotech stocks are bound for this level of glory, there are going to be times when holding on through a temporary down cycle will be rewarded with a big kickup in price once a key milestone is passed.

There are certain basic characteristics of excellent companies that transcend technology type or industry sector. They sound, for the most part, like basic common sense.

TABLE 22.1   Characteristics of Quality Biotech Companies

- Great management with relevant experience
- Ties to top academic centers
- A strong technology platform that will support multiple product opportunities, not a single product play, and protected by a strong IP portfolio
- Access to financing alternatives to the stock markets, including significant corporate partnerships
- Product development strategy that will yield high-value products in our lifetime
- Location, location, location
- The ability to articulate science as a business opportunity
- Avoidance of fads

WHAT MAKES A QUALITY COMPANY?

The eternal quest among biotech CEOs is finding the magical business strategy that will convince investors to open their purse strings. Every few months, there seems to be some new buzz phrase that folks think will guarantee a steady flow of investment dollars. For a while, it was *genomics*, then it was adding *dot.com* to the company name. Biotech execs and investors who try to catch the current fad will inevitably find themselves jumping in too late to ride the wave up, but in time to ride it down.

Are investors really that fickle? Do the characteristics of great companies and good investment opportunities really change that frequently? Years of talking to long-time industry investors suggests that there is a short list of desirable characteristics that have remained constant throughout years of constantly changing business fashion.

Management: At the top of everyone's list is management. Great management is especially important in entrepreneurial technology companies, where the chief asset for at least a decade is the technical team slaving away to create the first product. In a stock market that places a premium on product revenues rather than sexy science, companies need to be led by management with hands-on experience in converting discovery research into drugs and merging academic scientists with business folks.

Over the years, in essentially every technology sector, we have seen great science die a painful and pitiful death because of a weak management team. Alternatively, a great team can pull together a survival strategy even in the face of failure in the company's primary technology. Dr. George Rathmann's big pharma experience and ability to keep Amgen forging ahead even during those dark days of

$3.50/share, then to convert that company into the top biotech stock, is why savvy investors were willing to give his next company, Icos, big chunks of cash.

As an investor, you want to have confidence that the management is experienced enough to plan for failure as well as success. There should be evidence of strategic thinking, not just reactive thinking.

But how can an individual investor tell a great team from a shaky one? One hint is to look at the pedigree of the executives. Do the people running key parts of the company—research, product development, clinical and regulatory, manufacturing, sales and marketing, business development, finance—bring real-life experience? Did they come from big pharma or biotech companies? Or are they straight out of school or consulting companies and thus learning on the job? Did they spend time at other quality companies, or are they refugees from failed firms?

Keep in mind that just because someone excelled in another industry does not mean she or he will also excel in building a successful biotech company. Over the years, BioVenture Consultants has worked with companies that were formed or funded by enthusiastic entrepreneurs with no relevant biopharmaceutical background. Although this enthusiasm is important, the lack of relevant experience often means that companies take too much time and/or money to make progress. So far, we have no reason to believe that a fabulously successful Wall Street career improves the odds for building a successful biotech company. And if the CEO, CFO, and head of R&D share the same last name—watch out!

The board of directors is an extension of the management team and benefits greatly from the inclusion of folks with relevant industry experience. The board should provide the CEO with access to a network of important contacts to help the company grow, including personal introductions to potential additions to the executive team and potential investors, corporate partners, bankers, and other service providers. There should be enough diversity—in background, gender, and race—on the board to challenge the assumptions of management and provide differing views on problem solving.

Some of this information shows up on company Web sites or in offering memoranda. A call to the company's corporate communications office can yield a company backgrounder kit that includes management biographies. Attending annual shareholder meetings or industry conferences can give you a chance to see management in action, and to get a feel for its ability to articulate the company's strategy.

Successful biotech management teams must evolve as the company evolves. The skills needed to drive a young company forward through the proof-of-concept stage, to keep the venture investors supporting the company, and to manage a rowdy group of scientists are not the same skills needed by an operating business with products in the clinic and a sales force to build.

In the early days of a biotech company, there is usually a strong focus on beefing up the technical parts of the team—loading up on excellent scientists and managers with science management expertise. As time goes by, executives with deal-making experience are needed to put in place those crucial corporate partnerships with other companies. A great CFO can make a huge contribution in helping a company get ready for the IPO, and also in exploring new financing vehicles as market conditions fluctuate. Look for an influx of executives with leadership skills and real-life experience as the company grows up. Stagnant management might be a red flag.

Ties to top academic centers: No matter how powerful a company's internal R&D team may be, the rapid pace of research progress means that no one company can cover all the bases. Early in a biotech company's evolution, essentially all of its technology probably comes from its academic cofounders and collaborators. But even well-established companies benefit from strong academic ties to researchers who can contribute new inventions, assays, tools, and compounds that might lead to new products.

Scientific collaborators also provide a valuable service by sitting on the company's scientific advisory board (SAB). The SAB keeps the company honest by critically evaluating the R&D plan down to the level of experimental design and result analysis. Just as a board of directors provides valuable input simply by including (theoretically) objective outsiders, an SAB challenges the company's scientific staff to question their assumptions and tighten up their research.

By top academic credentials, I mean science centers such as Harvard, Stanford, Yale, Johns Hopkins, the University of California at San Diego/Berkeley/San Francisco, Columbia, Rockefeller, California Institute of Technology, and MIT. There are other great schools involved in the sciences, such as Duke, that are rapidly climbing up the ranks, but as in all other pedigree issues, working with the best provides instant credibility.

Although having Nobel Prize laureates on the SAB is impressive, most investors realize that what the company really needs are researchers and clinicians who are actively engaged in research and who are willing to devote time and energy to the company.

Information on a company's scientific advisory board can be found in offering memoranda, on Web sites, or from the company's PR department.

Strong proprietary technology with a business opportunity: The most exciting science in the world isn't a great investing opportunity unless it can be used to create important products with clinical relevance. For example, it's not enough to have discovered a new genetic mutation in tumor samples from patients. You have to also show that there is a direct connection between that mutation and what happens to the patient. And there must be some way to use that new information to change current patient treatment. Otherwise, the discovery has no commercial value—nobody will pay to use it.

Sometimes the technology buzz gets generated too far in advance of the business opportunity.

Geron Corp. is a good example of technology looking for a commercial opportunity. This California-based biotech company saw its stock price almost triple to $17 a share after announcing in August 1997 that its scientists had cloned a gene encoding telomerase, a protein involved in cell proliferation.

There was evidence that telomerase may be important in the uncontrolled cell proliferation in cancer and the loss of cell growth in aging. But when the stock jumped, the company had not identified a product candidate based on its discovery—much less moved such a candidate into the development pipeline. It will probably take the usual 10 years or so for the first therapeutic product to emerge from this very exciting research. In the meantime, telomerase remains an intriguing technical tool for studying cell behavior.

In stocks like Geron, the savvy institutional investors tend to take profits off the table when they see a premature price run-up way in advance of the technology evolving into a product opportunity. And the individual investors, who may have seriously overestimated the commercial impact of the scientific discovery, get stuck with an eroding stock price until the product promise catches up with the scientific enthusiasm. The closer a program is to showing it works in humans, the higher the value.

Keep in mind that not all technology deserves to become a company. Even with lots of snazzy science and world-class researchers attached to it, some technology is just not enough to drive a business forward. Companies need critical mass—there has to be enough technology to channel into products that will generate enough revenue flow to grow a sustainable business. Otherwise, management better be looking at in-licensing complementary technology to bolster the business, or at out-licensing the technology to a partner that can integrate it into a larger entity and generate a royalty stream of revenue.

Another important technology issue is intellectual property—the patents and trade secrets a company uses to keep other groups from competing directly in its area. As an investor, you want to be sure that the company actually owns the technology it plans to use for product development. This may sound intuitively obvious, but many young companies do not realize that a handshake agreement with a scientific founder doesn't guarantee access to that founder's academic research. Amgen Corp. took Millennium Pharmaceuticals by surprise in 1995 when it snagged the red-hot obesity gene project out of Rockefeller University—right out of the lab of a Millennium cofounder!

Companies must actively pursue a strategy for protecting their intellectual property and blocking competition. This means working with experienced patent agents and attorneys to apply for patent coverage and to build a wall of protection around the original invention. It includes putting agreements in place with academic institutions and collaborators to ensure that the company will have rights to use the technology and rights to future related inventions. It can be pretty frustrating to build a company around an initial invention, then to find a competitor has leapfrogged past you by licensing an improved invention that can circumvent your technology.

Often, the patent situation for a given technology is unknown at the time of investing. Until patents actually issue from the U.S. Patent and Trademark Office or its foreign equivalents, which can take several years, companies and their shareholders won't have any guarantees.

Cadus Pharmaceuticals (Tarrytown, New York) saw its market valuation erode to essentially nothing after it lost a patent fight in U.S. District Court in early 1999 with competitor Sibia Neurosciences over technology that was at the crux of its business. Although Cadus researchers had built a very favorable reputation for using genetically engineered cell assays to uncover gene function and for drug discovery as early as 1995, that expertise lost its value when the company lost its proprietary position. The company's assets are being sold off, and the team is essentially disbanded. Sibia went on to be acquired at a nice premium by Merck & Co. in the summer of 1999.

Companies that have focused all of their resources on a single product are treading a dangerous path. Although it is important to have product focus and not be running projects all over the map, the rules of universal product risk mean that most projects won't make it all the way to the marketplace. Without a fallback position, the company will die. Cadus is an example of a single technology speed bump killing a company.

Alpha-Beta Technology, Inc. (Worcester, Massachusetts) started 1997 sitting comfortably in the middle of the BioVenture Consultants' *Stock Report* list with a market cap of $190 million and its lead product, Betafectin, in Phase III trials to prevent infection in surgery patients. The one red flag raised by analysts was that the company's future depended upon on the success of Betafectin. The other company programs were so far behind in development that a nasty surprise in the Phase III study could knock the stock out of the box.

Sure enough, the FDA wasn't satisfied with the Phase III data on Betafectin and asked for a confirmatory study. Alpha-Beta started 1998 at the bottom of BioVenture Consultants' stock list with a market cap of $49 million, cash that would carry it an estimated 6 months, and a significantly reduced workforce. Management was hard-pressed to find the resources to work on the less-developed projects. There just wasn't enough time to bring any of them far enough along to help support the company's valuation.

By early 1999, the confirmatory study had been discontinued after an interim analysis showed insufficient evidence that Betafectin worked. The company announced it would pursue an out-of-court liquidation and that there would not be any residual value for stockholders once liabilities were dealt with.

The moral of this story? Your investment is safer if the company's technology can yield multiple product opportunities.

Access to money: We saw in earlier chapters that it can take around $150 million (at least!) and a decade to take a discovery all the way into the marketplace as a revenue-generating product. Given the vagaries of Wall Street, smart investors should look for signs that a biotech company has access to funding that is independent from Wall Street. For the most part, that means corporate partnerships.

The typical means for biotech corporate partners are big pharma companies, although technology firms, including Motorola, and manufacturing companies like BF Goodrich and Unilever have been getting into the partnering act as they see ways to apply the growing biotechnology realm to their business.

The potential partners are looking for the same characteristics as any other investor group: quality in people, technology, and strategy. Biotech companies able to make significant deals that provide capital to run and grow their business are able to make decisions based on what's best for the business rather than what Wall Street wants (not always the same thing).

One of the best public biotech dealmakers is Millennium Pharmaceuticals (Cambridge, Massachusetts). This company began life as one of the first genomics companies, hoping to tap into the potential of the human genome. The CEO, Mark Levin, and his team were savvy enough to realize that although the genome would produce oodles of interesting genetic information, it would take years before any therapeutic products could emerge from the data.

The team decided to pursue a strategy of using corporate partnerships to pay for building the research infrastructure, and of retaining rights to the technology and applications outside the defined scope of the agreements. That approach has worked well for Millennium, which now consists of a technology division (informatics and technology development), a pharmaceutical division (small-molecule drugs), Millennium Biotherapeutics Inc. (therapeutics based on proteins, antibodies, vaccines, gene therapy, and antisense), and Millennium Predictive Medicine Inc. (applications of genomics in patient diagnosis and care).

Millennium has drug target discovery deals in different clinical areas with Roche, Eli Lilly, Pfizer, and Wyeth-Ayerst; a $218 million agriculture genomics deal with Monsanto; a huge target discovery deal with Bayer AG (worth at least $465 million); a protein/antibody deal with Lilly; and a diagnostic genomics alliance with Becton Dickinson. In all cases, the partner pays for the people, resources, and equipment, and Millennium retains a significant portion of the end result for its own product development activities. All of these deals will bring in an estimated $1.2 billion to the company and helped make Millennium profitable for 3 years in spite of the lack of conventional product revenues.

Product development strategy: To generate a huge amount of revenue fast, a drug needs to be so novel, so incredibly effective at treating life-threatening disease, that price is no object even in a tiny patient population. Alternatively, the drug could be reasonably priced but very effective in treating a large patient group that will use the drug regularly for years (such as Warner-Lambert's Rezulin for Type II diabetes).

For either strategy to work well, the drug has to make a real impact on the disease. In the best of all possible worlds, the drug should have the potential to treat patients with other diseases, thus extending the potential market with follow-on studies. A biotech company may be able to convince the FDA to approve a less effective drug aimed at a desperate patient population, as long as the drug is very, very safe.

Chronic diseases, which last for years, can provide the best opportunity for creation of a blockbuster $1-billion drug. This is why so many biopharmaceutical companies have programs aimed at cardiovascular, neurological, and chronic inflammatory diseases. The downside is that the cost of the needed clinical trials skyrocket. The longer the anticipated treatment, the longer the clinical trials have to be to look for long-term toxicity and loss of effectiveness.

A popular route to rapid market launch and revenue accumulation is to aim for diseases where patients are so critically ill that the extent and duration (and thus the cost) of animal and clinical testing is reduced compared to treatments for less terminal diseases. Cancer drugs don't usually require animal reproduction or carcinogenicity studies, and the clinical trials usually include patients whose life expectancy on conventional treatment is measured in months.

This strategy has its drawbacks. The patients are often so sick and have so many other health problems that the drug would have to have a miraculous effect to work. Often, the patients must also be on so many other medications that the effects of the new drug being tested are hard to measure.

A problem that recently arose in the AIDS area shows how a clinical population can rapidly evolve from one supporting fast, simple trial design to a much more complex and extended process. In the early days of developing AIDS drugs, the lack of treatment and the viciousness of the virus kept the clinical trials short, and there was a highly motivated patient population desperate to enroll in a clinical study.

The current crop of AIDS drugs is so effective that patients are living as long as a decade after diagnosis, making the treatment chronic. Consequently, unexpected long-term effects of the antiprotease drugs are slowly showing up. These include strange redistribution of fat mass and "pill-fatigue"—patients losing interest in taking 35 pills a day under strict regimes. As a result, the regulatory agencies are now looking at requiring longer-term animal and clinical testing for all new AIDS drugs as well.

Location, location, location: The refusal of venture capitalists and Wall Street analysts to fly more than 4 hours at a time is one of the most frustrating aspects of trying to raise money for biotech companies. It's like pulling teeth to get these folks to visit any biotech company that is not located in the Seattle-to-San Diego or Boston-to-Washington, D.C., corridors. This may sound crazy, but it's a very real problem for biotech companies in Texas, North Carolina, or Florida. In spite of the presence of fabulous academic and clinical research centers, places like Houston and Raleigh-Durham have struggled to convince the VCs and bankers to pay attention to their emerging companies.

Part of the problem is time. If it takes a day of connecting flights to reach a company and another day to return home, busy venture capitalists won't have the time to attend regular board meetings. And they are antsy about investing if they can't babysit the company. Another big piece of the problem is supply versus demand. VCs and bankers can find plenty of deals begging for their attention right in their own back yards. There's no need to travel long distances.

This resistance feeds back into the pedigree problem. Companies located off the beaten path may find themselves going public with a less-than-sterling investment bank, because the top-tier bankers won't travel to see a company that doesn't have top-tier VCs in the deal. The less-known bank may be able to raise the IPO money but probably won't provide the analyst coverage that would help expand the investor base and provide after-market support. The share price may stall out for years, in spite of real progress by the company.

SunPharm Pharmaceuticals Corp. of Jacksonville, Florida, found itself in just such a bind. In spite of a broad technology platform with the potential for products aimed at multiple markets, two products in the clinic, a corporate deal with Warner-Lambert, a CEO with experience in several biotech start-ups and venture investing, and a sterling board packed with experienced retired big pharma execs, SunPharm was unable to get the attention of the broader market.

The company went public with a small regional bank and watched its market cap refuse to budge, in spite of real progress. SunPharm was acquired in 1999 by GelTex (Waltham, Massachusetts), which plans to use SunPharm's rich product portfolio to bolster its product pipeline.

Fads in biotech: Every time the stock market and the venture community make it tough for biotech companies to raise money at favorable valuations, an interesting trend occurs. First, there is the emergence of a new type of company pursuing an innovative technology aimed at a novel market opportunity. Often, these companies are founded by a seasoned team and are able to make a compelling case for investment in their new scheme. Existing companies, perhaps struggling a bit as their cash balance creeps down and investors remain elusive, become jealous of the attention being grabbed by the latest hot new thing. Management tries to find some way, no matter how far-fetched, to tie the new buzzword to the struggling company.

How can you, the investor, tell the difference between the real thing and a buzzword chaser? Read through the company's past annual reports and press releases. If the fad phrase shows up for the first time in the past 6 months or so, it probably hasn't been an integral part of the company's strategy. If the newly announced strategy makes you scratch your head and wonder how the heck it fits in with the existing business, you've found a fad. If the management team and research staff have no background in the newly announced area of emphasis, duck and take cover.

Of course, there are always exceptions. Some companies have made 90-degree course corrections apparently overnight after a major disaster in a critical program. But they tend to be the exception, not the rule.

Biotech has seen several fads come and go. Remember when almost every company tried to get the word *genomics* into its mission statement? Then came 50 versions of "genomics"—pharmacogenomics, proteomics, diagnomics, and so on.

As the stock market remained cold to biotech therapeutic companies in the 1990s, the private companies were being urged by their venture investors to find a low-burn-rate business model. The goal was a model that would generate revenue faster without the long time frame and high cost of drug development. This gave us accelerated commercialization (in-licensing drugs already in development, but all too often in areas outside the company's focus), "tool" companies that sold access to their technology to generate revenues faster and with less risk (the downside was that the return, although near-term, was significantly lower than for a therapeutics play), and the nutraceuticals boom of the late 1990s (these don't even have to go through FDA!).

Most of these fads originated with quality companies that built successful businesses around the original concept. The problem came when shakier firms tried to use the buzzwords to generate interest in their stock, even though the strategy implied in the fad didn't really fit at all with their company.

My particular favorite fad is the recent rush to add "dot.com" to a biotech company's strategy, no matter how far-fetched the connection. Procept Inc. (Cambridge, Massachusetts) won the prize in September 1999 when it ran a press release announcing a new Internet business strategy. Procept had been working on antimicrobial drugs and chemosensitizers that would make cancer cells more susceptible to chemotherapy.

Somehow, Procept's management came to the conclusion that the way to maximize shareholder value was to plan a merger with Heaven's Door, a Web site service that provides one-stop shopping for the funeral services industry. Yes, simply by clicking on www.HeavenlyDoor.com, you, too, can tap into a database of over 27,000 funeral homes, get information on the funeral process, place your obituary (or presumably that of a loved one) on-line, and make a "virtual visit" to a loved one's burial site without leaving home!

According to John Dee, president and CEO of Procept, this is a tremendous opportunity for the company to tap into the phenomenal growth of the Internet and e-commerce to create value for his shareholders. The plan is to add products and services aimed at the elderly and the aging baby boomer population—moving right down that food chain! I think it's safe to say that this particular course alteration is probably not based on any relevance to the Procept technology and may well be a sign that Procept has fallen out of our definition of a quality company.

PRACTICAL ADVICE

Every long-time biotech analyst and industry insider will tell you the key is picking a basket of stocks and holding them for the long term. This allows you to diversify away from that nasty product risk and to ride through the market fads to reach product launch for at least part of your portfolio. Remember, today's big winners, such as Immunex, MedImmune, and IDEC, were all floundering in the lower biotech tiers in the mid-1990s in spite of having late-stage products in development. The bear market in biotech back then let brave investors pick up those stocks at bargain basement prices. Investors who bought IDEC at the end of 1994 and sold in mid-1999 got a whopping 3,526% increase in stock price. Not bad, and certainly better than the S&P index or NASDAQ.

But how to pick the stocks to put in the basket?

Richard van den Broek, senior biotech analyst at Hambrecht & Quist, suggests keeping an eye on the product pipeline while making investment decisions in the biotech arena. "Those who win, win big and sustained. The key is to park your cash in quality assets and let it run for a sustained time."

Van den Broek outlines two approaches to biotech investing: "Pay for assurance" by stocking up on the companies with product candidates in the final stages of development—Phase III trials revenues and big market caps to match—and "speculate for free" by investing in the cheaper small cap stocks.

In the "pay for assurance" approach, the investor reduces risk substantially by waiting until the company reports positive Phase III clinical trial data or even until a favorable FDA advisory panel review. Van den Broek and his team chose a group of 54 biotech companies that had happy endings to their pivotal clinical trials. By plotting the average stock performance of that "winner" group versus the NASDAQ index, they found that waiting until the results were reported and buying only those stocks with favorable results provided a return of almost 15% over the 6 months postreporting. The NASDAQ index average booked about half that performance in the same time (see Figure 22.1).

Even if you wait until the FDA advisory panel meeting to reduce further risk of product approval, you can still make a decent return of 10% over the next 6 months (see Figure 22.2).

If you had taken the risk and bought these same stocks 6 months before the pivotal trial results were announced, you would have made a 60% return by the end of the 6 months after the trial announcement. So why not just do that?

Because you can't know ahead of time which companies will have positive trial data or good news from the advisory panel. And the

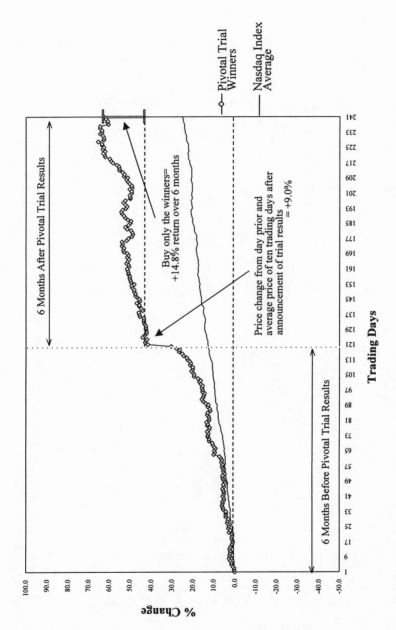

FIGURE 22.1 Payoff from Pivotal Trial Winners (*n*=54)
SOURCE: Hambrecht & Quist

212

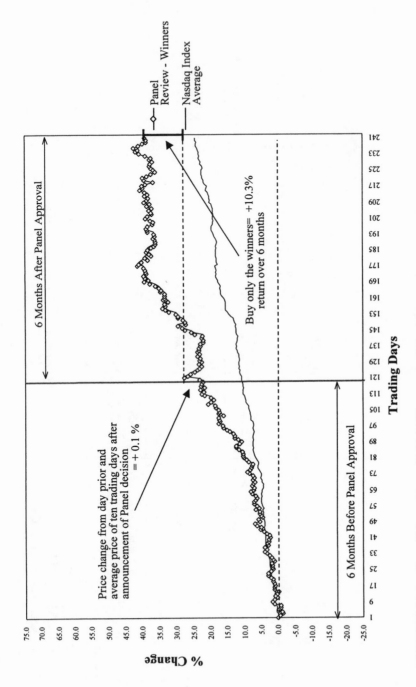

FIGURE 22.2   Payoff from Pivotal Trial Winners (*n*=54)

SOURCE: Hambrecht & Quist

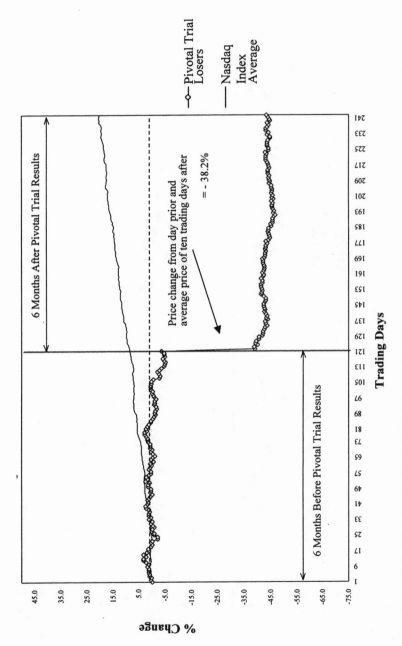

FIGURE 22.3 Penalty for Pivotal Trial Losers (*n*=49)
SOURCE: Hambrecht & Quist

214

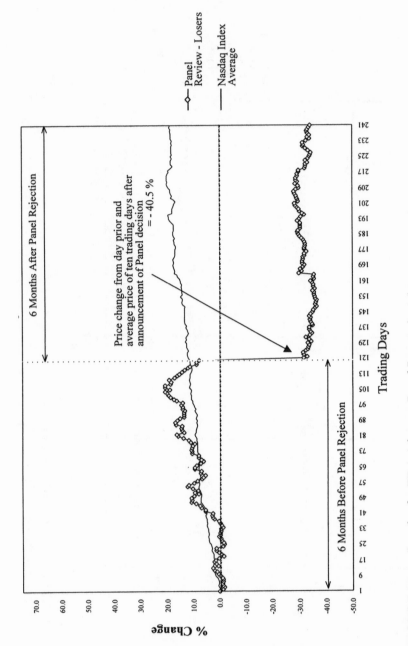

FIGURE 22.4   Penalty for FDA Advisory Panel Losers (*n*=16)
SOURCE: Hambrecht & Quist

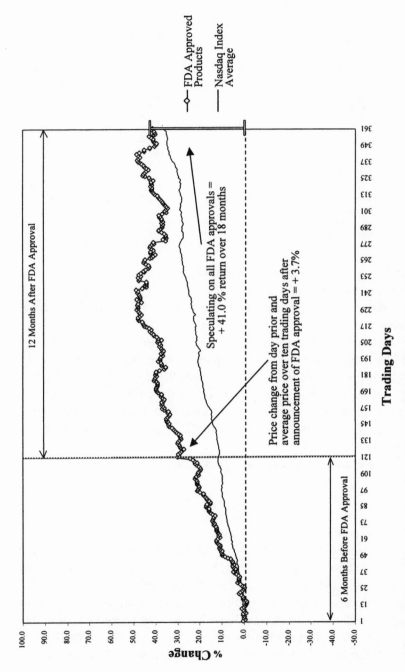

FIGURE 22.5   Biotechnology Products with FDA Approval (*n*=48)

SOURCE: Hambrecht & Quist

TABLE 22.2   The Smooth-Sailing Team

Symbol	Company	Price 12/30/99	Price 6/30/99	% price change
AGPH	Agouron	5.63	60.00	967%
ALKS	Alkermes	2.13	23.13	988%
BXM	Biomatrix	1.75	21.56	1,132%
GILD	Gilead	9.50	52.25	450%
ICOS	Icos	3.69	40.81	1,007%
IDPH	IDEC	2.13	77.06	3,526%
IMCL	Imclone	0.94	25.38	2,607%
IMNX	Immunex	7.44	127.44	1,613%
INCY	Incyte	6.94	26.44	281%
MEDI	MedImmune	1.75	67.75	3,771%
QLTI	QLT Phototherapeutics	5.63	55.00	878%
SEPR	Sepracor	4.13	81.25	1,870%
Average price performance				1,591%

source: Hambrecht & Quist

penalty for bad news from the pivotal clinical trials is an average drop of around 45% at the 6-month posttrial mark (in a group of 49 stocks); the loss is an average 35% for a group of 16 stocks that got bad news from the FDA advisory panel.

What happens if you try to reduce risk even further and wait for the final FDA response to the advisory panel recommendation? After all, a couple of companies have found out the hard way that FDA advisory panel support for your product doesn't guarantee market approval. Van den Broek and his team found that waiting until the final FDA green light to invest still gave you the chance to outperform the NASDAQ index average.

So, being conservative can pay off in biotech stocks.

SPECULATE FOR FREE!

But perhaps you're a carefree risk taker! Maybe you're just not satisfied with a measly 40% return. None of this wimpy risk reduction for you! You want to get in there early and realize the entire run-up in stock price, not just the last bit. Well, this is a risky stance.

The good news is that investing in a basket of biotech stocks with product candidates in late-stage development can bring incredible returns, if you are both informed and lucky. Van den Broek et al. went back to December 30, 1994, and picked a dozen stocks that fit this description.

TABLE 22.3   Bumpy-Road Group Performance

Symbol	Company	Price 12/30/99	Price 6/30/99	% price change
ATIS	Advanced Tissue Sciences	8.25	3.25	–61%
ALLP	Alliance	6.00	2.63	–56%
AMLN	Amylin	6.00	1.13	–81%
AIMM	Autoimmune	5.75	2.38	–59%
CEPH	Cephalon	8.25	17.38	111%
CORR	COR Therapeutics	11.00	14.75	34%
IMUL	Immulogic	7.25	1.88	–74%
IMNR	Immune Response	6.00	5.38	–10%
IPIC	Interneuron	4.88	2.75	–44%
LIPO	Liposome Co.	8.38	19.13	128%
MAGN	Magainin	2.69	2.56	–5%
REGN	Regeneron	3.00	7.81	160%
Average price performance				4%

But wait—what if we didn't pick winners? What if you managed to pick companies that had late-stage product candidates but had product disappointments that walloped their stock? Things are still not so bad:

The bottom line? Even with a portfolio full of disappointments, the investors essentially got all their money back. In a mixed portfolio, one that contained both the "smooth-sailing" winners and the "bumpy-road" losers, investors would have realized a return of 749% in the period from December 30, 1994, to June 30, 1999. This outperforms the NASDAQ index (250%), the Russell 2000 index (80%), the AMEX Drug Index (269%) and the PSE Semiconductor Index (241%) during that same time.

What this all suggests is that taking a chance on the small cap biotech stocks could pay off if you do your research carefully and don't mind enduring the nail-biting risk. This also assumes, of course, that you invest in a basket of stocks s and that you hold onto them for significantly longer than the current 7-day average reported by *Business Week* for holders of Amazon.com stock!

Clearly, biotechnology stocks are not for the faint of heart, but like the industry itself, the profits are a wild ride with huge upside potential in the long run.

APPENDIX A

BIOTECH TIMELINE

1866:
-Gregor Mendel published his studies of the rules of trait inheritance—how progeny inherit characteristics from their parents in a regulated way—with his pea plants

1944:
-Oswald Avery and colleagues reported the first clear evidence that the DNA found within bacterial chromosomes, not the protein component, carried genetic information. This was confirmed in 1952 by Martha Chase and Alfred Hershey in experiments with viruses that infect bacteria by injecting their DNA core, which leads to creation of progeny viruses.

1953:
-Using X-ray crystallography, James Watson, Francis Crick, and Rosalind Franklin developed the double-helix model of DNA that still holds true. The model explained for the first time how DNA could carry the genetic code in the linear sequence of chemical building blocks (A, T, C, and G), and how the two mirror-image helices use very specific base pairing between the chains to maintain the structure and to protect the correct sequence during replication of chromosomes during cell division.

Also in 1953: Frederick Sanger determined the linear sequence of amino acids, the building blocks of proteins, that make up insulin, a protein hormone. This was the first time anyone showed that a protein had a specific, defined sequence.

1961:
-Jacques Monod and Francis Jacob proposed the concept, proven experimentally, that a new class of genetic information—termed *messenger RNA*

(mRNA)—is synthesized when genes are turned on. This mRNA carries the genetic information encoded in a gene from the cell's nucleus into the cell body, where it is read and translated into a unique protein chain by "protein factories" termed *ribosomes*.

1965:

-Pehr Edman developed chemistry that removes one amino acid at a time, chewing in from one end of a protein and allowing scientists to determine the specific amino acid sequence of a whole protein by repeating the reaction. This chemistry became the basis for automated protein sequencers, developed initially by the Hood/Hunkapiller team at Cal Tech, which enabled young biotech companies to move at light speed.

1966:

-Genetic code determined. Researchers, especially Gobind Khorana and Marshall Nirenberg, figured out the sequence of DNA building blocks that encodes each of the 22 amino acids—the building blocks of proteins.

1967:

-Arthur Kornberg and his team at Stanford used a single strand of viral DNA to create synthetic infectious viral DNA.

1969:

-Leonard Herzenberg and his team at Stanford developed the fluorescence-activated cell sorter, which is able to scan cells flowing past its laser light and separate them based on cell surface markers. This instrument became a crucial component of the biotech toolbox.

1973:

-First recombinant DNA molecules formed: Stan Cohen (Stanford) and Herb Boyer (University of California-San Francisco) used specialized enzymes—essentially molecular scissors and glue guns—to "cut" genetic information from one organism and "paste" it into the chromosomes of another organism. This invention, which built on important work from several other labs, is the basis of the entire biotech revolution.

1974:

-Hybridoma technology: By fusing a cell that is churning out a valuable antibody protein, with an immortal tumor cell line, Cesar Milstein and Georges Kohler were able to create a cell line that would pump out vast amounts of the desired antibody—termed a *monoclonal antibody*—essentially forever. This invention is what led eventually to the important anticancer monoclonal antibody products being sold now by Genentech and IDEC Pharmaceuticals.

-At the request of the National Academy of Sciences, Stanford's Paul Berg and 10 colleagues wrote a letter published in *Science Magazine* calling for the National Institutes of Health to set down guidelines for experiments using recombinant DNA techniques, and to ask that scientists avoid certain experiments until safety issues are resolved.

1975:

-A 4-day meeting at Asilomar, California, near Monterey, was attended by 140 academicians and other researchers to debate how scientists should make use of, and guard against problems arising from, the new gene-splicing methods. The recommendations become the basis for the NIH (National Institutes of Health) guidelines, approved in 1976.

1976:

-Herbert Boyer and Robert Swanson founded Genentech, Inc., the first biotechnology company based on recombinant DNA technology—and the beginning of the industry.

1977:

-Allan Maxam and Walter Gilbert (cofounder of Biogen) devised a chemical cleavage/gel separation method for determining the sequence of DNA building blocks relatively rapidly. This chemistry was incorporated into the first automated gene sequencers.

-Genentech researchers reported expression of somatostatin, the first human protein produced by a bacterium.

1980:

-Biotech's first IPO: Genentech went public October 14 at $35/share, raising $35 million. Within an hour, the stock leaped to $89/share and closed the day at $71.25.

-The U.S. Supreme Court ruled in *Diamond vs. Chakrabarty* that genetically engineered organisms can be patented, paving the way for biotech companies to protect their inventions.

1981:

-Dr. Leroy Hood and his team at Cal Tech invented an automated gene-sequencing machine that can read 7,000 DNA building blocks in a day.

1982:

-Eli Lilly got FDA approval to sell the first genetically engineered drug—human insulin, cloned by Genentech in 1978. This approval allowed patients to take the human protein, and thus to avoid the allergic reactions caused by the pig protein they had been forced to use. Lilly's Humulin had 1998 sales of $702 million.

-Oncogenes—cancer-causing genes—were identified in human tumors, and genetic engineering was used to create transgenic animals, which make foreign proteins. The ability to make transgenic animals allows the study of human diseases and production of complex proteins.

-Applied Biosystems, spun out of Amgen around technology from Lee Hood and others, marketed the first gas phase protein sequencer, which allows the rapid analysis of amino acid sequences in very small amounts of protein samples. This instrument plays a huge role in allowing biotech teams to move rapidly from protein isolation to gene cloning.

1983:

-PCR (polymerase chain reaction) gene amplification technology allowed the study of small amounts of DNA by generating millions of copies in hours. PCR made a big impact on the diagnostic world also, by allowing detection of low levels of infection. Also, the first tumor suppressor gene was identified.

1985:

-Genentech got FDA approval to sell the first biotech industry product—recombinant human growth hormone, which allowed patients to stop taking the cadaver-derived product previously available; 1998 sales were $214 million

-The Human Genome Project began: The international community and the U.S. federal government (Department of Defense) began to pour funding into an organized attack on sequencing the entire human genetic library—the genome. This project, expected to be completed in the new millennium, should yield information supporting a deeper understanding of health and disease and, hopefully, new therapeutic approaches.

1986:

-Genetically engineered alpha interferon became the first recombinant protein approved for cancer treatment in the United States. Chiron received FDA approval for the first genetically engineered vaccine, aimed at hepatitis B.

-Press reports of unapproved experiments by Advanced Genetic Sciences (AGS) Inc. (Oakland, California), spraying its "ice-minus" bacteria on rooftop plants, led to stronger EPA regulation of field trials for genetically engineered microbes. AGS later merged with DNA Plant Technology and, in the late 1990s, was found to have been working secretly on projects to increase the nicotine levels in tobacco.

1987:

-Advanced Genetic Sciences conducted the first field trial of a recombinant microbe, testing its "ice-minus" bug for the ability to protect strawberries from frost.

1988:

-The "Harvard mouse," engineered to be a model of human cancer, became the first mammal to be patented. This patent set off a huge debate on the patenting of living creatures, which continues today.

1989:

-The first food product engineered to resist rotting, Calgene's tomatoes, began field testing.

1990/1:

-The first human gene therapy studies were conducted in severe combined immunodeficiency patients and brain cancer patients. Also, Chiron introduced the first blood-screening test for hepatitis C, a major threat to the safety of the blood supply.

1992:

-Interleukin–2 was approved for advanced kidney cancer.

1994:

-The BRAC1 gene was identified and linked to breast and ovarian cancer.
-Calgene gets okay to sell its FLAVR SAVER genetically engineered tomato.

1997:

-FDA approved IDEC's Rituxan, the first monoclonal antibody treatment for cancer.
-PPL Therapeutics produces Dolly, the first cloned animal.

1998:

-Isis gets FDA okay to market Vitravene, the first antisense drug.

APPENDIX B

BIOTECHNOLOGY-DERIVED PRODUCTS ON THE MARKET

TABLE B.1

Product	Indication	Date Approved
Humulin, Humalog (insulin, Eli Lilly)	Diabetes	10/82
Protropin, Nutropin (hGH, Genentech)	Dwarfism; Short stature-renal disease	10/85, 11/93
Intron A (alpha interferon, Biogen/Schering-Plough)	Cancer, hepatitis B & C, genital warts; melanoma; lymphoma	6/86, 2/91, 12/95–8/98
Roferon A (alpha interferon, Hoffmann-La Roche)	Cancers	6/86, 10/95
OKT3 (MAB, Ortho)	Graft rejection	6/86
Recombivax (Merck/Chiron)	Vaccine—hepatitis B	7/86
Humatrope (hGH, Eli Lilly)	Dwarfism; Adults	3/87, 8/96
Activase (t-PA, Genentech)	Heart attack, Pulmonary embolism, acute MI, stroke	11/87, 6/90, 4/95, 6/96
Epogen/Eprex (erythro-poietin, Amgen and J&J) Procrit (Amgen and J&J)	• Anemia in renal disease • Anemia from AZT • Chemo-induced anemia in cancer	6/89 12/90 4/93
Engerix-B (Wellcome/Biogen)	• Hepatitis B vaccine • treatment for chronic Hep. B	9/89 8/98
CytoGam (immune sera, MedImmune/Connaught)	• Prevention of CMV infection • Prophylaxis	4/90 12/98
Actimmune (gamma interferon, Genentech)	Chronic granulo-matous disease	12/90
Neupogen (G-CSF, Amgen)	• Chemo-associated neutropenia • Bone marrow transplants	2/91 '94–4/98
Leukine/Prokine (GM-CSF, Immunex/Hoechst-Roussel)	Bone marrow transplants; AML	3/91, 9/95

(continues)

TABLE B.1 *(continued)*

Product	Indication	Date Approved
Ceredase (beta-glucocerebrocidase, Genzyme) Cerezyme (rDNA version)	Gaucher's disease	4/91 $411M '98
Proleukin (rDNA IL-2, Chiron)	metastic kidney cancer; melanoma	5/92–1/98
Recombinate (rDNA Factor VIII, Genetics Institute/ Baxter)	Hemophilia A	12/92
Oncoscint (MAB, Cytogen/ Knoll)	colorectal/ovarian cancer imaging	12/92
Kogenate (rDNA Factor VIII, Genentech/Cutter)	Hemophilia A	2/93
Betaseron (beta-interferon, Chiron/Berlex)	Multiple sclerosis	9/93
Pulmozyme (rDNA DNAse, Genentech)	Cystic fibrosis in mild–severe and infants	12/93–3/98
Oncoaspar (PEG-asparaginase, Enzon)	Acute lymphocytic leukemia	'94
ReoPro (MAB against the gp IIb/IIIa platelet receptor, Centocor/Lilly)	Restenosis after angio-plasty, angina	12/94, 11/97
Havrix (SmithKline)	hepatitis A vaccine	3/95
WinRho SD (antibody-based, Univax)	Blood clotting disorders, Rh disease	3/95, 4/95
Bio-Tropin (rDNA growth hormone, Bio-Technology General)	Growth hormone deficiency	5/95
Norditropin (rDNA growth hormone, Novo Nordisk)	Growth hormone deficiency	5/95
DaunoXome (liposomal daunorubicin, NeXstar)	Kaposi's sarcoma	6/95
Epivir (3TC oligo, Biomira, Glaxo)	AIDS	11/95
Photophrin (light-activated antitumor agent, QuadraLogic)	Head & neck cancer	12/95

(continues)

TABLE B.1 *(continued)*

Product	Indication	Date Approved
Abelcet (liposomal ampho-tericin B, The Liposome Co.)	Serious fungal infections	12/95
Doxil (liposomal doxorubican, Sequus)	Kaposi's sarcoma	12/95
Respigam (RSV immune globulin, MedImmune/AHP)	RSV prevention in infants	1/96
DaunoXome (liposomal daunorubicin, NeXstar)	Kaposi's sarcoma	4/96
Avonex (beta interferon, Biogen)	Multiple sclerosis	5/96
Confide (Chiron, J&J)	HIV blood test	5/96
Vistide (IV oligo, Gilead)	CMV retinitis in AIDS	6/96
CEA-Scan (Te-MAB fragment, Immunomedics)	Colorectal cancer imaging	6/96
MyoScint (MAB, Centocor)	myocardial necrosis imaging	7/96
Serostim (hGH, Serono)	AIDS wasting	9/96
Verluma (MAB-based diag., Neorx)	Lung cancer diag.	9/96
Photofrin (light-activated cytotoxin, QLT/Sanofi)	esophogeal cancer	9/96
ProstaScint (MAB, Cytogen)	prostate cancer imaging	10/96
Truquant (MAB-based Biomira/Immunex)	breast CA diagnostic	11/96
Ambisome (liposomal amphotericin B, NeXstar)	Serious fungal diseases	8/97
Benefix (F. IX, Genetics Inst./AHP	Hemophilia B	2/97
DermaGraft TC (tissue engineered human dermal replacement, Advanced Tissue Sciences	Burns	3/97

(continues)

TABLE B.1   *(continued)*

Product	Indication	Date Approved
Viracept (HIV protease inhibitor, Agouron)	HIV	3/97
Carticel (tissue engineered cartilage, Genzyme)	Cartilage replacement in knee	8/97
Graftpatch (tissue engineered soft tissue, Organogenesis)	Soft tissue replacement	8/97
Infergen (consensus IFN, Amgen)	Hepatitis C	10/97
RITUXAN (Mab, IDEC/ Genentech)	Lymphoma	11/97
Rabies vaccine (Chiron)	Rabies	11/97
Neumega (IL-11 platelet growth factor, Genetics Institute)	Platelet reconstitution	11/97
Zenapax (Mab, Protein Design Labs/Roche)	Graft vs. Host disease in transplants	12/97
Regranex (PDGF, Chiron/ J&J)	Diabetic foot ulcers	12/97
Refludan (rDNA lepirudin??, Hoechst)	Thromboembolism	3/98
Simulect (Hu-MAB to IL-2 receptor, Novartis)	Prevent acute rejection of kidney transplants	5/98
Integrilin (Iib/IIIa inhibitor of platelet aggregation, COR Therapeutics, Schering-Plough)	Heart attack and angioplasty	5/98
Apligraf (Organogenesis Inc.)	Skin replacement for leg ulcers	5/98
Simulect (MAB, Seragen-Ligand/Novartis)	Prevent acute rejection of kidney transplants	5/98
Synagis (Passive immuno-globulin, MedImmune)	Prevents RSV disease in high risk pediatric patients	6/98
Rebetron (Interferon A + ribavarin combination, Schering-Plough)	Chronic hepatitis B pat. w/liver disease who failed IF-A	6/98–12/98

(continues)

TABLE B.1   *(continued)*

Product	Indication	Date Approved
Thalidomid (single enantiomer thalidomide, Celgene)	Leprosy	7/98
Certiva (DTP accellular vaccine, North American Vaccine)	Diphtheria, tetanus, pertussis	7/98
Remicade (TNF antagonist, Centocor)	Crohn's disease	8/98
Vitravene (antisense to CMV, Isis/Ciba Vision)	CMV retinitis in AIDS patients	8/98
Herceptin (MAB to Her2, Genentech)	Metastatic breast cancer	9/98
Thyrogen (rDNA thyroid hormone, Genzyme)	Thyroid disease diagnosis	11/98
Enbrel (TNF antagonist, Immunex)	Moderate to severe Rheumatoid arthritis	11/98
LYMErix (recombinant Lyme protein, SmithKline)	Vaccine for Lyme disease	12/98
Provigil (modafinil, Cephalon)	narcolepsy	12/98
Thymoglobulin (polyclonal Ab, SangStat)	Prevent acute rejection of kidney transplants)	12/98
Agenerase (protease inhibitor, Vertex/Glaxo)	Combination treatment for HIV	4/99

APPENDIX C

BIOTECH WEB SITES
AND RESOURCES

NEWSLETTERS AND INDUSTRY/
BUSINESS WEB SITES

- **www.BIO.org**

This Web site is produced by the Biotechnology Industry Organization, the trade association that represents the biotech sector in Washington, DC, and around the world. The site contains news, information on the industry's impact (products approved, legislation, etc.), career services, and links to member company Web sites, press releases services, FDA activities, and worldwide organizations.

- **www.phrma.org**

This is the Web site for the Pharmaceutical Research and Manufacturers of America, the trade association for the big pharma companies. This group posts some very useful annual surveys on drugs in development for specific diseases and age groups, and on biotech drugs in general.

- **www.bioindustry.org**

The UK biotech industry is represented by the BioIndustry Association, which sponsors this Web site along with conferences and seminars.

- **www.bioventureconsultants.com**

BioVenture Consultants Stock Report (BVCSR) is published on the last Friday of each month and tracks the stock and earnings performance, market capitalization, and product status of the top 100+ public biotechnology companies. The report includes useful charts and figures that compare performance of the different biotech stock tiers versus the S&P 500, and graphically shows stock performance to date. The focus is primarily on the therapeutic and tool companies. Contact the company on-line.

- **www.biotechinfo.com**

The Institute for Biotechnology Information was founded 15 years ago by Dr. Mark Dibner. Its mission is to provide strategic business information to the biotechnology, pharmaceutical, and life science communities, including databases of products in development, partnerships, market research, competitor analysis, and more. The Web site includes a free biotechnology company "phone book" that includes contact information for more than 1,500 U.S. biotech firms.

- **www.Biospace.com**

This site combines access to the daily news wire stories and features from major business journals with original feature stories, links to sources of financial and industry news, directories of biotech companies, and chat rooms. There is also a daily "heads-up" service, called the Gene Pool, that alerts readers to key stories. Contact the company on-line.

- *Bioworld Today, BioWorld Financial Watch*, **and Bioworld.com**

BioWorld Today is a daily newspaper for the biotech industry that can be obtained by fax or on-line. *BioWorld Financial Watch*, published weekly via fax and on-line, covers the top financial and corporate partnering stories and provides an overview of biotech stock performance. BioWorld.com provides on-line access to current and archived issues of both publications, as well as special reports on the industry and market activity info. Contact the company at info@bioworld.com or at 800-688-2421.

- **Windhover Information, www.windhoverinfo.com**

This publishing group produces *In Vivo* magazine (industry trends, key developments, company strategies in the biomedical/ device/equipment/hospital supply/diagnostic industries; *Start-Up Magazine* (focus on emerging medical markets and young companies); *Health Care Strategist* (an annual review of deal-making activity and trends, the most active banks and companies, and other important aspects of business development); *Pharmaceutical Strategic Alliances* (an annual summary review of pharmaceutical deals); and Strategic Intelligence Systems (a computer-based subscription that allows you to monitor business and financial activity in the biopharmaceutical world). Several of these publications are available in print and on-line. Contact the company at 203-838-4401, X 232, or e-mail custserv@windhoverinfo.com.

- **www.recap.com**

Recombinant Capital, based in San Francisco, California, has an interesting Web site that combines original features with access to its own databases on products in clinical development and corporate partnerships. The company also hosts an annual meeting, the Allicense Conference, that provides a great overview of the corporate partnering issues and trends of the previous year.

- *Medical Technology Stock Letter*

Edited by James McCamant out of Berkeley, California, this newsletter, part of the biotech scene since the early 1980s, provides nontechnical descriptions of programs and products in development and tracks the performance of a model biotech stock portfolio. Contact the company at 510-843-1857.

- **www.bioportfolio.com/bio**

This site, organized by Bioportfolio Ltd. in Cambridge, England, includes a database of 5,500 global biobusinesses with 20,000 hyperlinks to stockbroker reports, news services, stock prices, the U.S. Patent Office, and company Web sites. The site is aimed primarily at companies needing information to support strategic analysis.

- **www.genengnews.com**

Genetic Engineering News publishes a newsletter and this Web site, which includes daily biotech news from press releases.

- **PJB Publications**

This UK-based biopharmaceutical publishing house produces a number of relevant newsletters and magazines, including the monthly *BioVenture View* (not related to BioVenture Consultants), *Biopeople Magazine*, and *Biocommerce Data Ltd.* Contact the company at www.pjbpubs.co.uk or call 212-262-8230.

- **www.techvestllc.com/newsletter**

Techvest LLC publishes a newsletter for individual investors interested in biotech and biomedical investments. A subscription form is on the Web site.

- **www.sec.gov/agi-bin/srch-edgar**

This site provides access to SEC documents filed by companies.

INVESTMENT SITES

- **www.morningstar.net, www.bloomberg.com, www.kiplinger.com**

You can search these sites for information on health or biotech stocks and funds and track their performance.

• **www.smallcapsonline.com**

This gives investors access to the free on-line investment research division of Bridge Technology Group LLC, which also handles public relations for biotech companies through another division.

• **www.nvst.com**

The *Venture Capital Journal* on-line version covers key players and events in the U.S. venture capital arena.

SCIENCE SITES

• **www.fda.gov**

This site gives you access to the Food and Drug Administration's full court press of information on regulations, upcoming advisory panel meetings, and events.

• **www.nih.gov**

The National Institutes of Health are the primary federally funded health care research institutes. This site will take you to all of the individual institutes, including the National Cancer Institute, and provides access to information on diseases, research, and ongoing clinical trials.

• **www.biomednet.com**

The Internet community for biological and medical researchers, including a daily news-and-views service, links to a huge database of medical and scientific Web sites, career services, access to the 9 million records in a free MEDLINE database of scientific articles, reports from scientific conferences, and all sorts of cool stuff!

• **www.aaas.org**

This is the Web site of the American Association for the Advancement of Science. The AAAS publishes a highly regarded scientific journal—although the articles are way beyond non-science-nerds, the overview of current events on the site and the interesting topics in www.scienceon-line.org, the AAAS's companion site, can provide a window into the most recent scientific advances and politics.

• **www.bis.med.jhmi.edu/Dan/DOE/intro.html**

"A Primer on Molecular Genetics," published by the Department of Energy (which funds the Human Genome Project). The site provides definitions of important terms.

• **www.citeline.com**

This San Francisco–based service allows you to search for information on different diseases, along with articles on treatments.

• **www.Drkoop.com**

This site gives you access to medical encyclopedias, disease directories, and basic health information.

• **www.med.upenn.edu/~bioethic/**

This site is sponsored by the Center for Bioethics at the University of Pennsylvania, and it links to pages covering many different areas of the impact of technology on biology and the ethical implications.

• **fbox.vt.edu:10021/cals/cses/chagedor/index.html**

Public Perception Issues in Biotechnology are found at this site, including the areas of transgenic plants and animals, ag biotech issues, and human cloning.

• **biotech.icmb.utexas.edu**

This biotech site has a dictionary.

• **web.indstate.edu/thcme/mwking/subjects.html**

The *Medical Biochemistry Subject List*, produced by Indiana State University, is a text-based introduction to biochemistry—proteins, DNA, metabolism—all that cool stuff that happens inside cells.

• **www.gene.com/ae**

The Academic Excellence site, maintained by Genentech, contains information, news, and activities for teachers and students.

• **www.cellsalive.com**

This site has color images of cells and bacteria

APPENDIX D

BIOVENTURE CONSULTANTS' BIOTECH *STOCK REPORT*

As of December 31, 1999

BioVenture Consultants
6 Norfolk Road
Chestnut Hill, Massachusetts 02467-1808
www.bioventureconsultants.com
Email: BioVenture@aol.com

Top 100 Biotech Companies, Alphabetical Listing

Company	#	Company	#	Company	#	Company	#
Abgenix	14	Adv. Tissue	80	Affymetrix	8	Alexion	43
Alkermes	18	Amgen	1	Amylin	45	Ariad	96
Aronex	94	ArQule	81	Avigen	50	Aviron	60
Axys	82	Bio-Tech Gen.	24	BioCryst	41	Biogen	4
BioMarin	47	Biomatrix	39	Biotransplant	93	Cell Genesys	46
Cell Pathways	71	Cell Therapeutics	86	Celtrix	90	Cephalon	20
Chiron	6	CollaGenex	69	Collateral	61	Connetics	65
COR	26	Corixa	56	Corvas	91	Coulter	51
Creative BioMol.	73	Cubist	55	Curagen	22	CV Therapeutics	36
Cyto Therapeutics	100	EntreMed	52	GelTex	68	Gene Logic	31
Genelabs	67	Genentech	2	Genome Therap.	58	Genzyme	9
Geron	70	Gilead	12	Gliatech	75	Guilford	49
Human Gen Sci.	10	Hyseq	66	ICOS	17	IDEC	13
Imclone	21	Immune Resp.	85	Immunex	3	Immunomedics	40
Incyte	15	Inhale	27	Interneuron	63	Isis	72
La Jolla	97	Ligand	29	Liposome Co.	35	Lynx	53
Magainin	99	Matrix	87	Medarex	19	Medimmune	5
Microcide	88	Millennium	7	Myriad	44	NeoRx	89
Neurocrine	37	Neurogen	62	NPS	78	Onyx	84
OSI Pharm	74	PathoGenesis	54	Pharmacopeia	42	Pharmacyclics	28
Progenics	38	Protein Design	16	Regeneron	48	Repligen	95
Ribozyme	83	SangStat	32	Scios	77	Sepracor	11
Synaptic	92	Targeted Genom	79	Texas Biotech	59	TKT	25
Trega	98	Triangle	34	Trimeris	57	Valentis	64
Vertex	23	Vical	33	Viropharma	30	XOMA	76

Top 100 Biotech Companies
Descriptive Information, Stock Performance, Income/Balance Sheet Data

Company	Staff	Yr. Incor.	IPO Date	Stock Symbol	Price 12/31/99	Price Perf. Y-to-D[1]	12 Month High-Low	Shares	Market Out[2]	12 Mo Cap	12 Mo Sales[3]	12 Mo Rev	12 Mo R&D	Cash Earnings
1 Amgen	5,300	'80	6/83	AMGN	$60.06	130.1%	67–25	1,021.0	$61,323.8	2,890.4	3,190	772.9	1,053.8	1524.0
2 Genentech	3,300	'76	10/80	DNA	$134.50	177.3%	143–58	254.6	$34,243.4	1,030.2	1,367	374.7	(934.5)	1,663.6
3 Immunex	1,100	'81	3/83	IMNX	$109.50	247.6%	121–28	164.3	$17,986.9	411.5	478.3	118.8	39.2	476.8
4 Biogen	1,200	'78	6/83	BGEN	$84.50	103.6%	91–38	150.0	$12,675.0	564.8	737.4	209.8	193.0	672.6
5 Medimmune	430	'88	5/91	MEDI	$165.88	233.6%	176–43	63.4	$10,512.8	257.6	282.5	34.9	96.2	159.3
6 Chiron	3,247	'81	6/83	CHIR	$42.38	61.8%	45–18	181.7	$7,697.4	429.5	793.6	310.3	485.7	905.3
7 Millennium	850	'93	5/96	MLNM	$122.00	371.5%	144–24	36.0	$4,392.0	0.0	186.5	147.0	21.8	225.2
8 Affymetrix	400	'92	6/96	AFFX	$169.69	596.2%	196–23	25.0	$4,242.2	65.3	84.2	39.3	(26.1)	229.8
9 Genzyme	3,700	'81	6/86	GENZ	$45.00	9.5%	64–30	84.1	$3,784.5	643.2	645.5	95.3	183.9	530.0
10 Human Genome Sci.	460	'92	12/93	HGSI	$152.63	329.2%	173–28	23.1	$3,530.7	0.0	35.1	55.9	(36.8)	281.5
11 Sepracor	325	'84	9/91	SEPR	$99.19	12.6%	141–55	33.1	$3,283.1	12.2	16.2	96.1	(157.1)	377.8
12 Gilead	742	'87	12/92	GILD	$54.13	31.8%	96–35	43.9	$2,376.1	43.2	71.5	83.4	(77.4)	307.3
13 IDEC	364	'86	4/91	IDPH	$98.25	109.0%	105–20	21.2	$2,078.0	89.0	117.0	37.4	41.1	230.0
14 Abgenix	60	'96	7/98	ABGX	$132.50	715.4%	149–12	15.0	$1,987.5	0.0	8.6	20.0	(14.8)	55.9
15 Incyte	1,100	'91	11/93	INCY	$60.00	60.5%	74–16	28.5	$1,710.0	0.0	149.1	131.8	(18.9)	82.1
16 Protein Design Labs	285	'86	2/92	PDLI	$70.00	202.7%	75–13	18.7	$1,309.0	0.0	34.1	33.7	(9.7)	134.7
17 ICOS	292	'89	6/91	ICOS	$29.25	(1.7%)	49–24	44.2	1,292.9	80.0	143.1	110.0	20.9	59.7
18 Alkermes	325	'87	7/91	ALKS	$49.13	121.4%	58–21	25.3	$1,242.9	0.0	44.5	66.2	(71.8)	181.7
19 Medarex	90	'87	6/91	MEDX	$37.25	1,128.9%	42–2	31.7	$1,181.0	1.2	10.4	22.2	(17.2)	20.1
20 Cephalon	365	'87	3/91	CEPH	$34.56	284.0%	38–7	32.4	$1,119.8	15.1	32.4	42.3	(59.1)	213.3
21 Imclone	142	'84	6/86	IMCL	$39.63	337.2%	44–8	25.5	$1,012.0	0.1	2.2	27.9	(33.8)	34.2
22 Curagen	290	'91	3/98	CRGN	$69.75	887.6%	71–5	13.9	$969.5	0.0	12.4	26.2	(26.4)	40.9
23 Vertex	350	'89	7/91	VRTX	$35.00	17.6%	38–19	25.5	$892.5	5.1	43.7	72.1	(55.2)	188.1
24 Bio-Tech General	289	'80	1/83	BTGC	$15.00	119.8%	18–5	52.9	$806.7	67.9	91.8	20.7	20.7	80.9
25 TKT	230	'88	10/96	TKTX	$38.50	51.7%	54–19	19.2	$739.2	0.0	2.9	41.0	(42.8)	80.8
26 COR	320	'88	6/91	CORR	$26.88	102.8%	31–8	27.0	$725.6	24.9	46.2	40.6	(35.9)	58.3
27 Inhale	185	'90	4/94	INHL	$42.56	29.0%	51–22	17.0	$722.8	0.0	33.4	48.6	(24.0)	58.3
28 Pharmacyclics	70	'91	10/95	PCYC	$41.25	61.8%	49–13	15.1	$622.7	0.0	5.7	20.7	(18.8)	125.9

(continues)

Top 100 Biotech Companies
Descriptive Information, Stock Performance, Income/Balance Sheet Data *(continued)*

Company	Staff	Yr. Incor.	IPO Date	Stock Symbol	Price 12/31/99	Price Perf. Y-to-D [1]	12 Month High-Low	Shares	Market Out [2]	12 Mo Cap	12 Mo Sales [3]	12 Mo Rev	12 Mo R&D	Cash Earnings
29 Ligand	380	'87	11/92	LGND	$12.88	10.8%	15–6	47.7	$614.5	9.0	33.8	66.3	(92.6)	45.8
30 Viropharma	84	'94	11/96	VPHM	$37.00	297.4%	47–5	15.0	$556.8	0.0	1.4	20.1	(32.3)	12.0
31 Gene Logic	185	'94	11/97	GLGC	$26.50	280.3%	32–3	19.9	$527.4	0.0	18.5	26.9	(18.2)	16.6
32 SangStat	150	'88	12/93	SANG	$29.75	40.0%	33–10	17.2	$510.8	50.7	51.1	16.5	(35.4)	34.4
33 Vical	108	'87	3/93	VICL	$29.94	111.0%	31–9	16.2	$485.0	0.0	8.3	13.5	(8.8)	38.9
34 Triangle	157	'95	11/96	VIRS	$12.81	(6.0%)	24–10	37.7	$483.0	0.0	5.5	76.6	(94.4)	161.5
35 Liposome Co.	301	'81	6/86	LIPO	$12.19	(21.1%)	29–6	39.2	$477.2	83.6	89.7	25.2	9.7	62.4
36 CV Therapeutics	69	'90	11/96	CVTX	$26.06	448.7%	28–3	18.1	$472.4	0.0	0.5	18.4	(21.8)	33.3
37 Neurocrine	155	'92	6/96	NBIX	$24.75	260.0%	30–3	19.0	$470.3	0.0	17.2	28.3	(19.9)	48.5
38 Progenics	44	'86	11/97	PGNX	$48.88	294.9%	60–10	9.6	$469.2	0.0	15.0	10.7	(1.6)	24.8
39 Biomatrix	383	'81	8/91	BXM	$19.25	(33.9%)	45–17	24.2	$465.9	65.3	78.9	9.1	21.7	27.7
40 Immunomedics	80	'82	11/83	IMMU	$12.25	197.0%	14–1	37.9	$464.0	5.6	7.2	9.6	(10.5)	7.7
41 BioCryst	56	'86	3/94	BCRX	$29.50	321.4%	36–6	15.2	$449.5	0.0	4.0	7.5	(6.4)	19.1
42 Pharmacopeia	550	'93	12/95	PCOP	$22.63	138.2%	24–5	19.8	$448.0	0.0	102.4	43.5	(0.8)	63.9
43 Alexion	89	'92	2/96	ALXN	$30.13	125.2%	34–8	14.7	$444.3	0.0	26.3	31.0	(7.9)	21.3
44 Myriad	280	'91	10/95	MYGN	$46.00	360.0%	51–8	9.4	$432.4	5.9	26.5	23.4	(9.6)	46.5
45 Amylin	53	'87	1/92	AMLN	$8.34	1,568.8	10–0	50.0	$417.2	0.0	2.0	18.4	(27.9)	10.7
46 Cell Genesys	115	'88	5/?	CEGE	$12.81	113.5%	15–3	32.4	$415.0	0.0	36.5	24.2	12.2	60.0
47 BioMarin	108	'97	6/99	BMRN	$11.75	(9.6%)	20–10	34.8	$408.9	1.0	6.2	21.5	(23.5)	72.2
48 Regeneron	429	'88	4/91	REGN	$12.75	72.9%	13–5	31.3	$399.1	0.0	35.8	48.3	(27.1)	87.4
49 Guilford	2,225	'93	6/94	GLFD	$17.00	19.3%	18–9	23.1	$392.7	7.2	16.8	39.8	(30.9)	144.7
50 Avigen	44	'92	5/96	AVGN	$31.00	296.8%	37–4	12.6	$389.2	0.0	0.4	6.3	(9.8)	12.7
51 Coulter	206	'95	1/97	CLTR	$22.69	24.4%	35–11	16.7	$378.9	0.0	37.2	32.7	(10.6)	100.9
52 EntreMed	59	'91	6/96	ENMD	$25.63	22.0%	36–12	14.7	$375.9	0.0	6.7	26.5	(26.6)	39.9
53 Lynx	90	'92	12/97	LYNX	$32.38	181.5%	40–8	11.2	$362.6	0.0	7.7	15.7	(10.8)	21.2
54 PathoGenesis	286	'91	11/95	PGNS	$21.44	(63.0%)	59–10	16.4	$352.6	58.5	60.1	28.9	(5.1)	40.2
55 Cubist	65	'92	10/96	CBST	$19.25	404.9%	22–2	17.7	$340.7	0.0	5.0	16.4	14.6	13.7
56 Corixa	260	'94	10/97	CRXA	$17.00	83.8%	19–7	20.0	$340.0	0.0	28.6	36.1	(26.7)	55.4
57 Trimeris	70	'93	10/97	TRMS	$23.63	101.1%	28–11	13.7	$323.7	0.0	10.3	18.7	(13.3)	45.7

239

58 Genome Therapeutics	GENE	5/82	'61	175	$16.13	486.4%	20–2	18.5	$298.3	0.0	25.3	26.0	(5.1)	25.1
59 Texas Biotech	TXB	12/93	'89	86	$7.94	60.8%	9–3	34.2	$271.5	0.0	3.4	13.2	(15.4)	19.0
60 Aviron	AVIR	11/96	'92	297	$15.81	(38.9%)	35–14	15.9	$251.2	0.0	23.3	61.5	(55.2)	44.5
61 Collateral	CLTX	7/98	'95	53	$19.13	173.2%	30–6	12.9	$246.7	0.0	7.0	9.6	(6.8)	41.1
62 Neurogen	NRGN	10/89	'87	170	$16.50	(5.7%)	21–9	14.5	$240.9	0.0	9.9	23.1	(13.8)	69.5
63 Interneuron	IPIC	3/90	'88	92	$5.72	74.3%	9–1	41.9	$239.6	0.0	1.6	35.7	(37.7)	21.8
64 Valentis	VLTS	9/97	'92	129	$9.00	75.6%	10–3	26.4	$237.6	0.0	4.6	19.9	(62.4)	3.8
65 Connetics	CNCT	1/96	'93	110	$10.50	78.7%	11–4	21.6	$226.8	13.7	23.0	17.4	(24.7)	15.1
66 Hyseq	HYSQ	8/97	'92	170	$17.00	223.8%	20–2	13.0	$221.0	0.0	8.6	19.4	(17.7)	31.9
67 Genelabs	GNLB	6/91	'84	93	$5.50	100.0%	6–1	40.0	$220.0	0.0	8.0	13.0	(9.5)	11.1
68 GelTex	GELX	5/95	'92	107	$12.81	(43.4%)	29–9	16.9	$216.5	0.0	32.6	35.2	(39.7)	62.2
69 CollaGenex	CGPI	6/96	'92	142	$25.00	159.7%	26–7	8.6	$215.0	12.9	13.5	3.9	(16.2)	17.3
70 Geron	GERN	7/96	'90	100	$12.63	16.1%	20–9	16.8	$211.9	0.0	7.0	20.2	(42.1)	41.7
71 Cell Pathways	CLPA	10/98	'90	57	$9.25	(58.0%)	30–5	22.6	$209.1	0.0	1.5	15.8	(19.2)	23.4
72 Isis	ISIP	5/91	'89	387	$6.25	(51.7%)	18–3	29.2	$182.5	0.0	34.1	61.3	(58.2)	43.9
73 Creative BioMolecules	CBMI	12/92	'81	43	$4.94	33.9%	7–2	36.0	$177.8	0.0	8.2	13.9	(13.7)	23.5
74 OSI Pharm	OSIP	4/86	'83	204	$7.94	149.0%	9–2.25	21.5	$170.7	1.2	22.7	24.5	(9.8)	27.0
75 Gliatech	GLIA	10/95	'88	90	$16.63	(44.6%)	32–7	10.0	$166.3	30.8	33.1	12.7	3.6	22.5
76 XOMA	XOMA	6/86	'81	170	$3.00	(5.9%)	8–2	54.3	$162.9	0.0	0.5	42.5	(48.2)	22.8
77 Scios	SCIO	1/83	'81	267	$4.19	(59.6%)	13–2	38.5	$161.2	36.4	57.8	39.7	(27.1)	96.3
78 NPS	NPSP	5/99	'86	100	$12.25	59.3%	14–3	12.7	$155.8	0.0	5.1	19.7	(20.3)	28.4
79 Targeted Genomics	TGEN	5/94	'89	80	$3.94	200.0%	5–0	34.0	$133.9	0.0	11.2	????	(22.1)	??
80 Adv. Tissue Sci.	ATIS	1/88	'87	209	$2.50	(3.6%)	6–1	52.7	$131.8	13.5	40.2	15.6	(21.8)	22.1
81 ArQule	ARQL	10/96	'93	225	$10.25	107.6%	13–3	12.7	$130.2	0.0	20.2	16.9	(13.9)	41.0
82 Axys	AXPH	11/93	'89	218	$4.06	(30.9%)	9–2	30.4	$123.7	0.0	45.5	64.8	(47.1)	43.1
83 Ribozyme	RZYM	4/96	'92	78	$10.50	140.0%	22–3	11.2	$117.6	0.0	10.3	15.1	(9.0)	15.0
84 Onyx	ONXX	5/96	'92	113	$10.00	42.9%	12.38–5	11.5	$115.0	0.0	9.4	22.6	(17.4)	14.6
85 Immune Response	IMNR	5/90	'86	114	$4.34	(60.1%)	14–3	25.9	$112.6	0.0	21.1	35.3	(19.0)	22.2
86 Cell Therapeutics	CTTT	3/97	'91	165	$7.00	133.3%	8–1	15.6	$109.0	0.0	4.9	29.7	(35.7)	22.2
87 Matrix	MATX	1/92	'85	97	$4.75	81.0%	10–1	22.5	$106.9	0.0	0.0	18.8	(21.6)	51.8
88 Microcide	MCDE	5/96	'92	114	$8.88	129.0%	9–3	11.3	$98.5	0.0	8.4	17.4	(11.9)	23.7
89 NeoRx	NERX	1/88	'84	63	$4.06	202.3%	5–0	21.0	$85.3	1.8	3.2	11.3	(12.7)	20.0
90 Celtrix	CTRX	2/91	'90	7	$2.88	70.4%	3–0	20.0	$75.4	0.0	0.0	1.3	(10.4)	2.1
91 Corvas	CVAS	1/92	'87	75	$4.44	57.8%	4–1	16.8	$74.6	0.1	7.5	15.2	(11.9)	19.3

(continues)

Top 100 Biotech Companies
Descriptive Information, Stock Performance, Income/Balance Sheet Data *(continued)*

Company	Staff	Yr. Incor.	IPO Date	Stock Symbol	Price 12/31/99	Price Perf. Y-to-D[1]	12 Month High-Low	Shares	Market Out[2]	12 Mo Cap	12 Mo Sales[3]	12 Mo Rev	12 Mo R&D	Cash Earnings
92 Synaptic	100	'87	12/95	SNAP	$6.75	(55.0%)	20-4	10.7	$72.2	0.0	3.0	15.3	(14.0)	45.5
93 Biotransplant	70	'90	5/96	BTRN	$8.38	235.0%	10-0	8.6	$72.2	0.0	9.6	15.2	(8.0)	18.8
94 Aronex	90	'86	7/92	ARNX	$3.13	56.3%	8-1	22.8	$71.3	0.0	18.2	24.9	(9.0)	24.3
95 Repligen	25	'81	4/86	RGEN	$3.13	143.9%	5-0	22.3	$69.8	1.6	3.0	2.1	(3.1)	10.9
96 Ariad	129	'92	5/94	ARIA	$2.81	66.7%	5-0	22.0	$61.9	0.0	12.9	32.3	(24.1)	7.9
97 La Jolla	54	'89	6/94	LJPC	$2.53	(43.8%)	6-0	20.2	$51.1	0.0	7.4	13.6	(8.6)	14.2
98 Trega	122	'91	4/96	TRGA	$2.34	10.3%	4-0	18.5	$43.4	0.3	12.3	18.0	(11.8)	6.5
99 Magainin	47	'88	5/92	MAGN	$1.81	(43.1%)	5-1	22.9	$41.5	0.0	0.0	12.4	(12.2)	9.4
100 Cyto Therapeutics	5	'88	3/92	CTII	$1.47	0.0%	3-0	19.1	$28.1	0.0	7.7	12.5	(12.6)	6.3

notes:

*Numbers in millions except price, 12 month high-low, and multiples.

1 Year to date performance from December 1998 or from IPO.

2 Shares Out: The actual common shares outstanding.

3 Sales include product sales and royalties. Revenues include sales, royalties, collaborative agreement and research payments and interest.

Top 100 Biotech Companies
Companies by Research Focus and Market Capitalization (millions)

Anti-Infectives		Cardiovascular		Genomics	
Medimmune	$10,513	EntreMed	$376	Millennium	$4,392
Viropharma	$557	IDEC	$2,078	Affymetrix	$4,242
Triangle	$483	COR	$726	Human Genome	$3,531
PathoGenesis	$353	CV Therapeutics	$472	Incyte	$1,710
Trimeris	$324	Texas Biotech	$271	Curagen	$970
Genelabs	$220	Corvas	$75	Gene Logic	$527
Microcide	$99			Myriad	$432
Magainin	$42	**Cell-based**		Lynx	$363
		Adv. Tissue Science	$132	Genome Thera.	$298
		Hyseq	$221		
Antibodies		**Combinatorial Chemistry**		**Hormone Regulation**	
Abgenix	$1,988	Pharmacopeia	$448	Amylin	$417
Protein Design	$1,309	ArQule	$130		
Medarex	$1,181	Trega	$43	**Immunology**	
Imclone	$1,021			SangStat	$511
Immunomedics	$464	**Drug Delivery**		Alexion	$444
Coulter	$379	Alkermes	$1,243	Biotransplant	$72
NeoRx	$85	Inhale	$723	La Jolla	$51
		Matrix	$107		
Carbohydrates		**Gene Therapy**		**Lipid Drugs**	
BioMarin	$409	TKT	$739	Liposome Co	$477
		Vical	$485	Aronex	$71
		Cell Genesys	$415		
		Avigen	$389		
		Collateral	$247		
		Valentis	$238		
		Targeted Gebetics	$134		
		Ribozyme	$118		
		Cyto Therapeutics	$28		
Novel Chemistry		**Small Molecule Rational Design**			
Sepracor	$3,283	Vertex	$893		
Pharmacyclics	$623	BioCryst	$450		
Biomatrix	$466	Ariad	$62		
GelTex	$217				
Nucleotide-based					
Gilead	$2,376				
Isis	$183				
Neurobiology		**Target Assays/Drug Development**			
Cephalon	$1,120	ICOS	$1,293		
Neurocrine	$470	Ligand	$615		
Regeneron	$399	Cubist	$341		
Guilford	$393	CollaGenex	$215		
Neurogen	$241	Geron	$212		
Interneuron	$240	Cell Pathways	$209		
Gilatech	$166	OSI Pharm	$171		
NPS	$156	Axys	$124		
Synaptic	$72	Onyx	$115		
		Cell Therapeut.	$109		

(continues)

Top 100 Biotech Companies *(continued)*

Rec. DNA Proteins, Peptides		Vaccines	
Amgen	$61,324	Progenics	$469
Genentech	$34,243	Corixa	$340
Immunex	$17,987	Aviron	$251
Biogen	$12,675	Immune Response	$113
Chiron	$7,697		
Genzyme	$3,785		
Bio-Tech. Gen.	$807		
Connetics	$227		
Creative BioMol.	$178		
XOMA	$163		
Scios	$161		
Celtrix	$76		
Repligen	$70		

INDEX

243